ROCKETS TANKS AND SUBMARINES

Cover painting: Chapman, Conrad Wise (1842–1910). *Torpedo Boat* David *at Charleston Dock*. 1863, The American Civil War Museum, Richmond, Virginia.

ROCKETS TANKS AND SUBMARINES

The Ingenuity of Civil War Texans

EDWARD T. COTHAM JR.

State House Press

Schreiner University · Kerrville, TX
325-660-1752 · www.mcwhiney.org

Cataloging-in-Publication Data

Names: Cotham, Edward T, 1953- (Edward Terrel), author.
Title: Rockets, tanks and submarines: the ingenuity of civil war Texans / Edward T. Cotham.
Description: First edition. | Kerrville, TX: State House Press, 2025. | Includes Illustrations, select bibliography, notes and index
Identifiers: ISBN 9781649670274 (soft cover); ISBN 9781649670298 (e-book)
Subjects: LCSH: Military weapons – Texas – History. | Military weapons – United States – History. | Military weapons – History – transportation.
Classification: LCC E605 (print) | DCC 973
2025943321 CIP

First edition 2025

Cover and page design by Allen Griffith of Eye 4 Design

Distributed by Texas A&M University Press Consortium
800-826-8911
www.tamupress.com

Necessity is the mother of invention.

—Old proverb based on a similar phrase in Plato's *Republic*

If necessity is the mother of invention, conflict is its father.

—Kenneth Kaye

CONTENTS

ACKNOWLEDGMENTS

Writers of history rely on those who have preceded them in a particular field of study. This work, which covers an unusually wide range of topics, has been greatly assisted by several important sources. Mark K. Ragan, who has written extensively and comprehensively on submarines and the Singer Secret Service group in Texas, is owed a great debt by every scholar who follows in these areas of study. Because Mark owns a submarine and teaches others to pilot them, I have always given particular weight and deference to his analysis when it comes to anything in those waters.

Similarly, Neil P. Chatelain, who has written extensively on Civil War naval topics, has provided valuable insights. I am particularly indebted to Neil for connecting me with the Wiggins family, who were kind enough to grant me permission to publish the Creuzbaur drawings for the *Avenger*, which are a vital part of this work.

I would also like to thank my friend Andrew W. Hall, who has provided his always valuable advice on a variety of nautical topics, including most notably the Triton submarine, which we continue to jointly research.

It goes without saying that Donald S. Frazier, director of the Texas Center at Schreiner University, has been a constant influence on my research and writing since publication of his iconic book *Cottonclads: The Battle of Galveston and the Defense of the Texas Coast* in 1996. Finally, I would like to thank the staff of the Galveston and Texas History Center at Rosenberg Library, who have for many years provided me with a comfortable research environment and invaluable assistance in obtaining access to primary documents and images.

ROCKETS TANKS AND SUBMARINES

INTRODUCTION

In the course of what has now been four decades of researching and writing about the subject of Texas in the Civil War, I have often been fascinated by how a small number of Texans responded by imagining and experimenting with weapons that now seem far ahead of their time. Even acknowledging that some historians regard the Civil War as the first "modern" war, it is remarkable just how far "outside the box" some Texans thought. Indeed, some of the weapons they designed are so reminiscent of Jules Verne or steampunk fantasies that these visionaries must hardly have been able to see the box at all.

As a few examples will soon establish, Texas was far from a backwater of technological innovation during the period preceding and including America's great internal conflict. This should not surprise anyone. The Lone Star State has always been a magnet for creative people. Many around the world associate Texas with the NASA Manned Spacecraft Center (now known as the Johnson Space Center), which was established between Houston and Galveston in 1961. But there was a time almost one hundred years earlier when the same general area was home to the continent's most active rocket design and manufacturing program. Like many exotic ideas that surfaced in Civil War Texas, the Confederate rocket program in Texas never really got off the ground. But that experience is familiar territory to anyone who has witnessed the rise and development of new forms of technology. Cutting-edge ideas almost inevitably tend to have a high initial failure rate.

Rocket tests were not the only experiments conducted deep in the heart of Civil War Texas. At the outset of the war, Texans were bursting at the seams with exotic ideas intended to help their forces achieve a rapid victory. Their prevalence does not mean that these ideas were all—or even mostly—good ideas. Indeed, many of these ideas had good reason never to even make it within sight of a drawing board. Others, like the rocket program, would virtually leap off the drawing board only to come crashing back to earth as abject failures. But a few ideas would prove themselves to be practical and successful, and at least one of those projects would surprisingly go on to revolutionize warfare.

The title of this book emphasizes rockets, tanks, and submarines for an important reason. Most readers will not associate these inventions with the Civil War. It is certainly true that those particular implements of war were not effectively employed at scale until well after the end of the war. But the same characteristics of those inventions that eventually led to their widespread adoption were present during the Civil War. It did not take much imagination to see that each of these weapons, if they could be made practical, would more than fill a critical military need. Union and Confederate war planners could readily see the advantage of a boat that traveled beneath the waves, a rocket that soared overhead, or an armored artillery battery that could be easily moved to where its guns were most needed. The question is how close necessity actually came to being the mother of these inventions during the war. This book is intended to explore the steps that Texans took, sometimes at great personal risk, to explore the possibility and practicality of inventions like these.

Not all the inventions described in this book were pipe dreams that had little practical impact. There was one important invention, floating mines called "torpedoes," that Texans produced and installed in record numbers across the Confederacy. Deploying these "infernal machines" with devastating effect, they damaged or destroyed large numbers of Union ships and trains. This toll put an enormous strain on the Northern war effort.

The Texas torpedo service, a secret group consisting primarily of a small band of men from Lavaca, Texas, ended up sinking more enemy ships than the entire Confederate Navy and Army combined. Their torpedoes, which started out as tiny experimental bombs floating in a gunsmith's backyard barrel, eventually forced military planners around the world to fundamentally reconsider the way they would wage war going forward.

The subtitle of this book applies the word *ingenuity* to Civil War Texans. Although that word has come to mean clever, crafty, and creative in the English language, it originated in a Latin phrase that implied the status of freedom by birth. This language transition makes perfect sense. People who are ingenious in the modern sense arrive at creative solutions only when they feel free to look at problems from many different angles and evaluate a wide range of potential solutions. As the reader will soon discover, it is clear from the nature of the projects discussed in this book that Texans felt free to explore wildly unconventional ideas to try and achieve their military goals. Sometimes these ideas worked out, and, unfortunately for those involved on the front lines, sometimes they literally blew up.

In the end, Texans could not invent their way into creating a new nation. Many of the unique projects on which they labored so diligently during the war disappeared without a trace following the war. The very existence of such projects soon became shrouded in a mist of obscurity and secrecy. As the years went by, Texas veterans would talk proudly about their charges at Gettysburg and their victories at battles like Chancellorsville or Chickamauga. None would boast about their ill-fated attempts to launch effective rockets or note how close they came to perfecting truly revolutionary new devices like submarines, flamethrowers, or tanks.

Even the men from Lavaca who achieved unbelievable successes with their explosive torpedoes did not feel free to openly boast about the extent and devastating impact of their accomplishments. The records regarding these secretive programs were often destroyed or lost. Strangely enough, much of what we know about these clandestine projects derives from lost letters that literally floated down the Mississippi River or fell into enemy hands on at least two separate occasions during the war.

Johann Wolfgang von Goethe once advised, "Dream no small dreams for they have no power to move the hearts of men."[1] It is the goal of this book to examine the atmosphere that led to the "big dreamers" with which Civil War Texas was populated. Such a study raises a number of questions. What made one man decide to invent a new type of underwater bomb and franchise its production across the South? What led another to use his knowledge of fluid dynamics to imagine an entirely new class of submersible vehicles? How close did Texans really come to developing a viable rocket program or a functioning submarine? How close were Texans to deploying machine guns, flamethrowers, or tanks?

This study raises many questions in areas where answers are inherently elusive. It is my hope to shed what light I can on projects that by virtue of their secret service origins tend to resist all attempts at illumination. As Lewis Carroll's walrus famously noted, the time has now come to "talk of many things."

CHAPTER 1

PREPARING FOR WAR

On November 17, 1860, the front page of Scientific American featured a diagram of what was described as an improved water wheel. Inventor Caleb Van Ausdol Littlepage of Austin, Texas, had secured a patent for this clever device in 1859. Robert Creuzbaur, another Austin friend and inventor, was also interested in fluid mechanics. He and Littlepage had already teamed up to jointly write a series of articles for Scientific American that defended the results of their experiments with fluids and criticized the sloppy testing procedures that were all too frequently employed by supposedly reputable Northern firms and learned societies in this emerging field of study.[2]

That two Texans were on the cutting edge of American technical achievement in 1860 may surprise some readers. After all, Texas had only become a state in 1845 and was still in many ways a frontier region. The city of Austin, in which Littlepage and Creuzbaur lived, had only been in existence for about twenty years. But to think of Texas as an agricultural and unsettled entity with little need or capacity for industrial creativity is to miss an important part of the Lone Star State's early story. Almost by definition, the people who scrawled "Gone to Texas" on their doors and made the long journey to settle in Texas were looking for new opportunities in a free and open land. Many were by nature unconventional and creative. They soon found that the wide-open spaces of Texas provided plenty of room to try different ways of doing things. As a couple of examples will illustrate, innovation soon became an essential part of the emerging Texas identity.

Gail Borden Jr. came to Texas from New York in 1829. In addition to farming and publishing a newspaper, he served as a surveyor and helped lay out some

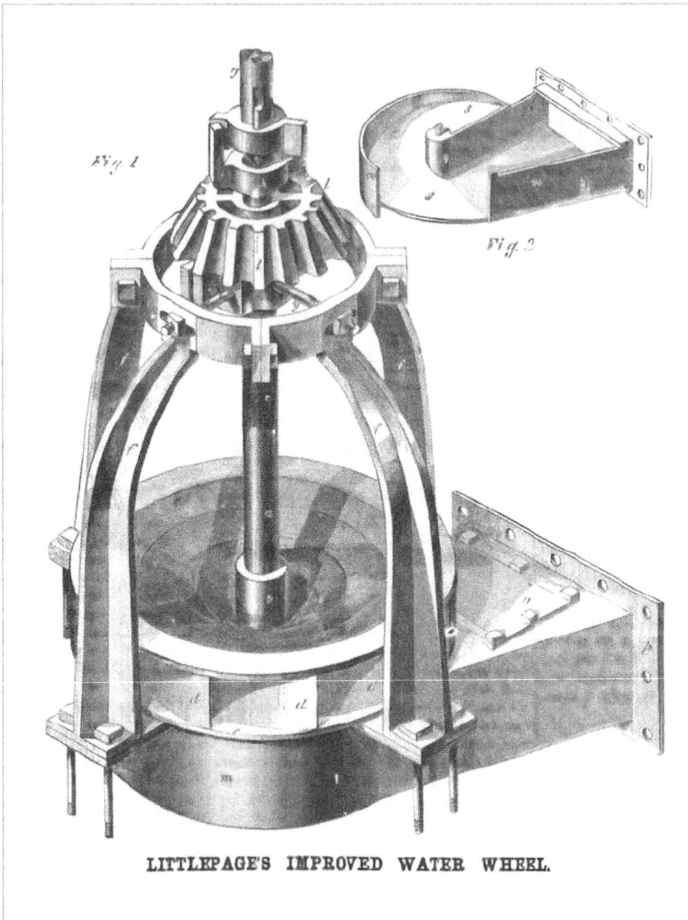

"C. V. Littlepage's Improved Water Wheel."
Scientific American, November 17, 1860.

early Texas cities. In 1839, Borden became the agent for the Galveston City Company and was instrumental in its early development.

In Galveston, he turned his hand to inventing. Like many early Texans, Borden had a vivid and Texas-sized imagination. He imagined a giant air-conditioning system that would protect Galveston from the heat and the ravages of yellow fever. Unfortunately for subsequent generations of sweltering Galvestonians, this appealing idea never came close to reality.[3]

Gail Borden Jr. (1801–74). Borden Name File-Photographic Collection, Rosenberg Library, Galveston, Texas.

Living on Galveston Island, Borden was surrounded by water. It is not surprising, then, that a number of his early inventions had aquatic themes. To help ladies bathe conveniently in the Gulf of Mexico, Borden proposed a "locomotive bath house" that would safely transport female bathers out into the water while shielding its occupants from view. Although this intriguing device was unsuccessful, Borden continued to be fascinated with innovative means of marine transportation.[4]

Borden's most exotic invention was undoubtedly his "terraqueous machine," which combined a wagon with a sailboat. This strange craft was intended to enable its driver to transition instantly from land to water as the wagon converted into a boat. Although the device functioned well on land, the invention had an unfortunate first test when it left the beach and reached the sea. On its first venture into the Gulf of Mexico, the machine capsized and left its unfortunate passengers helplessly swimming ashore to safety. Although severely disappointed that his machine did not work, Borden would probably feel vindicated by the fact that "duck" tours provided by vehicles similar to his original land–water concept are today popular in Galveston and other coastal towns.[5]

Bathing shelters and sinking wagons were just two in a long string of invention failures for Borden. After years of unrewarding effort, Borden eventually had to face the fact that he probably never would find success in transportation innovations. It was time to pursue something closer to his intellectual home, something that was more practical. Ever creative, Borden decided to turn his attention to food; in particular, he shifted his focus to ways to preserve consumer staples for extended periods. Knowing that food preservation was critically important in a big state with a warm climate, his first experiment involved turning meat into a biscuit. Borden did everything he could to promote his "meat biscuit" idea, even publishing a letter that he had written to Dr. Ashbel Smith touting his invention.[6] In the end, publicity was not enough. Borden's experiment was successful in creating a product that would last, but the terrible taste of the biscuit meant that it would never be something people chose to buy and eat.[7]

Borden soon realized that to make and market viable food products on the scale he needed, he had to at least temporarily relocate near production facilities in the North. The inventor moved his operations to New York in 1851. After experiments suggested that a liquid might be more suited to his food preservation objectives, Borden developed a process for condensing milk in a vacuum. The resulting product, "condensed milk," turned out to be a huge success. During the Civil War, Borden supplied condensed milk and other products to the Union military. The army found that condensed milk was the ideal solution to the problem of keeping milk available in the hot summers of the South. Although he returned to Texas after the war, Borden would end up being one of the few Texas inventors whose products would be used almost exclusively by Union rather than Confederate armies.[8]

Like many Northerners who came to Texas before the war, Borden had close connections to both sides during the great conflict. He had spent many years in Texas and considered himself, in most important respects, a Texan. On the other hand, his business interests at the outset of the war were solidly positioned in the North. Borden's family made the situation even more complicated. His youngest child, John Gail Borden, had gone north with his father when he was still young. When the war came, he served in the Union army, ending the war as a second lieutenant with the Forty-Seventh New York infantry. However, his eldest son, Henry Lee Borden, had much stronger ties to Texas and was living there when the war broke out. He chose to serve the Confederate cause as a corporal in the Thirty-Fifth Texas Cavalry regiment.[9]

Borden's story of years of failure culminating in a single huge success turns out to be relatively common in the history of innovation. For an invention to become truly significant, the invented product must not only work as intended, but it must meet an important need. Although this formula for success sounds simple, satisfying both these criteria is actually quite hard to accomplish in practice. A good example of this is provided by the case of Abraham Lincoln, On March 10, 1849, twelve years before he became president of the United States and its commander in chief, then Congressman Lincoln filed a petition seeking a patent for an invention to attach buoyant air chambers to vessels to help lift them over obstacles in the water. The wooden model he filed with his application is today in the collection of the Smithsonian Institution. Lincoln's petition was granted on May 22, 1849, and he remains the only American president ever to have a patented invention. Unfortunately, the device that Lincoln designed was impractical and it never came into use.[10]

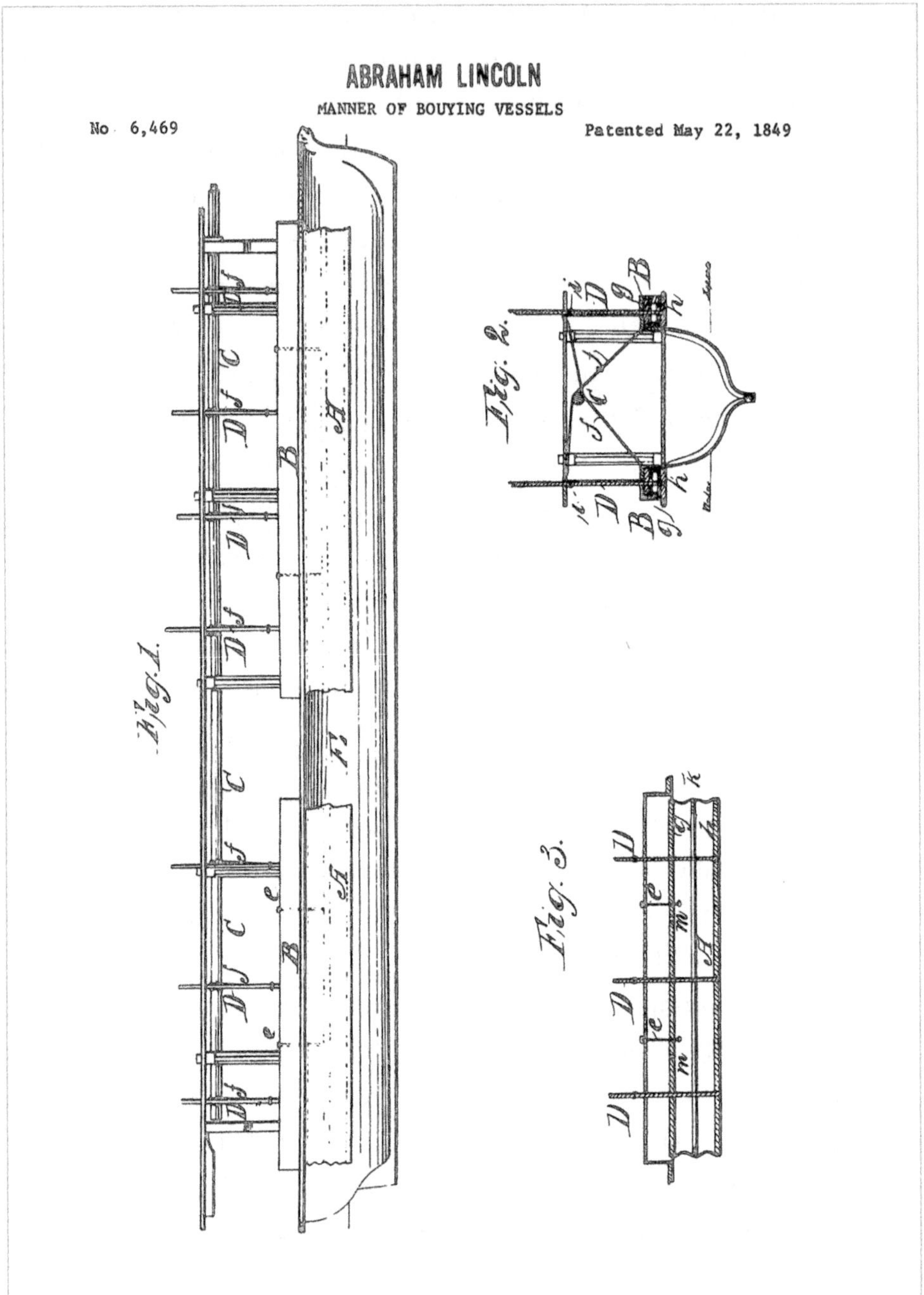

Drawing for US Patent No. 6,469, issued to Abraham Lincoln on May 22, 1849.
United States Patent and Trademark Office, Alexandria, Virginia.

The difficulties that both Lincoln and Borden experienced in finding users or consumers for their novel inventions highlight a problem that many inventors encounter. Finding eager users is particularly problematic for inventors of military hardware. An old and unfortunately true proverb holds that military planners are always preparing to fight the last war rather than the next war. This is because military bureaucrats and influential officers tend to stick with the military tools they know best and are notoriously resistant to change. Interestingly, early Texas provides one of the best contrary examples of how an innovative, game-changing weapon can develop that perfectly fits an emerging need.

In 1836, the year of the Texas Revolution, Samuel Colt of Connecticut patented a practical way to produce a revolving-cylinder handgun. At first, Colt found few interested buyers. In 1839, the Republic of Texas ordered

Samuel Colt (1814–62). Image no. 1215158, Miriam and Ira D. Wallach Division of Art, Prints and Photographs Collection, New York Public Library.

180 for its navy, making it the first large market for these guns. The Colts performed so well for the Texas Navy that they were later reissued to the Texas Rangers. Revolvers proved ideal for the type of mounted action that made the rangers famous. Colt continued to refine his guns over the ensuing decades, but he always recognized the important boost that Texans had given him by recognizing the value and viability of his invention. To commemorate this partnership, Colt engraved a stylized scene of the Texas Navy's 1843 Battle of Campeche on almost half a million of his revolvers.[11]

The development of revolvers is just one illustration of how the period from 1830 to the beginning of the Civil War saw ingenious developments in weapons and the way that wars would come to be fought. This was true not only in America, but also throughout the world. The Crimean War (1854–56) is sometimes described as one of the first modern wars because it featured technologies such as railroads, steamships, and telegraphs. To observe these developments, Secretary of War Jefferson Davis sent a delegation of army officers, including future Confederate General John Bankhead Magruder, to observe that conflict and report back any useful lessons. It turned out that the Crimean War that Magruder witnessed was the first conflict to see the use of naval mines, and the Virginian would certainly recall those devices when they were later built and employed in Texas during the Civil War.[12]

While weapons like revolvers were in development on land, there were also big changes in the military technology employed by the warships that dominated the water. The French ironclad *La Gloire* became the first ocean-going ironclad in 1859. The British responded by building their own armored vessel, HMS *Warrior*, shortly thereafter.[13]

Not only were surface vessels evolving, inventors experimented with submarine crafts. In Germany, a Bavarian inventor named Wilhelm Bauer built a submersible named *Brandtaucher* (German for fire-diver). It sank in an 1851 accident but was later salvaged. Today displayed in a Dresden museum, it remains the world's oldest surviving submersible. In addition to these exotic developments, there were equally dramatic advances underway in more conventional maritime weapons. More ships now featured rifled guns, which gave them longer reach and accuracy. Exploding shells became more accurate and were capable of doing enormous damage at ranges that naval officers just a generation before could not have imagined.[14]

The Mexican-American War of 1846–48, which was partly fought on Texas soil, provided additional opportunities to test new weapons and combat tactics. One of the biggest lessons learned from the war was the utility of light "flying artillery" batteries. Developed by Major Samuel Ringgold, US forces made use of a number of lighter guns mounted on special carriages, which were pulled by experienced crews and teams of horses. This resulted in batteries that could be quickly positioned and deployed to maximum benefit.[15]

"The Mode of Using Rockets in Bombardment from Earth Works." From Colonel William Congreve, *The Details of the Rocket System* (1814).

Bombardment of Vera Cruz. Print by Lossing and Barritt (1858), Image ID 809203, Miriam and Ira D. Wallach Division of Art, Prints and Photographs: Picture Collection, New York Public Library.

Not only did American artillery tactics evolve during the war, but the nature of artillery itself saw experimentation. The war with Mexico would be the first war in which the American army tested the use of rockets. Rockets were not new, of course. The first use of true rockets in a military sense is believed to be the "fire arrows" employed in China in the early 1200s.[16]

At first rockets were little more than colorful fireworks, but it eventually became evident that they would be useful supplements to more conventional artillery. After seeing the enemy in India use rocket batteries effectively in the 1790s, a British artillerist named William Congreve developed what became known as the Congreve rocket. These rockets were subsequently used by the British army in the Napoleonic Wars, including at the Battle of Waterloo.

Congreve rockets famously created "the rockets' red glare" that Francis Scott Key witnessed in the British assault on Fort McHenry in the War of 1812.[17]

The problem with deploying Congreve rockets was that they required use of long guide rods during launch and, despite being initially guided, tended to fly erratically and unpredictably. In the 1840s an Englishman named William Hale developed an improved stickless, or rotary, rocket. Hale rockets had tail vanes and secondary exhaust nozzles at their bases. This made the rockets spin, much like how a quarterback throws a football pass. The Hale rockets were more accurate and became the primary type of rockets used by the American military during the Mexican-American War.[18]

The American force that General Winfield Scott employed in 1847 to invade Mexico at Veracruz included a dedicated howitzer and rocket battery. Although never a critical factor in battle, this battery fired rockets in support of successful operations all the way from the coast to Mexico City. At the Battle of Contreras, the commander of the rocket battery was wounded, leading future Civil War generals George B. McClellan and P. G. T. Beauregard to take turns substituting for him.[19]

After the Mexican-American War, the prevailing view in the American military was that rockets showed promise but were difficult to effectively control and use except in special situations. Although many important future officers witnessed the performance of the rocket battery in Mexico, few seemed particularly enthusiastic about seeing rockets employed during the Civil War. An exception to this view was Beauregard, who in September 1861 actively tried to organize a rocket battery in Virginia. Problems involving the organization and selection of officers for this battery led to a bitter political feud between Beauregard and Jefferson Davis and kept this battery from achieving any success. It would be late 1863 before another attempt would be made by the Confederates to manufacture rockets and employ them in a dedicated battery. On that occasion, the rockets would be made and fired in Texas.[20]

CHAPTER 2

DESPERATE MEN INVENT DESPERATE THINGS

When sectional conflict appeared inevitable, military planners on both sides took stock of their respective resources and commenced assembling the means to wage war. There was a glaringly obvious mismatch. The North had vast advantages in measurables like military-age population and factories. The Tredegar Iron Works in Richmond was the only facility in the South where heavy ordnance and munitions could be manufactured. The economy of the South was heavily dominated by agriculture. It is not simplifying things too much to suggest that many Northerners made things while Southerners mainly grew things.[21]

If the numbers seemed unfavorable for the South as a whole, they looked particularly challenging for Texas. Against a Union population of roughly nineteen million, Texas in 1860 had a population of only a little over 600,000, with almost 200,000 of that number consisting of enslaved people. To make matters worse, it was obvious that many of the men Texas raised for Confederate armies would by necessity be sent out of state, leaving the state's vast coastline to be protected by relatively few men and very few large guns.[22]

Texans only had to look at a map to get uncomfortable about their defense prospects. Because of the way in which it had initially been settled, most Texas cities in the 1860s were relatively close to the coast or located on river systems that connected to it. Galveston, the state's largest city and most important port, was situated on a barrier island. Every Texas military leader was all too aware that a Union invasion force would almost certainly come by sea, and the time and place of such an attack could not be predicted.

The costal focus of Texas settlement was a key vulnerability, given the fact that the state had no real warships of any kind. Almost four hundred miles long, the Texas coast was also devoid of large protective fortresses like those that came into Confederate hands at Charleston, Mobile, or New Orleans. There was no getting around it. When the Civil War began, Texas probably had the least defensible coastline in the Confederacy. If Texas was going to defend itself, its citizens were going to have to step up and get creative. As later events would show, they were more than equal to the task.

Faced with the very real challenge of how to protect Texas against invaders from the sea, its inhabitants soon came up with many creative solutions. It did not take long for Jefferson Davis and Texas Governor Francis Lubbock to find themselves deluged with ideas from well-meaning and concerned citizens. Although these petitioners came from a wide variety of backgrounds, it is striking how many of the initial suggestions came from some of the earliest Texas settlers. In fact, there was so much unsolicited advice that it turned out to be a difficult job for public officials even to sort through the mail and separate the good ideas from the bad ones. A few representative examples will illustrate the challenge.

In 1829, at the age of eight, Leroy Alonzo Griffith arrived in Montgomery County, Texas. His family was part of Stephen F. Austin's second group of colonists. In June 1861, the forty-year-old Griffith wrote Jefferson Davis, signing his name "L. A. Griffith." He notified the president that he had invented a "portable breastwork" that would enable a light field battery to attack more powerful fortifications. Attaching drawings of his invention, Griffith offered to provide his invention and service free of charge if Davis thought it worthy. Davis thought it worthy only of a referral to the War Department to handle as it thought appropriate. Griffith was not alone in thinking that a portable breastwork might have utility. In 1863, *Scientific American* published an illustration of a portable breastwork for Union infantry attributed to S. M. Sherman of Plover, Wisconsin, which may have been similar to Griffith's original 1861 concept.[23]

S. M. Sherman's Portable Breastwork.
Scientific American, February 14, 1863.

Two other early settlers, who were veterans of the Texas Revolution, also sent Jefferson Davis their ideas. John Sutherland Menefee, who served as postmaster and county judge in the Jackson County community of Texana, had fought at the Battle of San Jacinto. He had also fought in 1842 against a Mexican incursion led by General Adrian Woll. Since Texana was located not far from Matagorda Bay, it is not surprising that Menefee's suggestion to Davis had a nautical theme.[24]

Menefee's bold idea was "to envelop the enemy's boat in a flame of fire by the use of [spirits of] Turpentine to be thrown in a stream from an engine and a flame communicated to it immediately after leaving the engine." In essence, Menefee was proposing the addition of a flame thrower to the bow of a boat. Davis referred this suggestion to the navy, which not only rejected the idea, but responded forcefully that it could not imagine even testing such a device. The navy's opposition was based on the extreme danger of fire to the boat from which the flame was to be thrown.[25]

Menefee's suggestion had the rare distinction of being both behind and ahead of its time. Devices to throw fire (sometimes called "Greek fire") from boats had been used by the Byzantine Empire as early as the seventh century AD. The first practical development of the modern flame thrower, however, is usually credited to the Germans in the early 1900s.[26]

Another creative early Texas settler, and certainly one of the most diligent inventors in terms of promoting his ideas, was Lucien Hopson. Born in Ohio, he arrived in Texas in 1836 at the age of thirty-three. During the Battle of San Jacinto, Hopson fought with the Mina Volunteers, a company of men raised in and around Bastrop. (In later years, Hopson would become a popular interview subject because he had been present when Santa Anna was taken before Sam Houston as a prisoner.) When the Civil War broke out twenty-five years later in 1861, the then fifty-eight-year-old Hopson was considered too old to fight. Like Menefee, however, Hopson spent a lot of time worrying about the fundamental problem of how to defend the largely defenseless Texas coast against powerful enemy warships. Hopson's solution involved not flames, but carefully designed guns that could fire his specially-shaped projectiles.[27]

Hopson's inventions arose from his belief that it made more sense to fire projectiles with points than objects shaped like balls. On September 25, 1862, Hopson obtained Confederate Patent No. 106 for an object described merely as a "projectile." Based on later US patents for similar projectiles, it seems that Hopson's 1862 invention had a triangular head, a conical base, and two outer bands to engage a gun's rifling grooves. Hopson's projectiles came both in a large size for artillery and one for small arms. The larger size was promoted as having important advantages for artillery pieces firing projectiles at armored ships. With samples of his inventions, Hopson made the long journey from his home in Lampasas, Texas, to Richmond, Virginia, where he held a series of meetings with Confederate ordnance and navy officials.[28]

At first things went well for Hopson. His new design for a small "ball" with a conical shape and a "driver" to be fired from rifled muskets was tested against the then prevailing Minié ball and found to have certain advantages

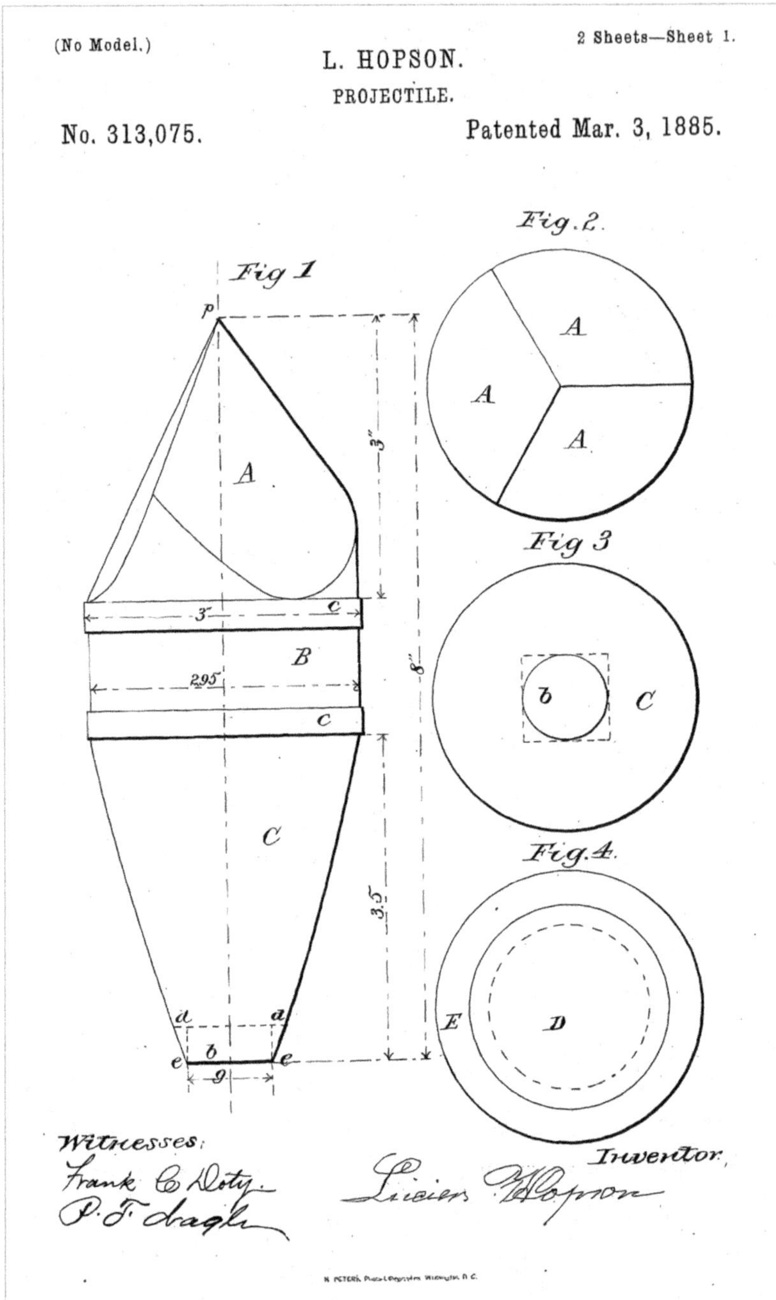

Drawing from US Patent No. 313,075 for projectile, issued to Lucien Hopson, March 3, 1885. US Patent and Trademark Office, Alexandria, Virginia.

in range and accuracy. Josiah Gorgas, chief of the Ordnance Department, was impressed enough with the preliminary tests to order that Hopson receive compensation while his new projectile underwent more rigorous tests. These tests only involved Hopson's small-arms inventions. To test his ideas for larger projectiles and guns, Hopson was referred to the navy.[29]

Here, Hopson found an unreceptive audience. He was not alone in receiving a cold reaction. This was the common experience of inventors pitching ideas to the Confederate Navy. It was the kiss of death for an inventor to have his idea forwarded to a naval review. Confederate naval officials tended to have their own pet projects and plans and were not particularly interested in hearing from outsiders. This was certainly Hopson's experience. Near the end of 1862, he reported to Jefferson Davis that he had arrived in Richmond in 1861 and conducted some successful tests of both his breech-loading rifles and cannons. But then communications from the navy largely ceased.

The Confederate naval officer assigned to review Hopson's inventions was Captain John M. Brooke. Brooke, the inventor said, "was down upon the inventions at the start," and "has labored to throw me and my improvements in the shade." Despite recommendations from the governors of Texas, Louisiana, and Mississippi, Brooke refused even to conduct tests on Hopson's six-inch cannon and completely ignored the inventor for four months.[30]

For his part, Brooke was not convinced of the merits of Hopson's triangular pointed projectiles in artillery pieces. He did a few experiments firing Hopson's artillery projectiles from a small smooth-bore gun and determined that they tumbled in flight. Although Brooke may have had legitimate concerns, Hopson's complaints about Brooke's possible conflicts of interest may well have been justified. Brooke would soon go on to design and produce his own brand of banded and rifled guns. Called "Brooke rifles" in their designer's honor, these guns turned out to be some of the finest guns in the Confederate arsenal.[31]

As Hopson frankly confessed in his pitiful 1862 letter to Jefferson Davis, his personal situation was growing increasingly desperate. He had now been

Commander John Mercer Brooke (1826–1906). NH 58902, US Naval History and Heritage Command.

away from his family in Texas for a year and was nearly destitute. The Ordnance Department had approved some limited stipend for him while the Confederate Army was actively testing his small-arms invention, but once his project shifted to the navy that early support vanished. As his funds dwindled away, the navy continued to ignore him. The old veteran confessed to Davis that he was now "sick and discouraged." Davis forwarded this distressing communication to the secretary of the navy with the notation, "please notice." Whether anyone from the navy ever subsequently noticed Hopson's work is unclear. It is unlikely that Hopson's projectiles and guns ever received the full attention that was due these unique designs.[32]

Some Texans with scientific experience chose to directly contact local military officials with their ideas. One such contributor was Dr. L. H. W. Johnson. Johnson was one of the earliest physicians in Texas, arriving in 1835. He was passionate about science and education. In 1851, he delivered a series of public lectures in Houston covering a wide range of topics extending from chemistry to electricity and natural philosophy. When the war broke out,

Johnson was living in Millican, which at the time was one of the larger cities in the state's interior. During the war, Millican would be a training site for approximately 5,000 Confederate soldiers.[33]

In the fall of 1861, Johnson suggested to Confederate officials in Galveston that they build a series of "submarine batteries" (underwater mines) and locate them strategically in the channels leading to the city. These batteries would consist of containers of gunpowder that would then be connected to the shore using copper wire. To trigger the explosion, a small platinum wire placed in the powder would receive current from a galvanic battery located on shore. The concentration of electricity on the platinum wire would cause it to be "heated to redness which will ignite the powder." If desired, Johnson explained, the galvanic battery used to ignite the explosives could even be located in Houston. Applying the current in Houston, Johnson claimed, would cause an almost immediate explosion in the water off Galveston because "electricity passes unobstructed at the rate of 200,000 miles per second."[34] Confederate officials found Johnson's suggestion intriguing but impractical. Although mines would be deployed at Galveston in 1863, they were never configured to be exploded remotely via an electronic signal from Houston.

One of the oddest stories involving a Texas inventor is that of Phidello William Hall. "Fidella" Hall, as he was called, had the unique distinction of being a Union cavalry officer who obtained a Confederate patent. How did such a strange combination occur? It starts with the inventor's place of origin. Hall was born in 1838 near a settlement that would eventually become Cave City, Kentucky. The town was named for a cave in the town as well as its proximity to Mammoth Cave.[35]

Hall immigrated to Texas and engaged both in farming and various lines of business. He came from a slaveholding but anti-secessionist family. In 1859, he was admitted to the bar in Robertson County by Judge John Gregg. While Gregg would go on to serve as a brigadier general in the Confederate Army, Hall resisted joining his sponsor. Instead, the lawyer turned his hand to inventing.[36]

Phidello William Hall (1838–88). Pictorial Monogram of the State Government of Texas, 1873, by H. B. Hillyer. Texas Photographs, Manuscripts and Imprints, Collection No. Ag2013.0005x, DeGolyer Library, Southern Methodist University.

Hall obtained the very first Confederate patent issued to a Texan, securing Patent No. 8 on August 10, 1861. The patent records describe Hall's claim merely as covering an "automatic breech loading gun."[37] It is unfortunate that Confederate patent records survive in only a fragmented and incomplete state. A more detailed description of the invention in an 1863 Richmond newspaper is more enlightening about the gun's true design and function:

> This invention consists [of] a combination of guns, so arranged that the barrels are secured on a frame parallel with each other, on a line with the centre of a revolving cylinder which forms the breech of the gun, and when revolving receives the loads and caps from the receptacles which contain the powder, balls and caps, each supplied in the proper place, when motion is given to the cylinder by means of a crank and a cam wheel which insures the capping, loading, priming and firing of the guns automatically.[38]

From this description it is apparent that Hall's invention was an early attempt at developing an automatic machine gun. Of course, Hall was not alone in trying to invent a gun that could be fired quickly and automatically. Inventors

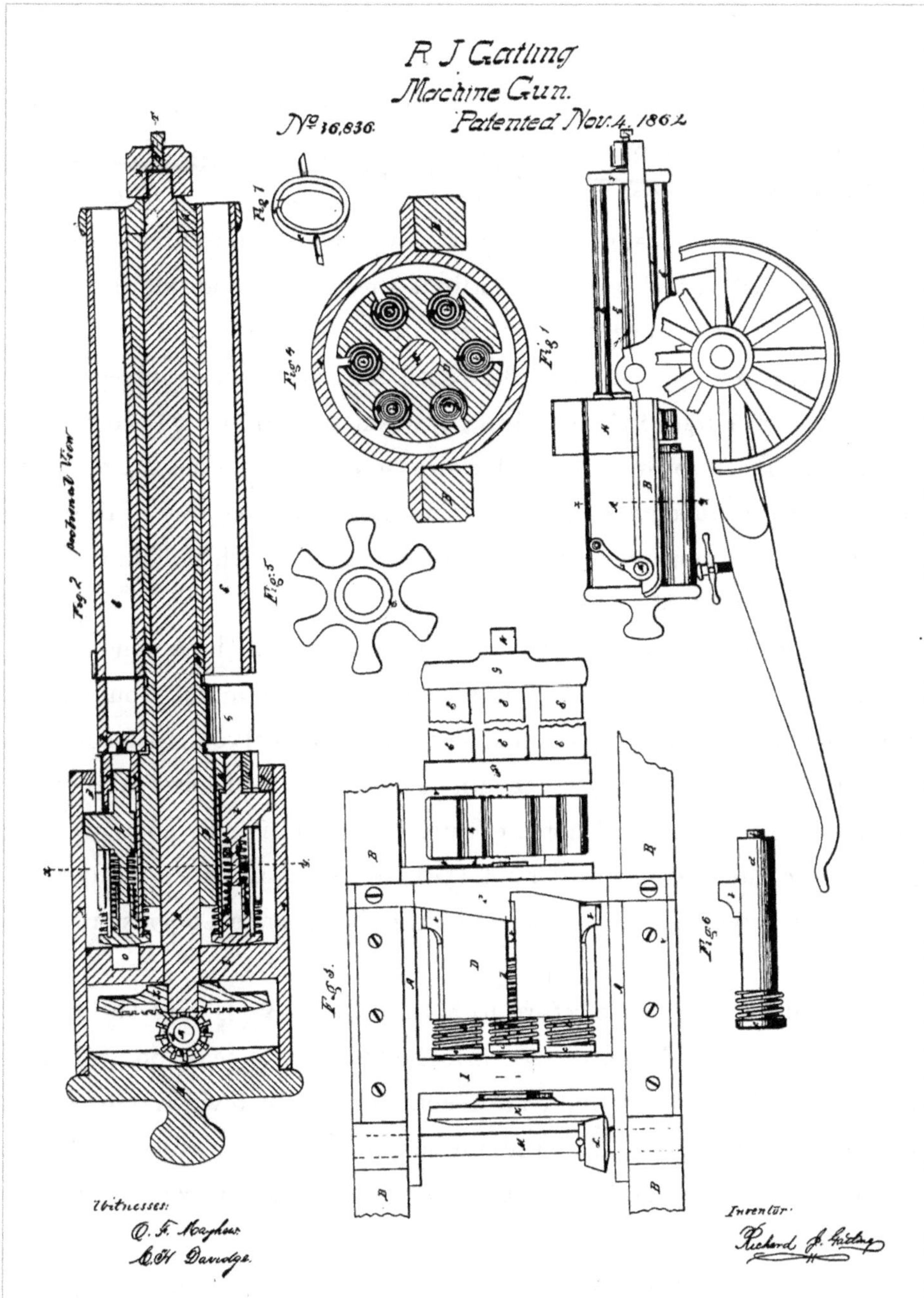

Drawing from US Patent No. 36.836 for machine gun, issued to R. J. Gatling, November 4, 1862. US Patent and Trademark Office, Alexandria, Virginia.

all over the world were busy thinking of clever ways to achieve precisely the same objective.

In November 1862, Richard J. Gatling of Indiana received a US patent for what he called an "improvement in revolving battery guns." The diagram attached to the patent described the weapon as a "machine gun." The "Gatling gun," as his new gun came to be called, consisted of a revolving battery of guns. As described and pictured, Gatling's invention sounds similar to the description of Hall's invention patented in the South the previous year. It is also worth noting that the widely used Maxim machine gun, patented by Englishman Hiram S. Maxim in 1891, was described in a US patent as an "automatic breech loading gun." This is exactly the same description used in Hall's 1861 Confederate patent. It is unknown whether any of the more famous machine gun inventors ever had any contact with Phidello Hall or even knew about his ideas.[39]

By 1863, when Hall's invention was described in the Richmond newspaper (as quoted above), its inventor was no longer present in the Confederacy. Instead, Hall would later explain that he had felt a sudden compulsion to leave Texas in the spring of 1862 "on account of my Union Principles." Apparently his "Union principles" had not prevented him from rapidly applying for a Confederate patent. Principled or not, Hall's move was almost certainly urged along by the conscription act passed by the Confederate Congress in April 1862.[40]

Why did Hall choose to return to his Old Kentucky Home? The answer probably had a lot to do with geography. The Bluegrass State lay on the border between North and South and its residents were deeply divided on the issue of secession. Although the state initially adopted a policy of neutrality, by the time Hall returned in 1862, it had become clear that Kentucky would remain in the Union.

Once he crossed the Kentucky line, Hall resumed work on his revolving gun design in preparation for submitting a US patent application. Hall would later falsely tell Union authorities that he invented his gun only after his move back to Kentucky, concealing the fact that he already held an 1861 Confederate patent for the identical weapon. Instead, Hall told Union authorities in an 1864 affidavit that while he was in Louisville, he "invented an Automatic Battery, which was examined by Major General [Ambrose] Burnside and others and favorably commended by them." The model of this battery, he assured them, was now awaiting a patent in Washington, DC. As it turned out, Hall would never secure a US patent for his invention, possibly because of the intervening Gatling patent.[41]

In September 1863, Hall was authorized to recruit a company of cavalry for the Eleventh Kentucky (US) Regiment. He was commissioned first lieutenant of Company L but never served in combat in any capacity. In March 1864, he reported to Union authorities that he had "never been engaged in any battles or skirmishes." Hall would eventually be dismissed from Union service in 1865 due to a variety of medical issues.[42]

As Phidello Hall proved by submitting his gun invention directly to the Confederate patent office, not every innovation was submitted to Jefferson Davis or state officials. Instead, some ideas went through far more indirect channels. To illustrate this point, consider the case of John G. Gooch, a successful businessman in Palestine, Texas. He advertised his business before the war as offering a variety of "Law, Collection & Exchange" services.[43] According to a Dallas newspaper, Gooch was "one of the best lawyers, and one of the most reliable businessmen, to be found in the State."[44] The multitalented Gooch was civic minded and is credited with organizing both the first Sunday school and the first public library in Palestine.[45]

Gooch's Sunday school connection probably helps explain a one-page letter he wrote on company stationery dated December 14, 1861. The letter was addressed to Confederate Major General Leonidas Polk, who was at that time involved in a critical campaign in Kentucky. Gooch addressed the letter to Polk at his headquarters in Columbus, Kentucky. Columbus was a small town, but it had a strategic location on the western edge of the state, less than a mile from the Mississippi River. Why did Gooch send his suggestion to a general in Kentucky? The answer almost certainly lies in Gooch's church connections. Before the war, Polk had served as a prominent Episcopal bishop and had visited Texas on multiple occasions in that capacity. It is likely that Gooch met Polk on one of these visits.[46]

Gooch wrote Polk, popularly known as "the Fighting Bishop," to recommend what he believed would be an effective defense against the enemy's "Lincoln Gun Boats." The first thing Gooch recommended was that Polk stretch a chain or group of chains across the Mississippi River to obstruct enemy vessels. Then, at the same location, the Confederates should sink "submarine batteries on wires attached to cans of powder." The chains at the surface, Gooch explained,

Portrait of General Leonidas Polk, officer of the Confederate Army. Brady's National Photographic Portrait Galleries, LC-DIG-cwpb-06714, Library of Congress.

were basically a diversion. While the enemy was occupied trying to cut the chains, "the electric spark would be transmitted to the powder," causing an explosion that would destroy everyone and everything in the vicinity.[47]

Gooch did not know it, but General Polk was already thinking along similar, and decidedly unholy, lines. On October 10, 1861, the "Fighting Bishop" wrote the secretary of war and requested the services "of an officer familiar with the subject of submarine batteries and capable of a practical application of this species of defense to the Mississippi River."[48] Although Polk requested the services of Matthew Fontaine Maury, with whom he had been corresponding about the subject of underwater explosives, Maury was unavailable. Instead, the navy sent Lieutenant Isaac N. Brown, an experienced naval officer who conveniently had been born in Kentucky and knew the area well.[49]

Brown met with Polk and decided that mines located on the river's banks would be more successful than trying to submerge torpedoes in the Mississippi River. In December 1861, about the same time that Gooch wrote

"Finding Infernal Machines in Fort Columbus, Ky." *Harper's Weekly*, March 29, 1862. Image NH 59015, US Naval History and Heritage Command.

his letter, Brown picked a location along the main road leading to Columbus and buried iron canisters filled with explosives. This is generally considered to be one of the first deployment of land mines in American history. Although the plan was to detonate the mines electronically, Union soldiers discovered and disabled them before they could explode.[50]

Although General Polk had obviously been thinking about deploying torpedoes long before receiving Gooch's letter, it may have influenced the manner in which Polk eventually installed them. By January 1862, a month after receiving Gooch's letter, the Fighting Bishop followed the Texan's suggestion and installed a chain across the river, and then he attached torpedoes to it. Not only did he follow Gooch's suggested plan, but he even used similar language in describing the work to his wife. "I am paving the bottom of the river with submarine batteries, to say nothing of a heavy chain across the river," he wrote, claiming that this would take care of what he and Gooch both called "Mr. Lincoln's gunboats." In the end, the chain and torpedoes did not make any difference. General U. S. Grant's army outflanked Polk's position at Columbus, and the Confederates withdrew by March 1862.[51]

Although Gooch's idea was creative, it did not really involve any new invention. There were others, however, who were eagerly seeking to take that next step. One of the more successful early Texas inventors was Caleb Van Ausdol Littlepage, the Austin resident whose waterwheel invention had dominated the front page of *Scientific American* before the war. As the war heated up, Littlepage quickly turned his attention to producing something with immediate defense applications. Before long, he had designed a bullet-making machine. Attached to a steam engine, the machine was theoretically capable of turning out up to sixty bullets per minute. He received Confederate Patent No. 79 for his invention on March 11, 1862. With his patent in hand, Littlepage obtained a contract from the Ordnance Department in Richmond, Virginia, to produce five bullet-making machines. According to his contract, when he delivered the first machine in San Antonio, Littlepage was to receive $3,000. He was then to receive $2,500 for delivering each of the remaining

C. V. Littlepage (1826–76). AR-2016–007, Caleb V. Littlepage Papers, Austin History Center, Austin Public Library, Austin, Texas.

four machines. By August, Littlepage had delivered his first machine and the chief ordnance officer in San Antonio pronounced himself satisfied.[52]

Littlepage was not the only Texan with important and productive ideas. Indeed, Texans may well have had more patented inventions per capita than any other Confederate state. Not all the inventors were in the Austin area, although that small city (the 1860 population was only 3,494) produced more Confederate patents than any other Texas city. Inventions were patented by residents in towns as diverse as Seguin, Henderson, and Lavaca. Surprisingly, larger and more familiar cities like Houston, Galveston, and Dallas produced relatively few patent awards.[53]

Not all of the patented inventions involved new and more effective ways to kill the enemy. Even during wartime, there were many inventions that had no military application whatsoever. In 1863, O. L. Bailey, the man who would later design the Dallas city seal, obtained a Confederate patent for a "gang plough," a plow designed to turn two or more furrows at the same time. In one productive week, John Hollander of Sutherland was awarded two separate patents. One was for his formula for "toilet soap composition." The other was for his "compound for expelling cattle worms." Although a war was raging, people on the home front still needed to find better ways to keep clean, grow crops, and keep their livestock healthy.[54]

CHAPTER 3

THE CAPTAIN NEMO OF TEXAS

In 1870, Jules Verne published his famous novel *Twenty Thousand Leagues Under the Sea*, which featured a visionary character named Captain Nemo and his futuristic submarine, the *Nautilus*. Nemo and his submarine were so popular that they appeared again in *The Mysterious Island* (1875). Given the times in which he wrote, it is not surprising that Verne was fascinated by the American Civil War. Verne's writings are filled with references to that war. *Mysterious Island* begins with a dramatic escape by five men from a Confederate prison in Richmond, Virginia. In 1871, he wrote a novel titled *The Blockade Runners*, and in 1887 he wrote a novella titled *North Against South*.[55]

Some Verne biographers believe that the wholesale destruction of commercial vessels by Nemo and *Nautilus* in *Twenty Thousand Leagues* is a deliberate literary reference to the Civil War commerce raids (just over twenty thousand leagues in distance) launched around the world by Captain Raphael Semmes and his famous cruiser, CSS *Alabama*. The context of the reference is reversed, however, since Semmes was a staunch Confederate while Verne's story tells readers that Nemo's cabin on *Nautilus* displayed portraits of both Abraham Lincoln and Frederick Douglass. Other references to the famous Confederate commerce raider in Verne's works are even more direct. CSS *Alabama* was constructed at Laird's Shipyard in Birkenhead, England, on the Mersey River opposite Liverpool. Verne says that the iron hull plates for *Nautilus* were made at "Laird's of Liverpool." This was no idle reference. Verne had personally visited that famous shipyard in 1859 and again in 1867.[56]

Although Verne's novels never featured a Texas visit by *Nautilus*, CSS *Alabama* did make a short but impactful visit to Texas waters. On January 11, 1863,

Alabama appeared off Galveston and after a short battle sank USS *Hatteras*.[57] To some Texans, this sinking proved that with the right mix of technology and stealth, Texas warships could be successful. In fact, some Texas inventors had believed in that possibility all along.

With the coming of the Civil War in 1861 it became evident to many Texans that it was just a matter of time before US Navy gunboats appeared in force and attempted to force their way into strategic waterways like Galveston Bay. General Paul O. Hébert, who was in command of the Confederate defenses of Texas, shared this concern. He did not believe that Galveston could be successfully defended. In fact, he was so anxious about the island's vulnerability that upon assuming command, he almost immediately began building a fort on the mainland and prepared to abandon Galveston to the enemy without much of a fight.[58]

Needless to say, abandoning the largest city in Texas to the enemy without a fight did not sound like a good plan to many of the state's inhabitants. Some Texans decided to devote their efforts to develop alternative strategies that might enable the state to even the odds and counter the expected influx of powerful Union warships. One of the most creative people to tackle this problem was an imported Texan named Robert Creuzbaur.

If Texas ever produced an equivalent to Captain Nemo, it was Robert Creuzbaur. Like many of the people discussed in this book, Creuzbaur did not start life out as a Texan. Creuzbaur had been born in Karlsruhe, Germany, in 1823. Located near the French border, Karlsruhe had a long history as a major science and technology hub. Creuzbaur studied engineering and technical drafting in the old country as a young man but, like many young Germans, had not completed his studies before immigrating to America with his family. He arrived in America in 1842 at about the age of nineteen.[59]

Robert Creuzbaur's family background was not the usual story for settlers to Texas. His father, Karl Friedrich Creuzbauer, had been a captain of artillery who served Napoleon with distinction in the disastrous Russian campaign.

His mother was the former Baroness Caroline von Hornig of Austria, whose family estates were confiscated during the series of conflicts following the War of the Austrian Succession (1740–48). His parents were full of interesting anecdotes but empty of wealth. The Creuzbauer family first settled in St. Louis, where Robert completed his training as an engineer.[60]

In 1846, twenty-three-year-old Robert Creuzbaur decided to make two important changes. The first was to change the spelling of his last name to delete the second "e." The second was to pack up and move to Austin, Texas, where he took a position as cartographer for the General Land Office. Creuzbaur quickly exhibited a natural talent for researching geography and generating high-quality maps. He became one of the most accomplished cartographers in Texas history; some of his maps still hang on walls today as pieces of art. His fame started in 1849, when he prepared a map of Texas for land promoter Jacob De Cordova. The resulting map, the first official map of the state of Texas, was a tremendous success. Sam Houston, who signed the map, called it "invaluable" and recommended it to "every person who desires correct geographical information of our state." The De Cordova map, recently named one of the six "landmark maps of Texas," is now extremely rare, and authentic originals seldom come up for sale. When one came up for auction in 2015, bidding closed at $149,000.[61]

Creuzbaur followed up his Texas map with a project that combined a more extensive map of the Southwest with a narrative based on notes compiled by legendary Texas Ranger and future Confederate cavalry commander John S. "Rip" Ford. This map showed sufficient route details, including the distance between water holes, to enable pioneer settlers to travel safely all the way from Texas through Paseo del Norte to California. It was included in a famous 1849 book titled *Creuzbaur's Guide to California and the Pacific Ocean*, which quickly became an essential resource for the "forty-niners" who were flocking overland to seek fame and fortune in California. Creuzbaur followed these maps up with an 1853 plan of Austin that remains one of the city's best early maps.

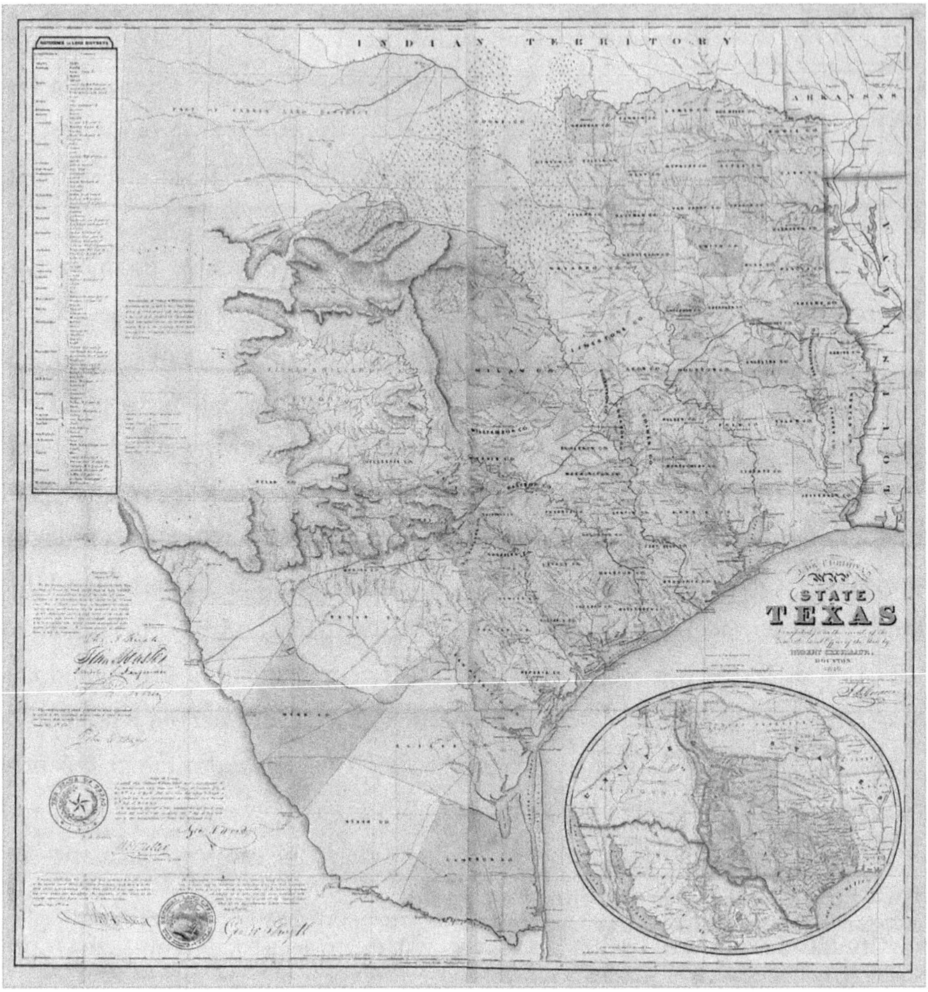

Above and opposite: Jacob De Cordova's map of Texas (1849) with detail of Robert Creuzbaur's name. Map #94026. Texas General Land Office.

In 1857, Creuzbaur also created maps of lands surveyed for the benefit of state asylums. The Texas General Land Office records contain so many famous early maps drawn by Robert Creuzbaur that they are too extensive to list. Creuzbaur's name is literally stamped on the early history of Texas.[62]

In the late 1850s, Creuzbaur decided to show the world that he was more than just a talented mapmaker. He began using his skills as an engineer, and

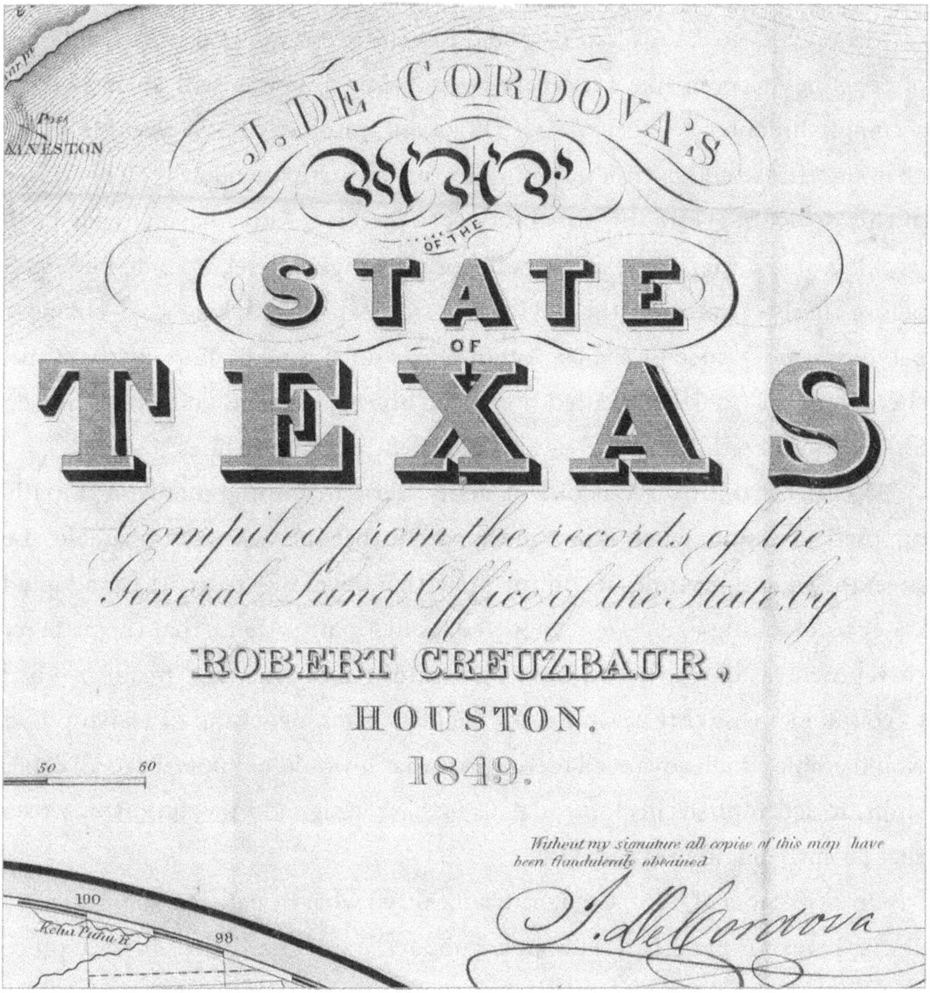

his extraordinary drafting ability, to come up with designs for revolutionary new inventions that could be patented. One thing that seems to have greatly assisted his progress in this regard was the presence of his friend and colleague Caleb V. Littlepage in the community. Together, these two Austin engineers must have debated the merits of their ideas for hours and fine-tuned their respective inventions. This friendship proved fruitful and would in time lead to their collaboration on a number of important technical papers and letters that were published in prestigious journals.[63]

Although Creuzbaur's first patented invention did not make the front page of *Scientific American* like Littlepage's water wheel, it was still an important accomplishment. Creuzbaur's first US patent, number 32,595, was for an air chamber that would permit pumping air into an airtight container. The nature of this device suggests the possibility that Creuzbaur may have already been working on a design for a submersible or watertight vessel of some kind well before the beginning of the Civil War. Ironically, Creuzbaur's air chamber patent was not issued by the US Patent Office until June 18, 1861. By that time, the Texas that Creuzbaur called home had already seceded and Creuzbaur no longer considered himself to be a resident of the United States.[64]

Although Creuzbaur was one of many German immigrants who initially opposed secession, when it became apparent that the war was inevitable, the inventor wasted no time in coming up with a novel way to assist his adopted state in defending itself. He recognized, as did many others, that the primary threat to Texas lay in the US Navy's powerful gunboats. What Texans needed to counteract this threat, Creuzbaur decided, was a new kind of warship that would employ such advanced technology that it would be superior to all other ships. To accomplish this lofty goal, Creuzbaur designed a revolutionary vessel that he aptly named *Sea King*.[65]

On November 11, 1861, Creuzbaur submitted what he called a "memorial" to Texas Governor Francis R. Lubbock. Lubbock was so newly installed in office that the memorial remains misfiled to this day in the papers of Sam Houston, the then recently deposed former governor. The memorial informed Lubbock that Creuzbaur had invented "a cheap and most effective substitute for a war navy to be placed at the service of the Confederate Government."[66]

Inviting Lubbock to appoint a committee of "scientific men" to examine the technical merits of his proposal, Creuzbaur suggested that if that committee's examination was favorable, the state should then take steps to support adoption of the inventor's plan by the Confederate government. Never short of confidence, Creuzbaur declared that "an early application of this plan would have the effect of a corresponding early close of the war." Creuzbaur signed

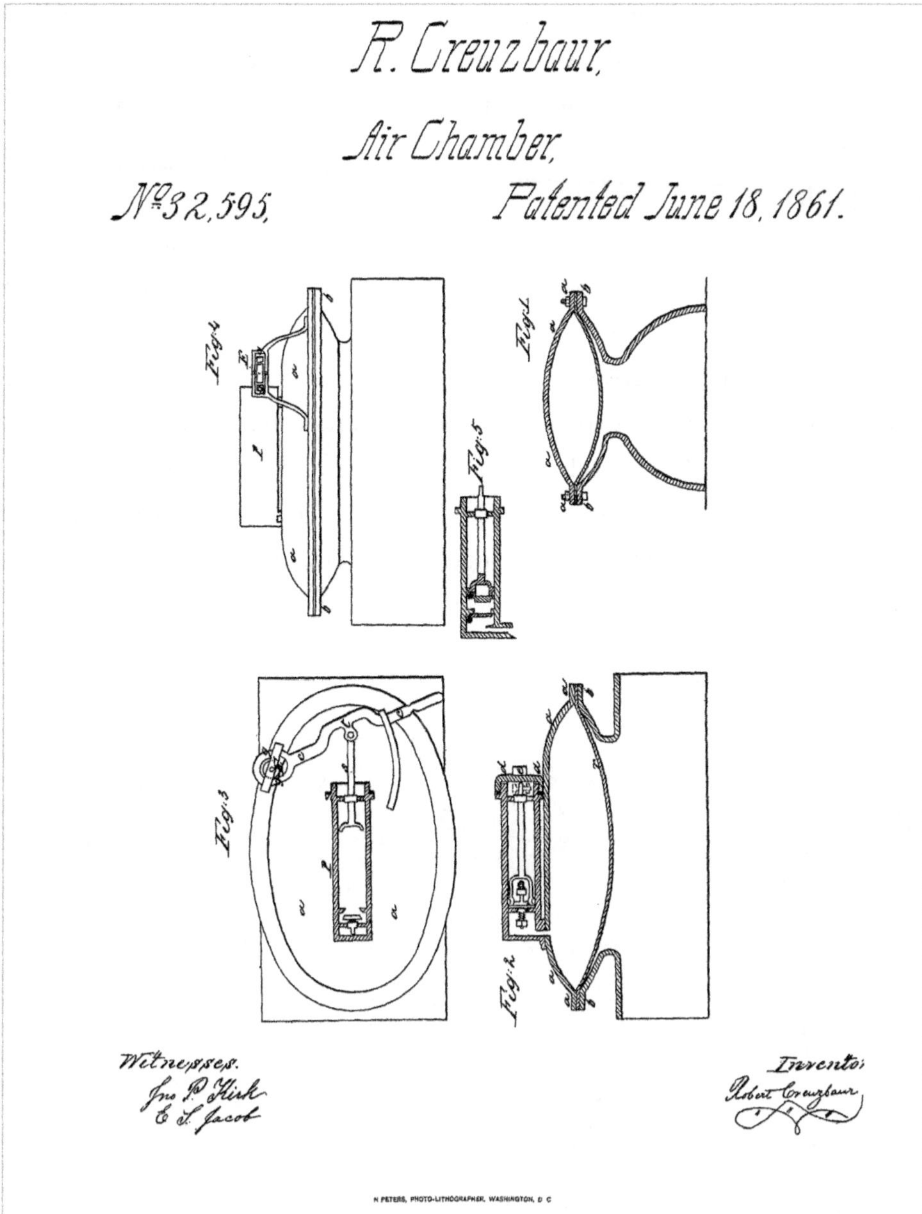

Drawing from Robert Creuzbaur's US Patent No. 32,595, for an air chamber, June 18, 1861. US Patent and Trademark Office, Alexandria, Virginia.

the memorial with his characteristic bold and elaborate signature and waited for a response. As it turned out, he would not have long to wait.[67]

What made Creuzbaur able to credibly assert that his invention could possibly serve as a substitute for an entire navy? To say that Creuzbaur's *Sea King* design was imaginative is to understate its long list of remarkable innovations. *Sea King* was designed to be a long cigar-shaped vessel with bow and stern propellers and a hot air (not steam) engine. It would have minimal exposure above the waterline and its hull would consist of a unique flexible structure of wood and cotton supporting an outer layer of iron plates. The armored plates were to be angled in such a fashion that they would deflect enemy projectiles. The vessel was to have three primary weapons systems: a breech-loading cannon mounted in a casemate on deck, an underwater cannon capable of firing shells through the water at an enemy vessel, and a mysterious "third mode of destruction" that prudence prevented Creuzbaur from describing in his memorial.[68]

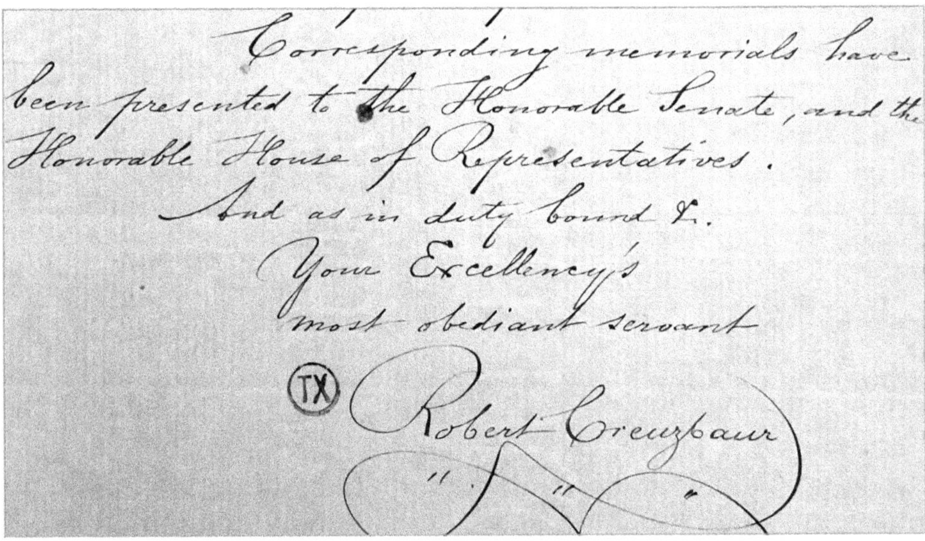
Corresponding memorials have been presented to the Honorable Senate, and the Honorable House of Representatives.
And as in duty bound &c.
Your Excellency's
most obediant servant
Robert Creuzbaur

Signature block from Robert Creuzbaur memorial, November 11, 1861. Texas Governor Sam Houston Papers, Texas State Library and Archives Commission.

Based on subsequent descriptions it seems likely that this third mode was what Creuzbaur would later call a "submarine battery" or a "torpedo cannon." This weapon was designed to send an explosive projectile that would either attach itself or get close to the hull of an enemy vessel and then explode.[69]

Creuzbaur's prominent position at the land office in Austin gave him not only credibility but also easy access to the new Confederate state government officials. He and his attorney had no difficulty convincing the new governor and key legislators to review his remarkable design. Everyone who examined his *Sea King* design was intrigued. They loved the concept of a single shot-proof vessel that, at least on paper, could potentially destroy an entire enemy fleet. Creuzbaur's project was immediately put on the fast track for approval. On the day after he received Creuzbaur's memorial, Governor Lubbock appointed a committee of three experts to review Creuzbaur's design and requested that they make an expedited report on its "usefulness and practical importance."[70]

On November 22, 1861, a mere ten days after its formation, the committee of experts issued a report containing favorable statements from each of the three committee members. In fact, it is hard to imagine a stronger set of endorsements. James Brown, one of the most prestigious engineers on the committee, said that in his judgment, *Sea King* had the potential to "destroy in a short time the whole naval power of our enemies."[71]

Governor Lubbock was delighted by the committee's unanimous support for the *Sea King* project. Forwarding the three statements to the legislature, he observed that, "It is very evident that the North is now relying on the superiority of its navy to subdue the South; we must therefore take some steps to combat the enemy on the ocean."[72] With the governor and key members of the legislature now firmly on board, an appropriation of $500 was soon authorized to fund Creuzbaur's travel expenses to Richmond to present his ideas to Confederate military officials. If all went well, the lawmakers dreamed, Texas might have the distinction of contributing the design for the project that singlehandedly won independence for the Confederacy.[73]

Creuzbaur was a talented engineer, but he knew that to promote his novel design in an unknown political environment he would need a skillful and experienced advocate. For this task, he chose attorney Ebenezer C. Allen. Because of his background and connections, Allen was a good choice. Born in Newport, New Hampshire, in 1804, Allen was a graduate of Dartmouth College. He studied law with a local lawyer and was admitted to the bar in Maine. After a number of years in private practice, the economic chaos of the Panic of 1837 encouraged Allen to relocate to Texas, a more financially promising location, which he did in 1840.[74]

At that time, Texas was still an independent republic. But continued threats from Mexico left its ultimate fate uncertain, and many residents believed Texas needed to join the United States to permanently escape this challenge. By 1844, Texas President Sam Houston had made Allen his attorney general. Soon after, under Anson Jones, the last president of the republic, Allen became both the attorney general and the secretary of state. Although Allen

Image 18: Matthew Fontaine Maury, USN (1806–73). LC-H261–7706, Harris & Ewing Collection, Prints and Photographs Division, Library of Congress.

personally opposed annexation to the United States, Texans voted strongly in favor of the union in 1845.[75]

The sixteen-year period between the date when Texas achieved statehood and the outbreak of the Civil War was not kind to Allen's personal fortunes. Although he was selected to be attorney general for the state in 1850 and was involved with the growing railroad network in Texas, by 1860, Allen found himself working as a lawyer in Galveston with a mountain of debt and very little net worth.[76]

When Allen saw Creuzbaur's design for *Sea King* in 1861, he was immediately impressed. He had never seen anything like it before and believed that no one else had either. He sensed that this opportunity could be something really big. He was confident that in the hands of a professional advocate (such as himself), it would be easy to sell his client's design to the new leaders of the Confederacy. He lost no time in going to Austin and assisting Creuzbaur in convincing the governor and legislature to appropriate funds for the inventor to travel to Richmond and present his design.

In Richmond, Creuzbaur conducted tests of his proposed "submarine cannon" under the watchful supervision of Commander Matthew Fontaine Maury of the Confederate Navy. Nicknamed the "Pathfinder of the Seas," Maury was a pioneer hydrographer and a highly respected former US naval officer. He is often credited with being one of the founders of the emerging science of oceanography. Maury had conducted his own experiments with torpedoes and was particularly interested in testing Creuzbaur's claim that he had found an effective way to launch exploding projectiles underwater.[77]

Starting in early May 1862, Creuzbaur began purchasing materials and putting together a working model of what Maury variously described as a "submarine battery" or "submarine cannon." As reflected in the large number of invoices Maury approved, Creuzbaur purchased items like copper cones, wire, caps, and priming tubes, as well as a large number of wooden frames. The frames were designed to hold wooden panels of varying thicknesses. These frames would serve as targets that simulated the hulls of enemy ships.[78]

Maury's tests involved firing Creuzbaur's model underwater cannon repeatedly at targets positioned at various distances and angles to determine the extent to which the projectiles penetrated the wooden surface. To keep them steady, the framed targets were mounted on the sides of a barge borrowed from the canal company. Each morning, Maury and Creuzbaur would board CSS *Teaser*, a tugboat, which would tow the targets and barge out from Rocketts Landing and Wharf in Richmond to a place where the test firings could safely be conducted. By their conclusion, the tests were successful enough that the navy had to pay for extensive repairs to the barge because it had been damaged during the experiments. Encouraged by these results, Allen and Creuzbaur decided to rename the proposed vessel *Avenger*.[79]

Allen later summarized the results of Maury's tests for the Confederate Naval Affairs Committee, noting that "at a distance of several feet, the effect of the submarine shot was such as to penetrate through the timbers of ordinary ships of war." Allen noted that even if the penetration was only slight, firing explosive shells would result in larger explosions that would then complete the damage to the enemy's hull. Finally, even if skeptics were correct that a submerged cannon had limited range, Allen argued that Creuzbaur's unique design called for the vessel to use its "third mode" system to deliver torpedoes as projectiles. These torpedoes were designed to exit through a tube and then penetrate or attach to an enemy vessel's hull, where they would subsequently explode.[80]

Creuzbaur was so encouraged by Maury's test results that he began preparing more elaborate scale drawings of *Avenger* to present to Confederate officials, While Creuzbaur was in the process of preparing these drawings, he came across a letter that resonated strongly with his ship-building instincts. Commander Thomas Edward Symonds, the son of a famous British admiral, wrote a letter to the *Times* of London on April 10, 1862, titled "Maneuvering Steam Rams and Iron-cased Ships." In his letter, Symonds complained that not one of the British fleet's screw steamers could be easily maneuvered from side to side, particularly in the type of slow-action military engagement that seemed now likely to occur between large, heavily armored ships. Symonds was convinced that if an armored vessel could be designed that could turn in its own length, that warship would have a decided advantage in virtually every potential military encounter.[81]

Symonds pointed out that the American Civil War then in progress showed that ramming might be coming back into favor as a part of naval warfare strategy. If so, "rapidity and certainty of maneuvering will be of still greater importance in these ocean tournaments; for a ram or, indeed, any other armour-plated ship possessing that quality may often avoid the blow of an adversary, or instead of receiving it at right angles (the only point at which it would be really effective), might be so turned on the instant as to receive it in an oblique or glancing direction, which would in a great measure, if not entirely, neutralize its effect, and, having thus diverted it, might turn on the passing ship and deliver a broadside into her stern, that would at such a distance stand a fair chance of crippling her screw and rudder (if not protected), or, at all events, doing her serious injury."[82]

Symonds's letter was music to Creuzbaur's ears, and he kept a copy in his files to show to potential backers. His *Avenger* was designed to be the most maneuverable ironclad of the Civil War era. In fact, it might well have been the most maneuverable boat of any description. To illustrate this point, in July 1862, Creuzbaur made some detailed drawings of what he expected *Avenger* to look like when completed. These were undoubtedly part of a sales effort to persuade the Confederate government to take the final step and commit to invest in the project. Although partially damaged, Creuzbaur's drawings have survived to provide a remarkable record of the inventor's vision.

Through the courtesy of the Wiggins family, and with the assistance of my colleague Neil P. Chatelain, who was first to publish many of them, copies of a number of Creuzbaur's drawings are included in this book.[83] From these drawings it is possible to take the reader on a brief tour of what *Avenger* would have looked like and explain how it might have operated if it had been successfully constructed according to Creuzbaur's plans.

Starting with the bow, the feature that made *Avenger* one of the most unique vessels designed during the Civil War was the horizontal propeller near the bow. To give an idea just how revolutionary this was, the first US patents for a "lateral thruster unit for marine vessels," a propulsion system employing a peripherally driven propeller, was not granted until 2010.[84]

Creuzbaur's bow propeller, depicted almost 150 years before the 2010 patent, would have enabled *Avenger* to present as slim a target as its operator wished while approaching an enemy ship and then, upon reaching the desired range, to maneuver so that its weapon systems were immediately aimed at the enemy's most vulnerable points (such as the stern, paddlewheels, and propellers). Creuzbaur knew that his bow propeller was unusual and that many would wonder how it could possibly be made to function. He therefore made a separate drawing showing the machinery that operated this propeller.

Moving back toward the center of the vessel, Creuzbaur provided a side and top view that conveniently has the vessel's name emblazoned on it. The center portion includes an oval casemate that projects above the deck. The detail shows a circular arched structure (m) at the front, which would provide

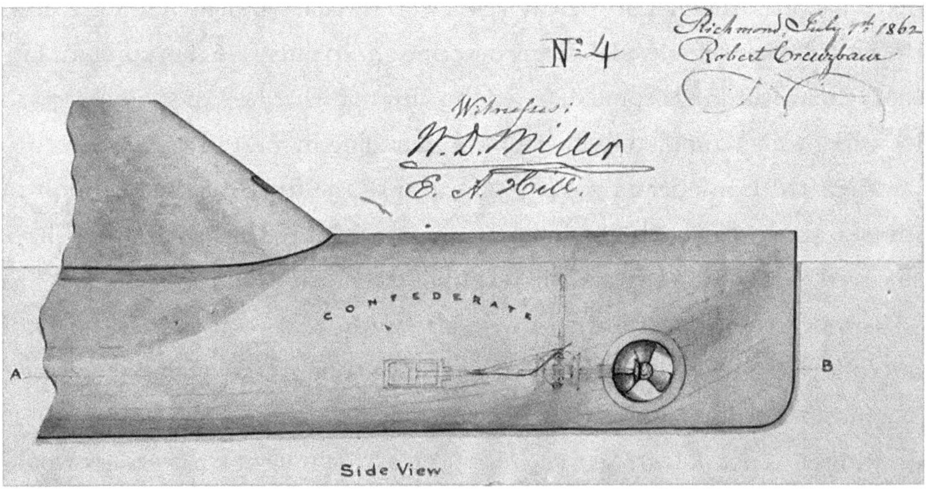

Robert Creuzbaur's drawing of *Avenger*, side-view showing bow propeller, Richmond, Virginia, July 1862. Courtesy of the Wiggins Family.

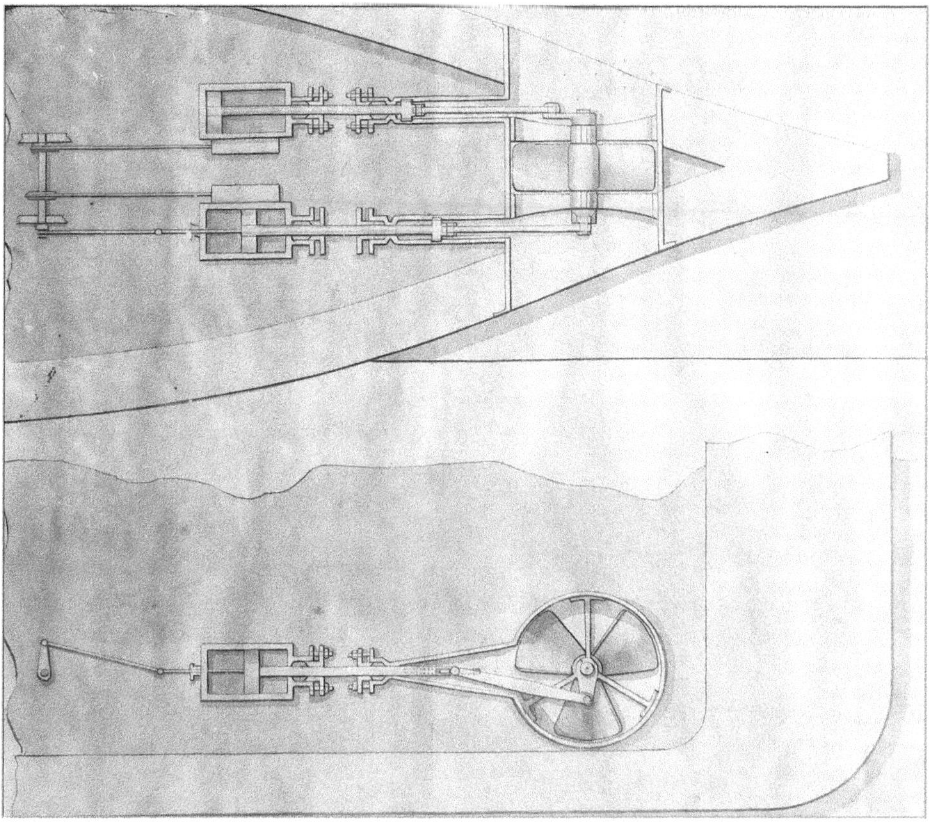

Robert Creuzbaur's drawing of *Avenger*, top and side-view showing bow propeller machinery, Richmond, Virginia, July 1862. Courtesy of the Wiggins Family.

a protected observation area or pilot house that presumably could by used by either the pilot or gunner. *Avenger* had a front-facing breech-loading gun (g) that is depicted in its retracted loading position. The fact that the gun is positioned to face only forward is not as big a disadvantage as it might first seem. This gun could be easily maneuvered to point in any direction with the aid of the nearby bow propeller. The stern of the vessel featured a propeller and twin rudders.

A figure inside the rear of the casemate is shown using a series of mirrors that functioned as a periscope. Like the bow propeller, this was cutting-edge technology. Although periscopes for naval military uses had been invented

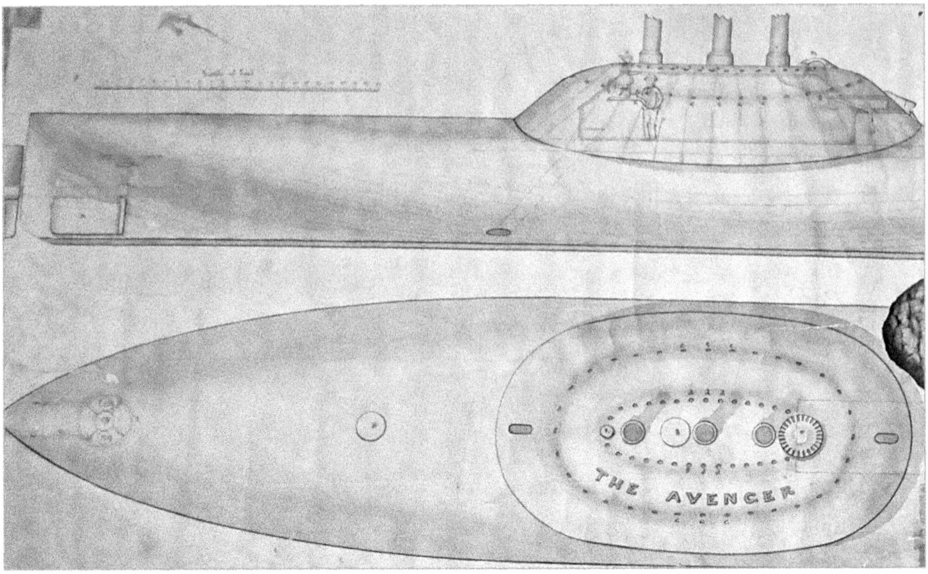

Robert Creuzbaur's drawing of *Avenger*, side and top view, showing operator and submarine battery tube, Richmond, Virginia, July 1862. Courtesy of the Wiggins Family.

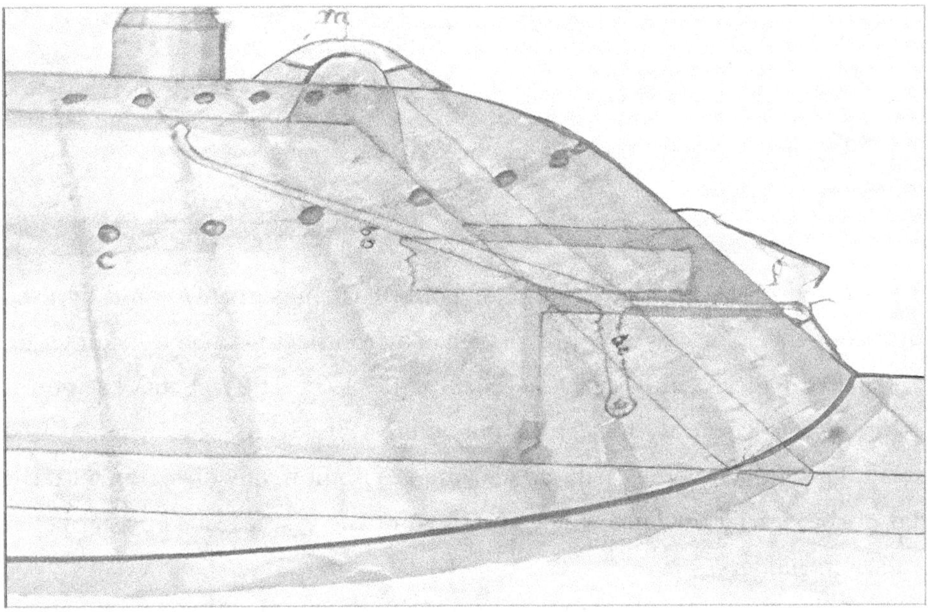

Detail from Robert Creuzbaur's drawing of *Avenger*, side view, showing pilot house (m) at top and retracted breech-loading gun (g), Richmond, Virginia, July 1862. Courtesy of the Wiggins Family.

by French scientist Hippolyte Marié-Davy in 1854, they would not be used in combat until a Louisiana battle in 1864, two years after Creuzbaur's drawings.[85] The figure using levers to manipulate the periscope is depicted next to a long tube extending to the left and out of the bottom of the hull. As will be explained shortly, this is the torpedo or "submarine battery" tube.

We now come to *Avenger*'s three weapons systems. In addition to the breech-loading gun shown in retracted position on top, the other two weapons that are depicted are the underwater cannon and the torpedo cannon. As its name implies, the underwater cannon fired a projectile below the waterline from a gun projecting horizontally through *Avenger*'s hull. This was the gun that Maury had tested with the barge targets at Richmond. Creuzbaur drew two drawings depicting these weapon systems. His cross-section drawing shows an underwater puff of smoke as the gun is fired and then shows the fired projectile partially penetrating the enemy's hull.

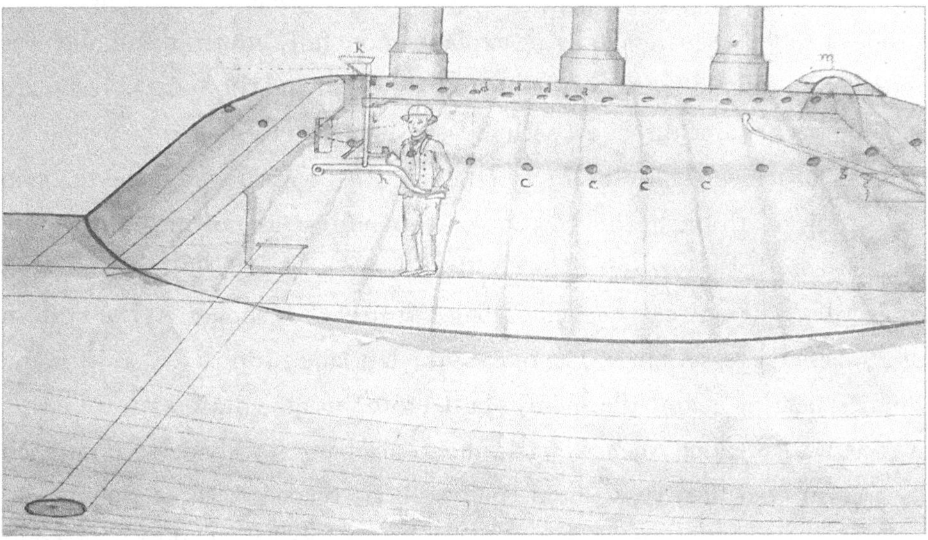

Detail from Robert Creuzbaur's side-view drawing of *Avenger*, showing periscope operator at left and submarine battery tube, Richmond, Virginia, July 1862. Courtesy of the Wiggins Family.

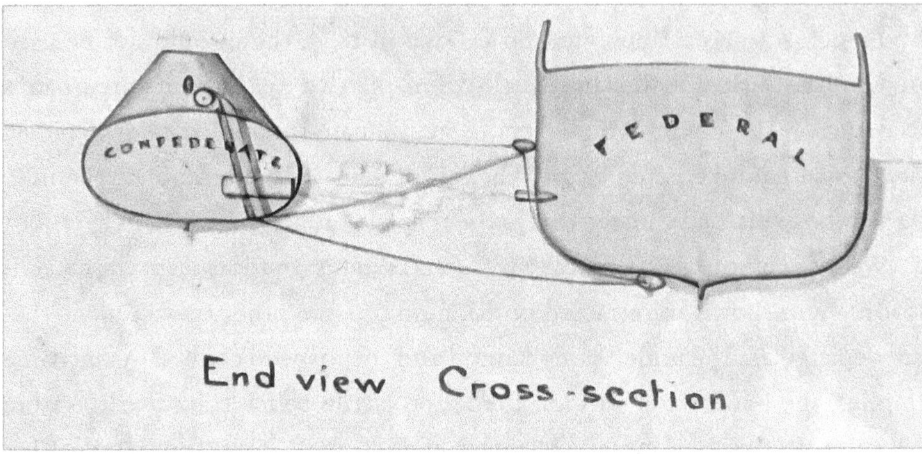

Robert Creuzbaur's end view and cross-section drawing, showing underwater cannon and submarine battery attack, Richmond, Virginia, July 1862. Courtesy of the Wiggins Family.

The torpedo cannon or "submarine battery" is more difficult to explain. Creuzbaur's cross section depicts two objects that have come out of *Avenger*'s lower submarine torpedo tube. The first is shown near the Federal ship's keel. The second is shown floating at the surface. The two objects are connected by a rope or cable. A separate drawing explains more fully how this assembly was intended to function. Arrows establish that *Avenger* and the Federal vessel are moving in the same direction with *Avenger* slightly in front.

Creuzbaur depicts the oval-shaped casemate, beneath which the torpedo tube projects through the bottom of the hull at an angle. Using some mechanism that Creuzbaur does not depict, *Avenger* has fired two connected projectiles. The one on the right, labeled "battery," is shown on the bottom of the Federal vessel's hull. The one on the left labeled "float," is, as its name implies, floating next to the enemy's hull. From this drawing it is apparent that *Avenger* was intended to employ its tube to discharge a torpedo accompanied by a connected float that would then pull the torpedo against the bottom of the enemy's hull as it surfaced. Whether this torpedo would be rigged to explode by hull contact or through some unexplained clockwork mechanism is uncertain.

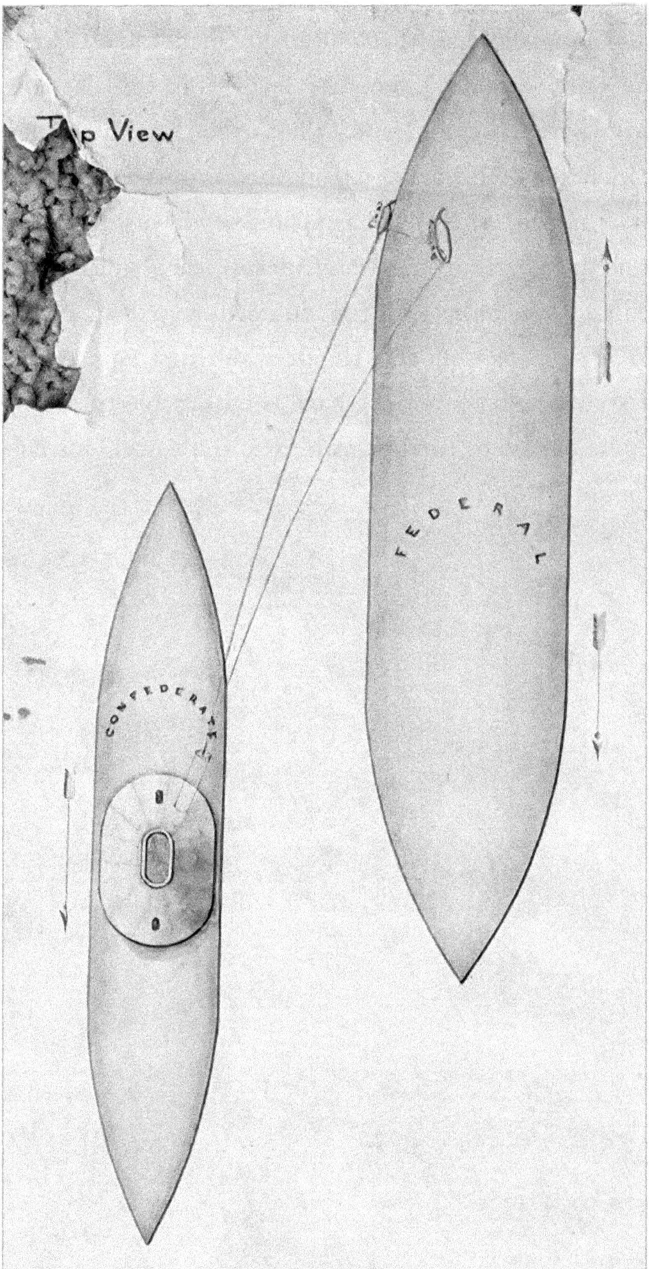

Robert Creuzbaur's drawing of top views of *Avenger* (Confederate) and Federal vessels, showing submarine battery attack, Richmond, Virginia, July 1862. Courtesy of the Wiggins Family.

The most detailed surviving drawing that Creuzbaur made of *Avenger* is a cross-section view. There are so many interesting features in this drawing that it is difficult to know where to begin. In order not to confuse the reader, this explanation will include Creuzbaur's unmodified original drawing followed by that same drawing with the author's explanatory labels. It should be noted initially that the drawing has two waterlines on each side, which are unfortunately difficult to see, indicating that the ordinary draft of the vessel was anticipated to be eight feet but that the draft during a fight would be nine feet. This suggests that *Avenger* might have been capable of taking on water or other weight as ballast to further minimize the vessel's surface area during combat.

Robert Creuzbaur's drawing of cross section of *Avenger*, Richmond, Virginia, July 1862. Courtesy of the Wiggins Family.

As the reader can see from these drawings, it is difficult to point to the most revolutionary element of *Avenger*'s design. Of course, the underwater cannon and submarine battery were absolutely unique for the time. The use of a periscope was also a major difference from conventional warships. Although not depicted in detail, the hot air engine that powered *Avenger* would also have been something that no other vessel of the period possessed.

One of the most innovative but easiest to overlook parts of the design was the bow thruster propeller, which would have enabled an incredible range of motion. It is no wonder that everyone who examined Creuzbaur's drawings found themselves captivated by his vision. As Jules Verne described Captain Nemo's *Nautilus*, if *Avenger* had been successfully completed and operated as its

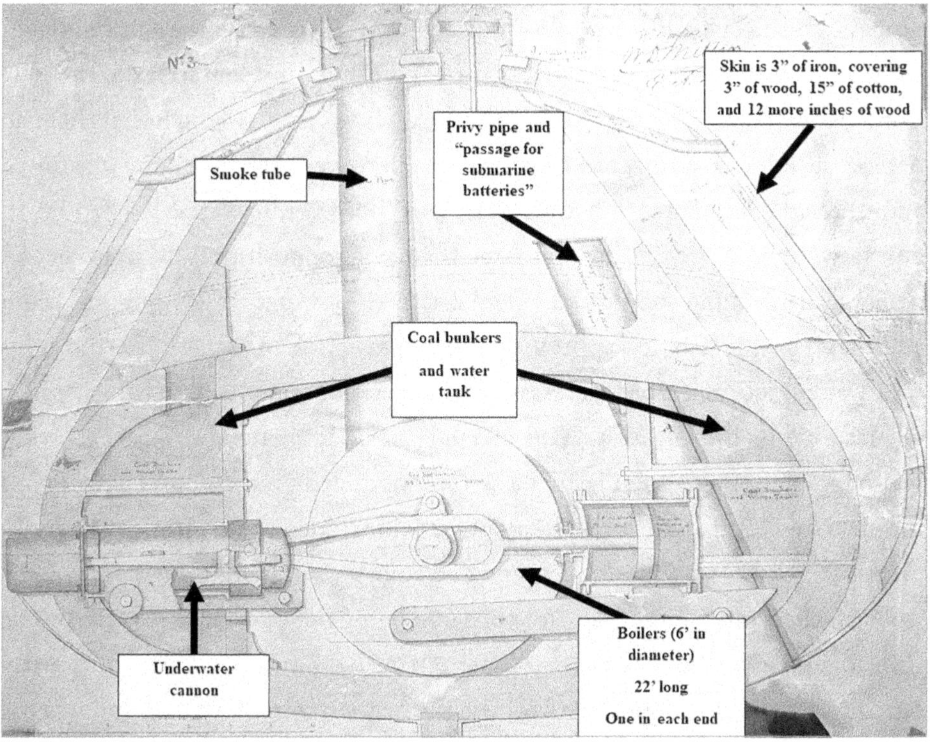

Robert Creuzbaur's drawing of cross section of *Avenger*, Richmond, Virginia, July 1862, with author's explanatory labels. Courtesy of the Wiggins Family.

designer intended, Creuzbaur's vessel might indeed have been a "masterpiece containing masterpieces."[86]

As it turned out, the only people who were not eager to build *Avenger* were the Confederate Navy officials who would be tasked with the job of actually constructing and operating the vessel. In the realities of the Civil War South, *Avenger* and its many curved iron components would have been a nightmare to construct. Whether Creuzbaur's dream vessel could ever have been successfully completed anywhere in the world in 1862 remains an open question. Deeply convinced of the merits of his design, the inventor completed the drawings shown above hoping to impress both naval officials and the Confederate government with his invention's usefulness. He also believed that enabling reviewers to see the details in full color might make them seem more practical and separate his designs from the many others then stuck in the navy's review process. In the end, the beautiful drawings and clever ideas were not enough.

After some initial success with Maury and other representatives of the new Confederate Navy, Secretary of the Navy Stephen Mallory concluded that the *Avenger* design was simply too impractical. There were just too many unproven and untried elements. Allen and Creuzbaur, however, had traveled too far to quit now. In order to try and overcome the navy's opposition, Allen succeeded in persuading some influential members of the Confederate Congress to go ahead and pass legislation approving the construction of *Avenger*. In hindsight, this was a tactical error. Secretary Mallory was furious about this attempt to circumvent his authority and alerted President Jefferson Davis to what had happened. Davis then issued a statement angrily refusing to sign the bill into law on the grounds that the navy had concluded that it had other, more practical, vessels on which to expend the country's scarce resources.[87]

With the Confederate Navy for the time being out of the picture as a buyer, Creuzbaur and Allen turned to South Carolina. Creuzbaur was constantly refining his design, hoping to find the perfect combination of elements that would make it both impossible to stop and possible to build. By the time the project reached South Carolina, *Avenger* was described as being 180 feet long and 40 feet wide. The vessel was still described as having an iron-plated skin suspended over an elastic surface like rubber or compressed cotton. This pliable armor, its boosters hoped, would enable *Avenger* to both absorb and disperse the force of any potential impact from shot or shell.[88]

As with early efforts to woo Confederate officials, at first there was considerable success in the Palmetto State. On December 3, 1862, South Carolina Governor Francis W. Pickens sent "Message No. 7" to the legislature recommending that they give serious consideration to building one of "Creuzbaur's shot-proof vessels of war."[89] Pickens noted that the Gunboat Commission of Charleston had already reviewed Creuzbaur's plans and pronounced them sound. The commission was said to have been particularly impressed by the report from Commander Maury summarizing his successful tests of Creuzbaur's underwater cannon.[90]

One of the main concerns about *Avenger*'s proposed underwater weapons was that the projectiles might explode at such close range that they would damage the vessel itself. Creuzbaur's design, however, minimized such an impact by sending the shots and torpedoes off at an angle. According to Maury's report, "there is no difficulty in causing the torpedo to sheer off at an angle quite sufficient to bring it alongside of an enemy's vessel for explosion, without danger to the vessel having it in tow."[91]

Although *Avenger* was unquestionably an interesting design on paper, there remained the issues of how and where it could be built. It would have come as no surprise to the South Carolina legislators reviewing Creuzbaur's proposal to learn that the men and material needed to construct *Avenger* simply were not available around Charleston in 1862. If such a vessel was going to be built, it went without saying that the builders would have to get creative.

To satisfy the state's concerns about the project's practicality, Creuzbaur's team announced that a new partnership called "Allen & Sprague" had been formed to build *Avenger* in some unspecified foreign port. This was all just window dressing. The Allen in this new partnership was Ebenezer Allen, Creuzbaur's lawyer and agent. The Sprague in the partnership was J. R.

Sprague, a Galveston friend who had been active in the leather business before the war.[92]

Avenger seemed to have so much potential that South Carolina, which faced enormous pressure from Union blockaders, quickly offered to purchase the vessel if the proposed builders could deliver on their promises. In December 1862, a purchase agreement was approved in a series of resolutions passed by both houses of the legislature. But the purchase arrangement they approved may be one of the strangest and least practical in the history of maritime construction. The state agreed to buy *Avenger* for $350,000, but only if two conditions were satisfied. First, the vessel, which had to be built in some foreign port because of the absence of men and material in Charleston, would have to fight its way through the blockade and tie up to a Charleston wharf. The second condition was that the newly delivered vessel would then have to pass a rigorous inspection by an independent engineer selected by the governor. Only if both these stringent conditions were met would the builders be entitled to any compensation. To make matters worse, the state reserved the option to pay the purchase price either in cotton priced at sixteen cents per pound or South Carolina state bonds with a 6 percent interest coupon.[93]

What this meant, of course, was that if the project were to move forward, the builders would have to find someone willing to risk a large amount of capital up front to build the experimental vessel abroad and then hope that *Avenger* could make it to Charleston, fight its way through an enemy gauntlet, and then pass inspection. Then, for his trouble, the investor might wind up being paid with over two million pounds of cotton in a blockaded port or bonds issued by a state then in the process of rebellion.

It is not surprising that even the smooth-talking Allen found it difficult to imagine finding anyone who would even talk about financing this project. But he certainly tried some unusual funding sources in the hopes of landing one anchor investor that might entice others to join. One of the more unconventional sources that Allen contacted was the Ladies' Gunboat Society of Mississippi, a charitable association that had previously raised funds to help the Confederacy build other gunboats. Unfamiliar with the ladies or their organization, Allen did not help his cause by addressing his initial solicitation to "Sir." He then implored the ladies to support the project, suggesting that eventually there might be as many as six *Avenger*-class gunboats, with at least one of them dedicated to driving the enemy from their dearly beloved Mississippi. The Gunboat Society apparently did not react warmly to Allen's request. If the ladies of Mississippi ever agreed to financially support *Avenger*, the author has located no record of it.[94]

It is likely that Creuzbaur and his companions realized from the outset that there was never any serious possibility of getting *Avenger* constructed under the ludicrous terms set by South Carolina. Instead, the wily Allen probably hoped that South Carolina's enthusiastic approval of *Avenger* might lead to reconsideration of the project's merits by the Confederate government. This interpretation is confirmed by the fact that on January 13, 1863, Allen reported to some friendly congressional representatives in Richmond about the project's latest stamp of approval. He said that "we hope the example of S. Carolina will have an effect to neutralize the hostility of [Secretary of the Navy] Mallory and also to encourage Congress to authorize the construction of enough of these vessels to retake the Mississippi River and inflict punishment in other quarters upon the enemy."[95]

Despite its novelty and potential, *Avenger*, as Creuzbaur originally conceived it, would never be constructed, either by South Carolina or the Confederacy. This did not mean that the project was a complete failure. Motivated by the submarine cannon's successful trials, Maury and the Confederate Navy continued experimenting with underwater torpedoes, including self-propelled torpedoes. Even John Brooke, one of the chief critics of Creuzbaur, was forced to admit later that the tests "developed the fact that projectiles may be thrown well under water, and I think an effective gun may be made."[96]

Brooke's relatively optimistic view took a lengthy period to be validated. It would be many years before the United States developed its own version of a reliable self-propelled underwater torpedo. An English engineer named

Robert Whitehead is credited with developing the first successful self-propelled torpedo in 1866. But it would not be until January 1878 that the Turkish steamer *Intibah* became the first vessel to be sunk by self-propelled torpedoes. America's own torpedo program began seriously in 1870, when Lieutenant Commander John Howell of the US Naval Academy began designing a torpedo that was more effective and reliable than the Whitehead models then in use. He finally achieved an improved working model in 1881, which won a contest sponsored by the navy in 1883. Although installed at the time on a number of navy vessels, only five Howell torpedoes still exist today. Two are on display in the US Naval Undersea Museum in Keyport, Washington.[97]

CHAPTER 4

MAGRUDER, MINES, AND TANKS

As many Texans had long feared and predicted, in the fall of 1862, Texas was well on its way to being dominated by the Union Navy. All of its major ports were either captured or firmly blockaded. The important port of Galveston was captured by a fleet of US naval vessels in early October, and Admiral David G. Farragut proudly reported to Washington that he had the Lone Star State almost entirely under his control. "All we want," he boasted, "is a few soldiers to hold the places, and we will soon have the whole coast."[98] Texas might well have ended the war as an early and easy Union conquest, and many of the inventions that form the core of this book would never have seen the light of day, except for one extraordinary development: the arrival in Texas of Confederate Major General John Bankhead Magruder.

If Robert Creuzbaur can be regarded as the Captain Nemo of Texas, General Magruder may well be considered the Lone Star State's ringmaster. Under his eccentric leadership, a circus of everything from rockets to exotic marine vessels would take turns upon the state's various land and water stages.

Because he was so instrumental to the events that will be described below, it is worth briefly discussing Magruder's background. He was born in Port Royal, Virginia, in 1807. In 1826, Magruder entered West Point, graduating fifteenth of forty-two in the class of 1830. (To provide some context with more familiar figures, Jefferson Davis was in the 1828 class and Robert E. Lee graduated in the 1829 class.) Following graduation, Magruder transferred to the artillery.[99]

Major General John Bankhead Magruder (1807–71). Magruder Name File—Photograph Collection, Rosenberg Library, Galveston, Texas.

After a series of relatively routine assignments, Magruder finally got the opportunity to demonstrate his ability as an officer during the Mexican-American War. He commanded a company of artillery during the march from Veracruz to Mexico City and was in the later stages breveted to the rank of lieutenant colonel for meritorious conduct. Magruder's experience in Mexico convinced him of the value of mobile artillery. It also gave him a ringside seat to witness the use of rockets by the battery that accompanied him. He would carry both of these experiences forward to influence his Civil War service in Texas.[100]

These experiences were not the only things Magruder carried with him to the Lone Star State: he also had a reputation as a flamboyant soldier who frequently drank to excess. The stories about his drinking were legendary even by the more lenient standards of the time, and they haunted him throughout his military career. It was not just that he was frequently inebriated, which he was. Even when sober, Magruder was known to all his old army companions as "Prince John" because of his elegant uniforms, theatrical mannerisms, and dramatic pretensions.[101]

When the Civil War broke out, Magruder tendered his service to his native state of Virginia and, because of his age and experience, he soon staked his claim to a responsible position. He started out well enough, commanding the small Confederate force that won the Battle of Big Bethel, on June 10, 1861. Although a minor skirmish, Big Bethel was arguably the first land victory of the war. Because of this early success, Magruder was promoted to the rank of major general and placed in command of a force tasked with defending the peninsula leading to the Confederate capital of Richmond. Magruder's position would be severely tested when, in the spring of 1862, Major General George B. McClellan landed his Union Army of the Potomac, over 120,000 men, near the tip of the peninsula and began to slowly march toward Richmond.[102]

In command of a Confederate force that was only a fraction the size of McClellan's army, Magruder knew that the only chance he had of keeping the enemy from advancing was to use deception and take advantage of unique features of the peninsula's terrain. Magruder's line from Yorktown to the James River, and the manner in which he proceeded to defend it, was a masterpiece of creativity. He used dams to flood some of the land to restrict enemy movement. He then drew on his theatrical training to create formidable looking defenses that featured logs painted to look like cannons. To further add to the illusion that he had a vast force, Prince John ordered his men to build extra campfires at night and to march around in circles blowing bugles as though they might be preparing to attack.[103] Confederate General Jubal Early's postwar memoirs summed up Prince John's performance in glowing terms: "The assuming and maintaining [of] the line by Magruder, with his small force in the face of such overwhelming odds, was one of the boldest exploits ever performed by a military commander."[104]

Magruder employed more than mere deception to delay his enemy. Military historian and *New York Times* contributor John Grady reports that Magruder "was the first commander to actively employ mines ("torpedoes") on a large scale during the American Civil War" because of some of the deadly explosives his soldiers concealed in the sand around Yorktown.[105] The individual primarily responsible for designing and burying these explosives was Brigadier General Gabriel James Rains. Rains had graduated in the West Point Class of 1827, three years before Magruder. He had been an active participant in the Mexican-American War and had seen action in Texas at the battles of Palo Alto and Resaca de la Palma. Because of his experience and passionate advocacy for land mines and marine torpedoes, Rains specialized in designing and installing these weapons. Rains would later go on to become chief of the Confederacy's Torpedo Bureau in 1864.[106]

"Explosion of a Torpedo." Alfred R. Waud's depiction of an incident at Yorktown, Virginia, *Harper's Weekly*, May 24, 1862.

With the assistance of Rains and his mines, Magruder's delaying tactics worked so well that McClellan advanced only slowly and cautiously toward Richmond. Major Baker P. Lee, one of Magruder's soldiers, said after the war that his commander "was equal to it all. Here, there, everywhere, by night and by day, he showed himself to the enemy in a magnifying glass, not only exaggerating the numerical proportions of his army, but in making illusive and confusing dispositions of his troops, in carefully concealed changes, and in transformations as deceptive as a juggler's tricks." The strategic genius of Magruder, Baker Lee concluded, caused General McClellan to "see a mountain that was but a molehill in a mirage."[107]

Magruder's delaying tactics were effective, but he knew that his conjuror's tricks could only occupy his meandering spectator for so long. Eventually, even the overcautious McClellan would wake up to the fact that he had comparative strength and hasten his army up the peninsula to the outer defenses of Richmond. By May 24, 1862, McClellan had advanced to the outskirts of Richmond and deployed his army along a thirteen-mile front. A week later, a Confederate assault at the Battle of Seven Pines produced little more than heavy casualties, one of whom was commanding Confederate General Joseph E. Johnston. These events left little reason for optimism in the Confederate capital.[108]

The loss of Johnston meant that McClellan would now square off against General Robert E. Lee, who had suddenly come into command of the Army of Northern Virginia on June 1, 1862. Lee knew that his army was badly outnumbered and could not afford to directly confront McClellan's entire army. He decided to instead make a bold movement that might give him a numerical advantage against a portion of it, separated from the main body. The advantage that Lee sought to exploit was available because the Federal troops were spread out on both sides of the Chickahominy River. Lee decided to take the bulk of his forces north of the river and launch a surprise attack against the smaller Federal force isolated on that side of the river. It was quite a gamble. Lee's departure would leave Magruder on the south side in command of a heavily outnumbered force that was all that stood between McClellan and Richmond.[109]

Outnumbered and in a desperate position, once again Magruder decided to put on a show. Officers again shouted orders at nonexistent soldiers. Units again moved back and forth between trees to magnify their numbers. He even arranged for enslaved people from Richmond to march around in circles beating drums.[110] As Lee and Magruder hoped, McClellan remained fixed firmly in position and watched the performance. It was Magruder at his finest. As General D. H. Hill later wrote, "No one ever lived whom could play off the Grand Seignior with a more lordly air than could 'Prince John.' . . . During the absence of Lee, he kept up such a clatter that each of McClellan's corps commanders was expecting a special visit from the much-plumed cap and the once-gaudy attire of the master of ruses and strategy."[111]

Lee's plan succeeded brilliantly in catching the Union forces north of the Chickahominy off guard. In a hard-fought campaign that became known as "the Seven Days Battles" because it featured six battles in seven days, Lee gradually forced McClellan to retreat down the peninsula, eventually ending the threat to Richmond. Lee's objective was not merely to force McClellan to withdraw, however. Lee correctly believed that for the Confederacy to stand a chance in this war he needed to so badly mutilate the opposing army that it could no longer pose a threat. Before he could destroy McClellan's army, however, he first had to catch it.

Because of his location south of the Chickahominy River, Magruder found himself in command of one of the forces best positioned to catch up with the retreating Federals, who by this point were moving steadily southeast toward their relocated base on the James River. On June 29, 1862, Magruder led an attack on the Union rear guard at Savage's Station, which was, as its name suggests, a station and depot of the Richmond and York River Railroad Line. Magruder's attack turned out to be wildly uncoordinated, and the results of the battle were inconclusive. Lee told Magruder afterward, "I regret much that you have made so little progress to-day in pursuit of the enemy."[112]

Although Magruder did not achieve much on the battlefield at Savage's Station, he did accomplish one thing that is relevant to one of the primary subjects of this book. To understand this achievement's importance, it is necessary to go back in time about a month before the battle. In the course of planning his defense of Richmond, General Lee had noticed that a rail line ran from Richmond directly through the expected site of the Federal lines. Lee thought that this line presented both a challenge and an opportunity. On June 5, 1862, Lee wrote to his chief engineer that "it has occurred to me that he [McClellan] is constructing a railroad battery, probably plated with iron, to push along the road and sweep the country."[113] Lee made the decision to try and beat McClellan to the punch and construct his own rail gun. He quickly

Major General Robert E. Lee (1807–70). LC-DIG-ppmsca-40660, Library of Congress.

instructed Chief of Ordnance Josiah Gorgas to coordinate with the navy to construct "a heavy gun, on trucks, the whole covered with iron, to move along the York River Railroad."[114]

Lee was very enthusiastic about his rail battery project. He saw it as the land equivalent of an ironclad warship sailing along a railroad track. He wrote to Captain George Minor of the navy's ordnance office that he was eager to get a naval gun "with one of your navy iron aprons adjusted to protect gun and men." "If I could get it in position by daylight tomorrow," he mused, we "could astonish our neighbors."[115]

Although he knew a rail gun could not be constructed overnight, Lee urged Lieutenant John M. Brooke, who was assigned by the navy to design the rail battery, to do everything in his power to ready it for service as soon as possible. Brooke decided that to save time he would build the rail battery in the same yard that had been used to recently construct CSS *Virginia*, the first Confederate ironclad. He would also have the rail car's protective armor built to the same specifications as the armor successfully mounted on *Virginia*. Because *Virginia* had been built on the hull of the captured USS *Merrimack*, some called the railroad battery that Brooke produced the "Dry Land *Merrimack*." This strange battery greatly impressed the Confederates who witnessed the heavy object being slowly pushed down the track by a railroad engine that was only lightly protected by cotton bales.[116]

Thanks to research by David H. Schneider, photographs in the Library of Congress of a railroad gun taken after the war have now been correctly identified as depicting the railroad gun originally employed by Generals Lee and Magruder outside Richmond in 1862. The distinctive railroad gun featured a rifled and banded thirty-two-pounder gun. It was protected by a wooden casemate that was two feet thick and angled at about thirty-six degrees. Fastened on top of the wood was four inches of iron armor. Although the casemate would provide strong protection in front, there was relatively little protection on the sides of the railroad gun. Based on other images of the rail gun, it is likely that some of the protection shown on the side of the gun in the photographs was added subsequent to the gun's initial construction and use.[117]

On June 24, 1862, the rail battery was ready for service. Since the battery had been constructed by the navy, Lee requested a navy gun crew to operate it. As it turned out, the crew that was best fitted for the job would consist of men from the United Artillery of Norfolk, who, despite not serving in the navy, had served in the gun crews on board CSS *Virginia* during her famous engagement with USS *Monitor*. On June 29, 1862, less than four weeks after Lee conceived of the idea, the rail battery rolled out of Richmond and slowly followed Magruder's force in pursuit of the retreating Federals.[118]

When Magruder decided to attack the Union rear guard at Savage's Station, both the enemy's lines and Lee's new rail battery were perfectly positioned to test the new weapon. Magruder was delighted to have the opportunity to be the first military commander to use a rail gun in battle. Several times the battery was pushed forward to shell enemy positions from a distance and silence Union artillery fire. As Magruder grew more confident in the battery,

Lee's Railroad Battery, Petersburg, Virginia. Right half of stereograph, LC-B811–1245B, Library of Congress.

Lee's Railroad Battery, Petersburg, Virginia. Right half of stereograph, LC-B811–1171A, Library of Congress.

he began to experiment with new ways to use it. At one point, when the enemy was firing from a deep cut under a railroad bridge, Magruder ordered the rail battery to be rolled forward to the very front of his line. He said that this unconventional movement enabled his battery to "fire upon the enemy's masses below, which was done with terrible effect." Impressed with the rail battery's performance, Magruder singled the battery out for responding to enemy fire "with effect" in his official report. The armor on the rail gun also served its purpose. Despite being in the advance position most directly exposed to direct enemy fire, none of the men behind the rail gun's armor were injured during the battle.[119]

Although his new railroad battery had been helpful, Magruder and his staff quickly realized that it could have been used to better effect. Joseph Lancaster Brent, one of the Confederate officers who watched the rail gun's performance, noted that it had a particular weakness. The iron armor plate

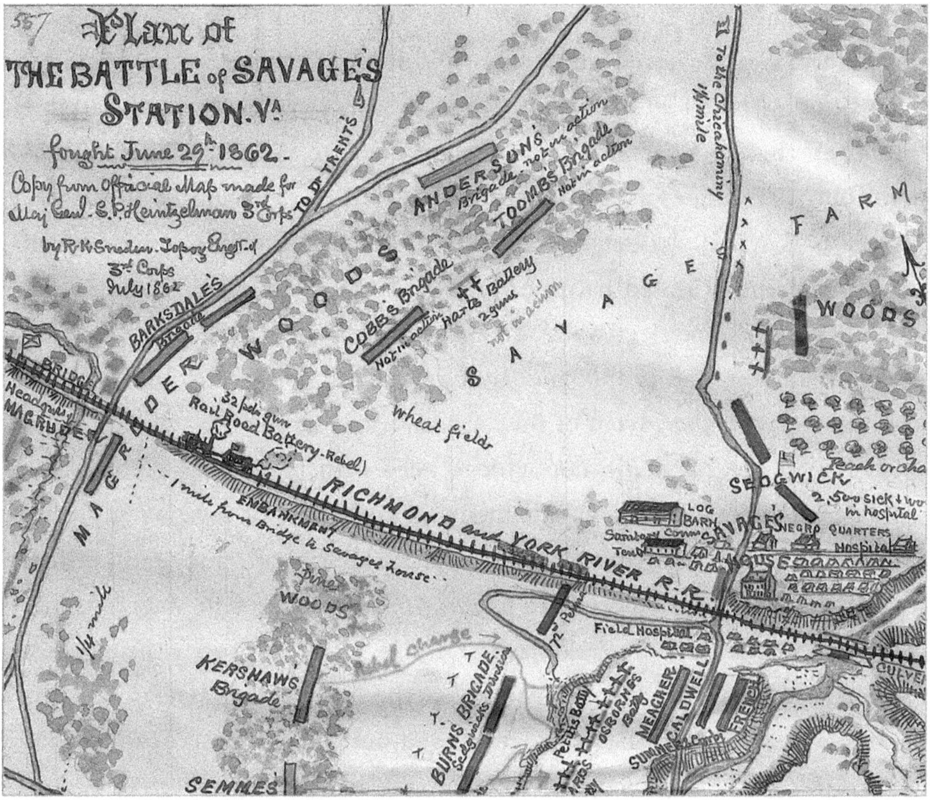

"Plan of the Battle of Savage's Station, Va., Fought June 29, 1862." Detail showing railroad battery at center left, Robert Knox Sneden Scrapbook, Image 1994.80.162.B, Virginia Museum of History & Culture, Richmond, Virginia.

was only present at the front of the car, leaving the sides and rear without any significant protection. Firing the gun through a casemate also meant that it had a limited field of fire confined to the area straight ahead. As Union skirmishers approached, the battery had to be withdrawn to avoid flanking fire. If the sides had been protected and the gun mounted so it could be traversed from side to side, the gun would have been unstoppable. Brent believed that "[i]f there had only been half a dozen such batteries, they could have easily broken the Federal line of battle, and have cut off their reserves, large numbers of which were stationed on the left of the track."[120]

Brent came away from the Battle of Savage's Station as a firm believer in the potential of armored gun platforms. In 1885, he wrote an important book titled *Mobilizable Fortifications and their Controlling Influence in War*, which forecasted that such weapons would soon come to dominate warfare. After describing Magruder's use of the rail gun in 1862, Brent said that this experiment was "beyond challenge a demonstration that there is no practical difficulty in using armored batteries and heavy guns on rails," noting that it would have achieved decisive results except for some "unskillful elaboration of details." Brent died in 1905, not living quite long enough to see his prophecy fulfilled with the advent of the modern battle tank.[121]

Although Magruder did not achieve Lee's principal military objective of inflicting a serious defeat on the enemy at the Battle of Savage's Station, he did emerge with the distinction of becoming the first commander in military history to employ an armored rail battery in battle. Although Magruder knew that not every battlefield would have a rail line running directly through it, he came away from the battle resolved to use the tactic again if the opportunity should ever present itself. As events played out, such an opportunity would appear on a Texas map far sooner than anyone could have expected.

Following the Battle of Savage's Station, Magruder continued to chase the retreating Federals. This chase did not end well when he finally caught up with them. The Battle of Malvern Hill turned out to be an unmitigated disaster for Magruder and the Confederates. The charge Magruder ordered into the teeth of enemy artillery proved catastrophic. The high casualty count resulting from the battle horrified General D. H. Hill, who had expressed such a complimentary opinion of Magruder's earlier deception strategy outside Richmond. "It was not war," he said about the charge Magruder directed at Malvern Hill. "It was murder."[122]

Hill was not the only critic of Magruder's performance during the Seven Days campaign. Rumors circulated almost immediately both in and out of the army that he had been drunk and grossly incompetent. This was the opinion of one of Lee's staff officers, who put the charge in writing and saw that it was forwarded to high Confederate officials, including President Jefferson Davis. When Davis was apprised of these allegations, he revoked Magruder's next assignment, which had originally been to command the Trans-Mississippi department, which included Texas. Months went by as Davis sorted through the various charges and the evidence that Magruder submitted to refute them.[123]

After meeting with Magruder and sorting through all the evidence, Davis decided to sweep the charges under the rug and send the flamboyant general on to Texas. On October 10, 1862, Magruder was delighted to receive word of his restored assignment to the Southwest.[124] Although the general was not placed in charge of the entire Department of the Trans-Mississippi, as he believed he deserved, he was given command of the District of Texas, New Mexico, and Arizona. In some ways, this command was a better fit for Magruder. Commanding a department was frequently a desk job. Commanding the District of Texas, by contrast, meant commanding an army in the field that was in direct contact with the enemy. Magruder knew that in Texas he could finally make his own plans and see them implemented, free of the bureaucracy and politics of the army and government in Richmond.[125]

This sense of independence was important. It enabled Magruder to be creative, which was the one quality that had always made him most productive. As one of his staff officers wrote long after the war, "Magruder belonged partly to that class of men whose genius, being unshackled, was capable of achieving the most brilliant results; but when overshadowed by authority became paralyzed."[126]

In Texas, Magruder would have many opportunities to show what his creative genius could do when "unshackled," but he first had to confront a troubling reality. While Magruder had been busy in Richmond securing supportive affidavits and defending his reputation, Texas was in the process of being thoroughly dominated by the Union Navy. Magruder would not arrive in Houston until early November 1862. By that time, Admiral Farragut was in the process of boasting that he had Galveston in his pocket and was on the verge of controlling the entire coast. In fact, there was really only one place along the entire Texas coast where the navy had been relatively unsuccessful. As it turned out, that one place would be the key that unlocked a terrifying new weapon.

The Union fleet that captured Galveston in early October was headed by Commodore William B. Renshaw. His instructions from Admiral Farragut were to capture Galveston and then to proceed down the coast of Texas, entering its bays wherever possible and destroying whatever Confederate defenses he might encounter. Accordingly, on October 23, 1862, Renshaw entered Matagorda Bay with two gunboats, USS *Clifton* and his flagship, USS *Westfield*. On October 31, after surveying the shallow channels in the bay and running aground several times, Renshaw finally approached the town of Lavaca (today called Port Lavaca). Unlike other Matagorda Bay towns like Powderhorn and Indianola, where Renshaw had been cordially received, Lavaca had relatively few German immigrants. What it did have was a Confederate artillery battery stubbornly commanded by an Irish immigrant and steamship captain, Major Daniel D. Shea.[127]

Renshaw sent a surrender demand ashore, which Shea immediately refused. After a ninety-minute delay to allow women and children to evacuate, the Federals then attempted to teach Lavaca the error of its ways by bombarding the town from long range. When the Confederates did not immediately respond, Renshaw moved his vessels even closer to the city. At this point, Shea startled the Federals by returning fire, although his smaller guns fired erratically and were no match for the heavy guns on the Union warships. Renshaw responded by backing his boats out of the garrison's range and continuing to fire from long range until dark. As evening approached, the one hundred-pounder gun on *Westfield*, the largest gun in Renshaw's arsenal, burst. Although it did not kill anyone, it deprived the Federals of their most effective long-range weapon.[128]

On the next morning, the Federals again resumed their bombardment of Lavaca. Since they were out of range, all Shea's Confederate gunners could

“Bombardment of Port Velaca [Lavaca], Texas, Oct. 31st–Nov. 1st, 1862.” Daniel D. T. Nestell Papers, MS 310, Box 2, Folder 49, Special Collections & Archives Department, Nimitz Library, United States Naval Academy, Annapolis, Maryland.

do was watch as their town and lives were threatened from afar. After two and a half hours, Renshaw decided that he had taught the Rebels enough of a lesson and decided to move on. Over the course of the two-day bombardment, the Union warships had fired a total of 252 solid shots and shells at Lavaca. Fortunately for the Confederates, no one was killed. Mainly as a result of luck, Shea’s gamble of refusing to surrender had succeeded. The end of the battle left the town of Lavaca mostly intact and, more importantly, still in Confederate hands.[129]

No member of the garrison at Lavaca could possibly have been comfortable sitting helplessly while undergoing a relentless bombardment from enemy ships located out of reach. And here is where the story takes a strange and unpredictable turn. Serving as part of Shea’s defensive force in Lavaca during the two-day bombardment was Edgar Collins Singer. The presence of Singer, a thirty-six-year-old gunsmith, would have far-reaching implications both for this war and the course of military history.[130]

To say that Singer came from a uniquely colorful family background is to greatly understate the case. John Valentine Singer, Edgar’s father, was from New York, the eldest son of German immigrant Adam Singer. Edgar’s mother was John's first wife, Anna Collins Singer. Edgar Singer was born in Ohio in 1825. In the 1840s, the family moved to Lockport, Illinois, which was the headquarters for the Illinois and Michigan Canal. That canal, completed in 1848, linked the Great Lakes to the Mississippi River by way of the Illinois River.[131]

As of the 1850 census, Edgar Singer was employed as a clerk in Lockport. By that point, his seafaring father had abandoned the family and moved south, where he proceeded to engage in a number of shipping ventures. One of these ventures involved a ship operating out of Galveston. In 1852, Edgar moved with his wife and child to Texas, which they entered through Galveston. Whether this move was in pursuit of his missing father is unknown. In any event, Edgar soon settled his wife and child in Lavaca, where he found work as a gunsmith.[132]

By the time Edgar arrived at Lavaca, his father, John, had been shipwrecked down the coast on Padre Island and decided to make that place his home. The castaway and his second wife, Johanna, proceeded to create a second family that included seven more children. Given the difficulty of island farming, John and his extensive family made a living by raising cattle. He also supplemented his income by serving as "wreckmaster," a title which was a more pleasant way of saying that he salvaged items from the ocean to refurbish and resell. Business was apparently good, and the family steadily became wealthier. When the Civil War broke out, John was ordered off the island because of his Union sympathies. One of the enduring legends of the Gulf Coast has it that before John left, he buried a substantial fortune consisting of coins, silver, and jewels. Unfortunately for him, when he returned after the war, neither he nor members of his large family were ever able to locate the buried treasure.[133]

One legend about the treasure that John Singer buried on Padre Island was that it included the proceeds from an early investment that he had made in his much younger and more famous brother Isaac's sewing-machine business. Isaac Merritt Singer, Edgar's uncle, was born almost twenty years after his oldest brother, John (Edgar's father). Isaac became famous in his forties for developing and successfully marketing the first practical and commercially successful sewing machine. Indeed, his first Singer sewing machine, patented in 1851, was depicted on the cover of *Scientific American* later that same year. The sewing-machine model used to obtain this patent is today part of the collection of the Smithsonian National Museum of American History.[134]

Isaac Merritt Singer makes his key improvements to the sewing machine.
From *Genius Rewarded, or the Story of the Sewing Machine* (1880).

Although Isaac Singer became famous both as an inventor and marketing genius, he somehow managed to have an even more scandalous home and business life than his older brother John. Business historian Gary Hoover wrote an article for the American Business History Center titled "The Sordid Saga of Mr. Singer and his Sewing Machine." In that article Hoover systematically detailed how Isaac Singer developed his famous machine in large part due to the efforts of partners he hated and later cheated. Isaac also fathered at least twenty-four children with a series of wives and mistresses, the last of whom, a young French lady named Isabella Boyer, may well have served as the model for the Statue of Liberty.[135]

Although not envious of Isaac's personal situation, Edgar Singer seems to have been greatly influenced by the older man's technical skills and achievements. Edgar knew his famous uncle well. In search of employment, Isaac had come to live with Edgar's family in Lockport for a period beginning in 1839. At that time, Edgar was about fourteen years old, an impressionable teenager. While working on construction of the Lockport and Illinois Canal, Isaac designed a machine for drilling rock. He patented that invention on May 16, 1839. One source suggests that Isaac first started tinkering with sewing machines in Edgar's Lockport home. It is possible that Edgar may have been involved as an assistant in some of these early experiments.[136]

Whether he helped Isaac develop his sewing machine or not, by closely observing his uncle, Edgar received valuable exposure to inventions and the patent process. Shortly after he arrived in Texas, Edgar decided to create his own inventions. He started with sewing machines, the machines that he knew the most about. In 1859, Edgar (listing his name as "E. C. Singer") obtained a US patent for what he called an "Improvement in Sewing Machines."[137]

It is unknown whether Edgar shared his father's reservations about the Confederate cause, but it is certainly the case that in 1862, when the Union Navy came calling at his home at Lavaca, Singer was serving either officially or unofficially with Shea's artillery battery. Perhaps it was because his own

Edgar C. Singer circa 1870. *San Antonio Express*, July 30, 1916.

father had deserted his family, but Edgar Singer reacted strongly to the bombardment he endured at Lavaca. He knew that it was only a matter of time before the Federal warships returned and completed their deadly mission of destroying his home. Singer was absolutely determined to find some creative way to protect his town and his family against this threat.

Unlike Robert Creuzbaur, a fellow Texas inventor, Singer did not think that the key to a successful defense lay in creating some type of futuristic vessel with revolutionary weapon systems. As Creuzbaur was in the painful process of finding out, that alternative would take too long and cost too much. Instead, Edgar Singer thought the solution was to be found in something much simpler and more cost effective to deploy. It might be said that Singer saw himself as a modern David in search of a slingshot. Modern commentators use the term "asymmetric warfare" to refer to efforts that a smaller or weaker combatant may employ to even the odds with a more powerful foe. Today such efforts might involve the use of drones or improvised explosive devices. However, as Singer was soon to prove, there is nothing new about this concept.

Edgar Singer and his associates would exit the Civil War as undoubtedly the most successful practitioners of asymmetric warfare during that conflict. Singer was not the only person, or even the first person, to conceive of using floating mines, then called torpedoes, to threaten enemy vessels. Robert Fulton had conducted experiments on them as early as 1797 and had unsuccessfully proposed their use by the United States during the War of 1812. Naval mines had also been used in the Gulf of Finland during the Crimean War. But it was only in the American Civil War that mines showed their true destructive potential. As Admiral David Dixon Porter wrote in 1878, "it is only since the year 1861 that it has been generally adopted as an engine of war, a tardiness in great measure due to the false sentimentality which, until a recent period, banned the torpedo as an inhuman and unchristian means of destroying an enemy."[138]

As soon as the Civil War started, inventors across the nation began designing their own torpedoes and seeking creative ways to solve their inherent problems. As many experimenters had learned since Fulton's time, there were a number of challenges confronting anyone trying to create a truly functional torpedo. The first obstacle was that it was difficult to keep explosive powder in a submerged torpedo dry for an extended period. It was also difficult to reliably trigger an explosion from outside a watertight powder chamber. Compounding this problem was that to be effective, a torpedo needed to be installed beneath the water's surface so that an enemy ship could not simply see and avoid it. Finally, torpedoes had to be capable of being manufactured efficiently and at scale. Only with large numbers could a defender stand any chance of creating a field of obstacles that would provide an effective screen against a fleet's entry to large bodies of water. Given these problems, it seemed highly unlikely in 1862 that the road to creating effective torpedoes ran through the backyard of an angry gunsmith with sewing-machine experience in tiny Lavaca, Texas.

Undaunted by the challenges, Singer first experimented with ways of exploding small floating containers filled with gunpowder in a barrel of water behind his house. These simple experiments proved promising, but the inventor soon ran out of powder. When he attempted to requisition more powder to conduct larger experiments, he was told there was none to spare. He persisted in begging for powder and Major Shea finally relented and gave him eight pounds to conduct a demonstration. Singer made a torpedo with all the powder he had been given and invited Shea to watch while he floated his small torpedo into contact with an old boat lying in the bay. When the target boat was "blown to atoms," as Singer later recalled, Shea was astounded. He immediately ordered Singer to report his work to General Magruder, who had recently arrived at his new command in Texas.[139]

Although Singer eagerly made the trip from Lavaca to Houston, he did not have a chance to demonstrate his device for General Magruder for some time. This was because Magruder arrived in Houston in November determined to launch a bold plan to recapture Galveston from the Federals as soon as possible. Magruder was convinced that without control of Galveston, the Confederates could not hold on to Texas. Still smarting from the demeaning treatment he had received in Virginia, Magruder arrived in Texas determined to recapture Galveston and make a name for himself.

As the new year of 1863 approached, there was a Federal fleet in Galveston Harbor, but only a small body of infantry occupied a wharf near the shore. Confederate scouts were able to move through the city at night relatively easily. Magruder's ambitious battle plan, inspired by an engineer named Caleb G. Forshey, was to conduct a simultaneous surprise attack by land and water in the middle of the night. The improvised naval force would consist of two river steamers armored with cotton bales lining the sides to protect the vessels' machinery and crews. The land force would include approximately twenty-one pieces of artillery, six of which were large enough to be considered siege pieces. Magruder made plans to launch the attack on the night of December 31, hoping to find his enemy distracted and disabled by an evening of raucous celebration.[140]

The most difficult part of Magruder's plan involved transporting his large artillery pieces from the mainland to the island's waterfront, where they would be spaced at regular intervals for a distance of about two and a half miles. To get to the places where the artillery was to be deployed, he would have to transport his guns over back roads a distance of up to nine miles. This challenging movement would be complicated by the fact that it had to be to be accomplished in the dead of night. Moving the guns across the island to the city would be difficult enough, but first, he had to get to the island. The only bridge from the mainland to the island in 1862 was a railroad bridge. That bridge would need to be planked over so the guns could be hauled over to their intended positions.[141]

Many elements of Magruder's plan went wrong from the very beginning. The first obstacle turned out to be the railroad bridge. The idea to plank the bridge over was fine, but the mules that were intended to haul the guns over these planks declined to participate. A great deal of time was lost using manpower to maneuver the guns over the bridge. This meant that the land bombardment that was originally scheduled to start at midnight did not start until five hours later.[142]

There were other aspects of Magruder's plan that went farcically wrong, as when a body of five hundred Confederates waded out into the water to attack Union troops on a wharf, only to discover that the ladders they carried were too short. Evening the scales, the Union Navy made more than their own share of mistakes, including the last act of the battle, when Commodore Renshaw intentionally blew up his flagship and, unintentionally, himself.[143]

After this chaotic series of events, what was left of the Union fleet streamed out of Galveston Bay. Against all odds, the Battle of Galveston ended as a dramatic victory for the Confederates. Letters of thanks and congratulations poured in from across the Confederacy. It was a remarkable accomplishment. Galveston would be the only major port city ever recaptured by the Confederates and would remain in Confederate hands for the remainder of the war.[144]

Because of the unusual—indeed unique—sequence of events that defined the Battle of Galveston, there is one aspect of that battle that is often overlooked. It involves the railroad bridge that Magruder had to plank over to transport his guns to the island. It turns out that there was actually one gun that did not require support planks. Well before the battle, Magruder had closely examined a map of Galveston. He had also personally scouted the outskirts of the city during the night. He quickly noticed that there was a railroad line extending from his position on the mainland over the bridge to

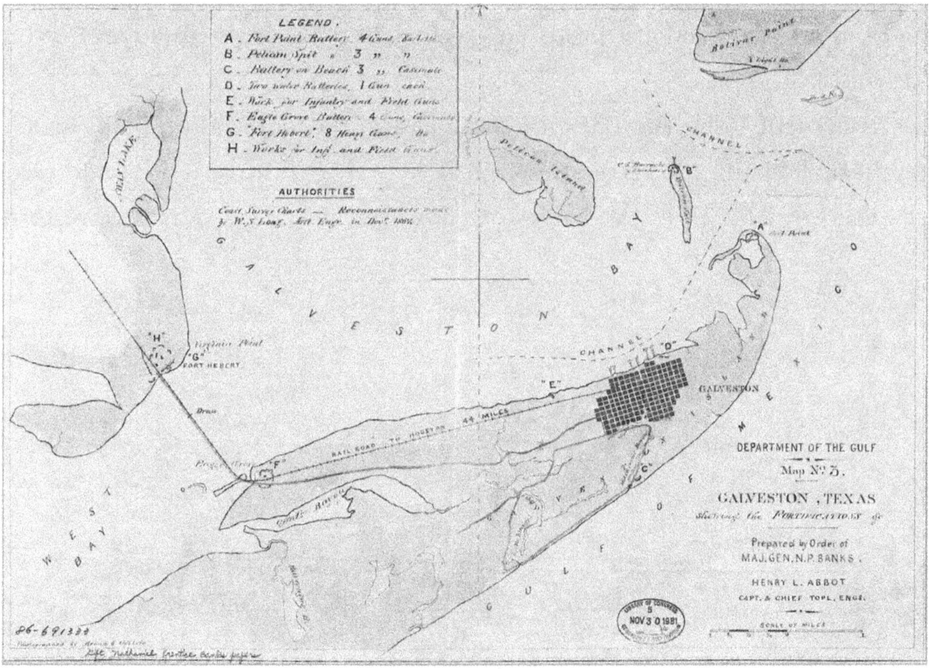

Image 37: Map of Galveston Island showing fortifications and railroad bridge from the mainland, prepared by Henry L. Abbot, captain and chief topographical engineer, undated, G4034.G3S5 1862. A2. Library of Congress.

a rail station in the western part of the city. This station was located within probable firing distance of the westernmost Union gunboats in the harbor. The direct nature of the rail line and its end point near the enemy reminded him of his experience with the railroad battery at Savage's Station in Virginia. He quickly decided that the rail-gun experiment was worthy of repetition.[145]

After getting all his other guns over to the island, Magruder's men rolled over a railroad flat car, on which he had mounted a heavy eight-inch rifled Dahlgren. Such a gun weighed close to 6,500 pounds and would have been virtually impossible to quickly move to the waterfront by more conventional means. Magruder did not have either the time or the iron to armor his new rail gun the way the navy had done in Richmond. So Magruder did what he did best and improvised. One thing that he always had in surplus near Galveston was cotton bales. Magruder ordered that a large quantity of these be stacked surrounding the gun to serve as a protective barricade. If Magruder had employed a "Land *Merrimack*" in Virginia, he would now employ a "Cotton *Merrimack*" in Texas.[146]

As it turned out, the rail gun at Galveston did not end up being much of a factor during the battle. In Virginia his rail gun had been located near the center of his lines. At Galveston, however, it arrived near the western

"Surprise and Capture of the United States Steamer *Harriet Lane* by the Confederates under General Magruder, and the Destruction of the Flagship *Westfield* in Galveston, Texas, January 1, 1863." From *The Soldier in our Civil War*, vol. 2 (1886).

end of the Confederate line. Its opportunities to fire were limited because USS *Harriet Lane*, the only enemy vessel close to the rail gun's position, was attacked by two Confederate steamers during the battle. One of those vessels succeeded in ramming and capturing it.[147]

Although his cotton-protected rail gun was only of limited value during the Battle of Galveston, Magruder was still fascinated by the possibilities of mobile armored guns. He demonstrated his faith in them on an even larger scale in his next major project. Recapturing Galveston was unquestionably a major accomplishment, but the general knew that it would all be meaningless if the enemy returned with an even larger fleet and reconquered the island. To keep that from happening, Magruder had to find a way to quickly build an enormous system of fortifications protecting the city. He had, at most, three or four weeks.

Magruder had an excellent staff of engineers, and he knew he could use his authority to impress large numbers of construction laborers (enslaved people) from the agricultural regions not far away. Given sufficient time, the Confederates could build walls and position guns at strategic locations. His top engineers, all European immigrants, were experienced in designing and building large fortifications. The defensive works that his engineers designed looked impressive on paper. The problem was that Magruder did not have anywhere near enough guns to fill the required gun positions. Even worse, he feared that he could not protect the few guns that were available to him.

To many commanders, these problems would have seemed insoluble, but to "Prince John" Magruder, finding creative solutions was all in a day's work. He instructed his engineers to go ahead and build the fortifications with gun emplacements spaced in carefully positioned bastions that projected from the walls. There was still the issue of how to fill these batteries. How could he create guns from nothing? Like many commanders, Magruder's actions tended to be strongly influenced by what he had seen work in the past.

On the peninsula in Virginia, Magruder had effectively used painted wood cannons ("Quaker guns") to simulate artillery pieces. He wasted no time in creating a wooden gun factory near Galveston to create that illusion again on an even larger scale. One other trick he had now employed twice, in short order, was the use of armored rail guns. Magruder was not deterred by the fact that his latest rail gun had been of little use at the Battle of Galveston. There was nothing wrong with the concept; it was simply in the wrong position to be effective. This time, in the permanent fortifications of Galveston, he could position the rail guns to be exactly where he needed them to be.[148]

To protect his gun positions with armor, Magruder needed iron. Fortunately, one thing Magruder then had on hand was plenty of railroad iron, which had been stockpiled before the war for the purpose of building new rail lines. An 1862 report reflected that there was 977 tons of iron near Galveston.[149]

Using this surplus, the general ordered that the gun emplacements be covered with railroad iron, creating protective casemates. The result was that each of these gun positions was essentially a smaller version of Lee's rail battery. One important difference was that the Galveston casemates allowed the gun positions a much larger lateral range of direction. This still left the problem that the Confederates had more holes in casemates than guns to fill them.

The resourceful Magruder then ordered each of his new bastions to be connected with two sets of railroad tracks. This meant that a new gun (or painted log) could be rolled out and replaced during a given night. A gun that was test fired to impress the enemy from position one on Monday might fire again from position two or even three on Tuesday. It was like a con artist on the street performing the three-card monte. The Federals never knew where a gun might appear and fire next. The Confederate artillery order books for this period reveal the elaborate ballet that went on behind the scenes, with guns moving erratically almost nightly to keep Union blockaders confused about their numbers and exact locations. This tactic proved incredibly effective. Once these tracks were installed, and the movements skillfully executed, the Union Navy never was able to get an accurate estimate of how many real guns the Confederates had at Galveston.[150]

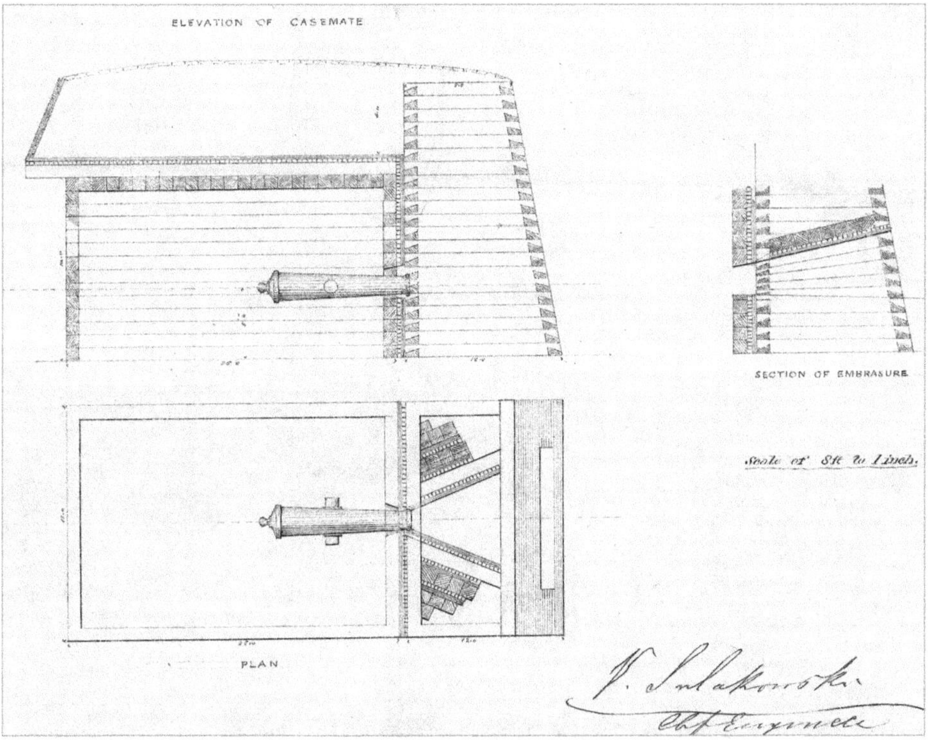

Iron casemate designed by Chief Engineer V. Sulakowski. Jeremy Francis Gilmer Papers #276, Southern Historical Collection, Wilson Library, University of North Carolina at Chapel Hill.

Counting the same gun many times at different positions, Commodore Henry H. Bell reported to Admiral Farragut in New Orleans after a few weeks that the defenses of Galveston had now become too "formidable to anything we might send against them."[151] Given the large number of reported gun emplacements, this news was both surprising and disappointing to Farragut. Although he did not order a renewed attack, Farragut was suspicious of this claim and remained puzzled about the source of the guns. As he told Bell, "I can not imagine where they got all the guns you speak of. They have been not only industrious, but where the guns came from is what puzzles me." Where they had come from, of course, was the creative imagination of "Prince John" Magruder and his clever engineers.[152]

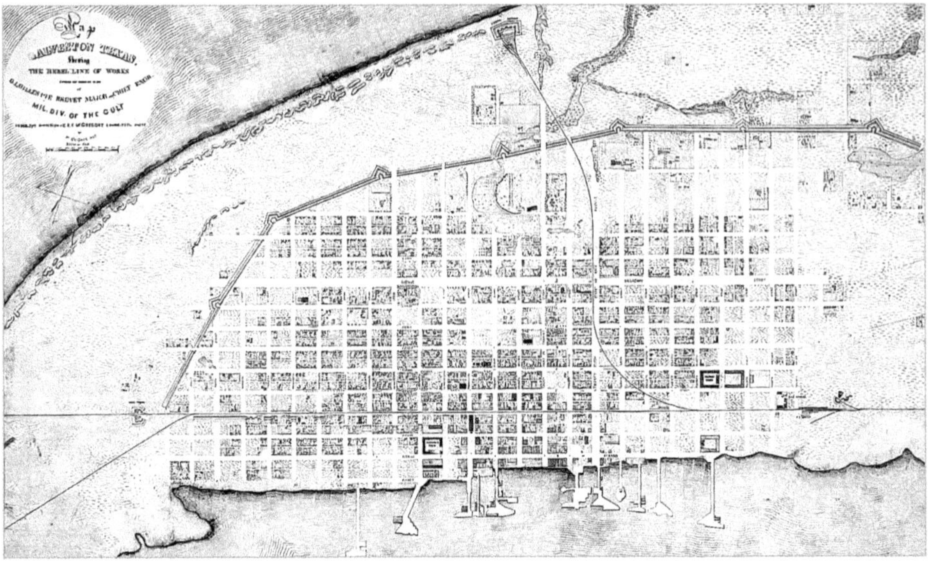

"Map of Galveston, Texas, Showing the Rebel Lines of Works." G. L. Gillespie. NAID 305667, National Archives and Records Administration.

In terms of results, Magruder's use of protected rail batteries at Galveston would turn out to be one of the most effective defensive strategies employed by any Confederate city during the Civil War. The fortifications surrounding Galveston would keep the Union army from attacking the city for the remainder of the war. Thanks to what was essentially a bold ruse, Galveston would end the war in 1865 as the last major Confederate port anywhere.

Although Magruder had finally found a way to effectively use mobile armored batteries, they were still confined to movement along fixed tracks. To create a true equivalent to a tank, his armored guns would need to be free to move wherever they were required. Magruder and his engineers began considering how this last step could best be accomplished. They were never short of ideas. As explored in detail later in this work, at the end of the war, several special service groups in Galveston were employed in a variety of secret projects involving everything from torpedo boats to submarines. There was one mysterious armored gun project, however, that was apparently completed but never used in battle. It was described in this tantalizingly brief account by a local historian:

> In contemplation of another attack on Galveston, and to aid in resisting it, a turret-car was built; the turret was constructed out of railroad iron and was made for one gun. James P. Sherwood, and other excellent mechanics and machinists, were engaged in the construction of this battery on wheels, but it was never called into requisition.[153]

James P. Sherwood, the mechanic charged with building the turret car, was a pioneer who had arrived in Galveston from Maryland around 1837. He built the first frame house in Galveston. On arrival, he became friends with Gail Borden, with whom he shared a natural love of invention. Like Borden, Sherwood was a uniquely creative and talented individual. Despite the absence of any formal engineering studies, he exhibited a natural talent for mechanics. He knew how to make things work and was a wizard at fixing them when they did not work. One of his earliest and most successful ideas was to develop a method of sinking wood pilings by hydraulic pumping. This made it possible to provide the foundations that supported Galveston's large houses and buildings. During the Civil War Sherwood was responsible for building or supervising many important projects, ranging from building gun carriages to installing the iron casemates used to protect the batteries of Galveston. Sherwood's experience made him a natural fit for the turret-car project.[154]

It is not surprising that Magruder was interested in developing an armored turret gun. He had been on the Virginia peninsula during the nearby confrontation between USS *Monitor* and CSS *Virginia* and may have witnessed part of that fight. *Monitor*'s unique rotating gun turret had to have made an impression on an experienced artillerist like Magruder. In February 1863,

Magruder expressed great interest in a "revolving battery" model that had been shown to him by Captain George W. Durant, an engineer and inventor who served in the Arizona Brigade. No information about the exact nature of this invention has come to light, but it may be related to the turret gun that Magruder later ordered James P. Sherwood to build.[155]

Given Magruder's fascination with guns in turrets, it is interesting to speculate about what Magruder's 1865 turret car might have looked like. How close was it to being an early prototype of the modern tank? Unfortunately, the available records do not provide much of an answer to that question. Although Magruder's turret car might well have come the closest, neither side in the Civil War produced a real tank prototype. The French and British would go on to experiment with self-propelled armored guns around the turn of the century. The first working tank in the world is generally considered to be the "Little Willie," which was developed by the British in 1915. The first tank to see serious use in battle, however, was the Mark I, which was employed by the British in 1916 during the Battle of the Somme.[156]

Scene from *The War Wagon*, Universal Pictures (1967). Courtesy of cola Images/Alamy Stock Photo.

The author confesses that for many years he tried to envision the appearance of Magruder's turret car. Something about its brief description, however, seemed vaguely familiar. Then, a poster for an old movie supplied the answer. In 1967, John Wayne and Kirk Douglas starred in *The War Wagon*, a popular Western film. Based on the 1957 novel *Badman* by Clair Huffaker, the movie's plot centers on an ex-con (Wayne) who enlists four men to rob an evil mine owner's armor-plated stagecoach (hence the movie's title). The film's unusual coach featured a Gatling gun mounted on top in a revolving iron turret. Although the war wagon and Magruder's turret car sound similar, the author has uncovered no evidence that the two were in any way related.[157]

According to motion-picture historians, *War Wagon* was filmed primarily on location in Mexico. This made its desert scenes look realistic. The wagon itself, however, was not particularly realistic. Built mostly of plywood and other lightweight materials, the upper parts of the coach were painted to look like iron. To add to the illusion, the movie's sound artists supplied appropriate "metallic" sound effects whenever the wagon's "heavy" iron doors were supposedly opened and closed. The author finds it ironic that Magruder and his Texas Confederates were building a real "war wagon" protected with real iron more than a hundred years before Hollywood designers resorted to fake materials to create a strangely similar vehicle. One movie history site notes that for many years, at least through the 1980s, the deteriorating remains of "The War Wagon" were displayed in "the Boneyard," a collection of discarded movie props at Universal Studios in California.[158]

CHAPTER 5

TORPEDOES AND THE SINGER SECRET SERVICE

The Battle of Galveston on January 1, 1863, left the Confederates in possession of the Island City. The question was now whether they could hold it. While Confederate engineers were busy creating fortifications with rail batteries around Galveston, Magruder finally found the time to immerse himself in the day-to-day demands of his new command. One of those demands was a persistent audience seeker named Edgar Singer, from Lavaca, who finally got his chance to present his torpedo ideas to the general. To gain a meeting with the busy general, Singer first presented Magruder with a communication from Major Shea recommending that Singer's floating mine-torpedo invention be tested. Many commanders would have rejected such a plea, but Magruder found the claim interesting given his prior experience with mines in Crimea and Virginia. Considering the continuing threat posed by the fleet of large Union warships hovering just offshore, Singer's ideas were certainly worth exploring.[159]

Although skeptical, Magruder authorized Singer to requisition twenty-five pounds of gunpowder to conduct a demonstration of his torpedo in the muddy waters of Buffalo Bayou. This was more than three times the size of the largest explosive device he had ever built. When the day finally came for the scheduled demonstration, the banks of the bayou were lined with soldiers and onlookers. Magruder and his staff secured prime positions to view the show. Singer placed his new torpedo in the bayou and floated an old scow over it. As Singer recalled long after the war's end, the demonstration could not have gone any better. When the boat struck the torpedo, "she was blown into kindling wood and the observers frantically sought trees for protection."[160]

After scrambling to safety, Magruder was so impressed by the violent demonstration that he immediately placed an order for torpedoes to be produced and installed at strategic locations in Galveston Bay. Back in Lavaca, Major Shea also received permission to order his own set of Singer torpedoes to protect the entrance to Matagorda Bay. Singer was suddenly in business on a large and increasing scale. In addition to buying torpedoes for immediate use in Texas, Magruder also told Singer that he would recommend the torpedoes favorably to Confederate officials in Shreveport and Mobile. With purchase orders in hand and the promise of significant business to come, Singer returned to Lavaca to assemble a team and get to work.[161]

Although the torpedoes that so impressed Shea and Magruder would take time to construct in large numbers, they were not very complicated from a mechanical standpoint. Singer's torpedo was termed a "percussion torpedo" because it exploded whenever it made contact with another object. It consisted of a watertight metal cylinder designed to be partially filled with gunpowder. It also featured a spring-loaded rod positioned facing the powder chamber. The device would be anchored to the sea bottom while the air in the

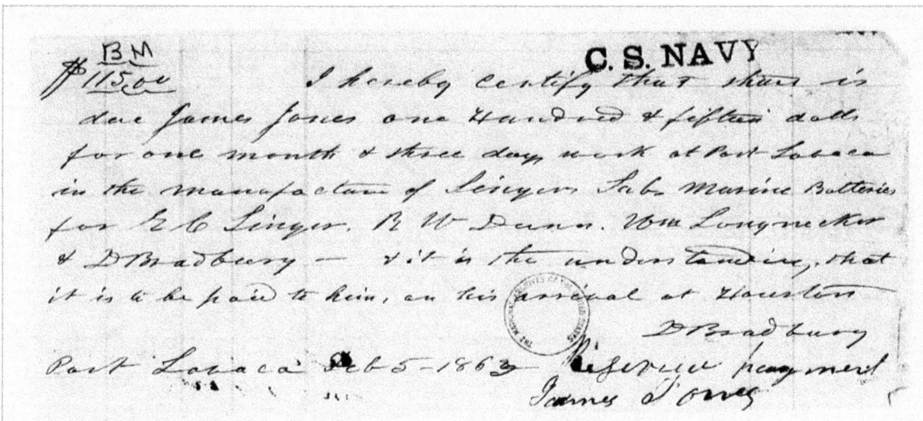
BM
C. S. NAVY
$115.00 I hereby certify that there is due James Jones one Hundred & fifteen dolls for one month & three days work at Port Lavaca in the manufacture of Singer's Sub Marine Batteries for E C Singer, R W Dunn, Wm Longnecker & D Bradbury — & it is the understanding, that it is to be paid to him, on his arrival at Houston
D Bradbury
Port Lavaca Feb 5 - 1863 Received payment
James Jones

Payment certification dated February 5, 1863, for work at Port Lavaca manufacturing Singer Submarine Batteries, BM-Mines and Torpedoes-Charleston-Miscellaneous, Record Group 45, National Archives and Records Administration.

powder chamber caused it to float several feet below the surface. When a large object like a passing vessel struck the torpedo, a pin would be jarred loose, and the spring would be triggered. This would cause the rod to forcefully impact a percussion cap situated just inside the thin wall of the cylinder. This cap would detonate in the powder and the torpedo would explode.[162]

It was not enough just to build torpedoes; they had to be deployed very carefully at the areas that most needed to be protected. This could be tricky. To keep a torpedo from exploding prematurely, there was a safety wire that kept the spring detonator from being triggered. This wire was then connected to a long piece of rope. When the torpedo was anchored in exactly the desired position, the rope would be pulled, and the safety wire withdrawn. This armed the torpedo. To prevent accidents, installers withdrew the safety wire only when they were at least fifty feet away. Laying a series of torpedoes was much more difficult than deploying one or two. If a field of

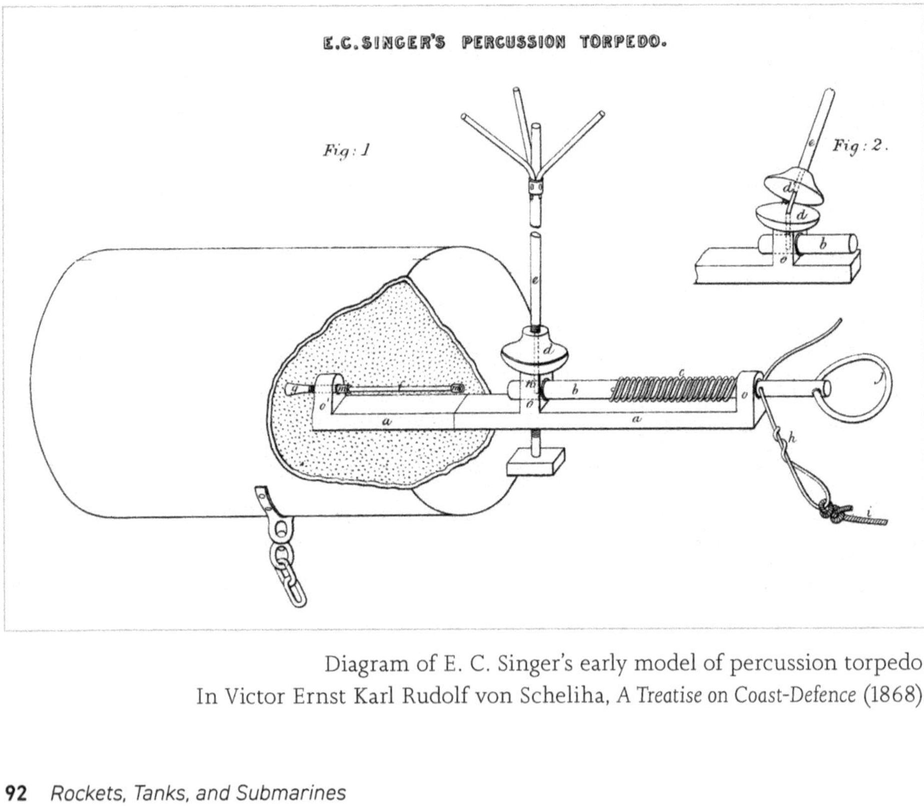

Diagram of E. C. Singer's early model of percussion torpedo.
In Victor Ernst Karl Rudolf von Scheliha, *A Treatise on Coast-Defence* (1868).

torpedoes was being created, they had to be distributed in a predetermined pattern spaced to avoid the inadvertent detonation of previously activated mines.[163]

Constructing and installing torpedoes was labor intensive. Singer knew that he would need a lot of help to get the job done, particularly if the job expanded as Magruder predicted to include torpedoes in waterways across the Confederacy. Because of the secret nature of the work, Singer needed to construct a team including only people he knew and trusted. For that reason, he gradually assembled a group of people with whom he was closely connected in Lavaca. Given Singer's need for trust and security, it is no accident that almost all of the chosen individuals were members of Singer's local Masonic lodge.

His first partner was John R. Fretwell, a fifty-one-year-old physician who had been born in Vicksburg, Mississippi. Fretwell was the ideal candidate to help direct this project for many reasons. First, Dr. Fretwell was the head of the local Masonic lodge and was trusted by everyone in the community. Although Singer would eventually get much of the credit for developing the torpedo that made him famous, Dr. Fretwell made his own valuable contributions. Indeed, it is likely that Fretwell provided the seed capital needed to get the torpedo business up and running.[164]

Not only was Fretwell a physician, but he was also a multitalented inventor who would eventually patent his own inventions. Fretwell had experience on both land and sea that would be very useful to the new enterprise. He was president of the Lavaca Navigation Company, which had recently surveyed and removed the obstacles in Matagorda and Lavaca Bays. In that capacity, he had undoubtedly made detailed studies of various waterways in Texas. Such a background would be extremely helpful in designing and installing floating mines to be placed in a marine environment.[165]

Realizing that the most direct way of protecting Texas waterways was artillery, in the summer of 1861, Fretwell supervised the establishment of a small foundry at Lavaca and produced two small iron cannons and the projectiles to be fired from them. These small guns were likely fired briefly during the Battle of Port Lavaca. Fretwell had also hoped to eventually produce a larger breech-loading gun, but lack of funds put this project on hold. Fretwell started the war by enlisting in a group called the Lavaca Guards but hoped to form or join an artillery company on the Texas coast. When Singer began developing his torpedo project at the end of 1862, Fretwell saw this as a better way to protect his town and jumped at the chance to lend assistance.[166]

As the war progressed, Fretwell became increasingly involved in assisting Singer in refining the original design of his torpedo. The new and improved

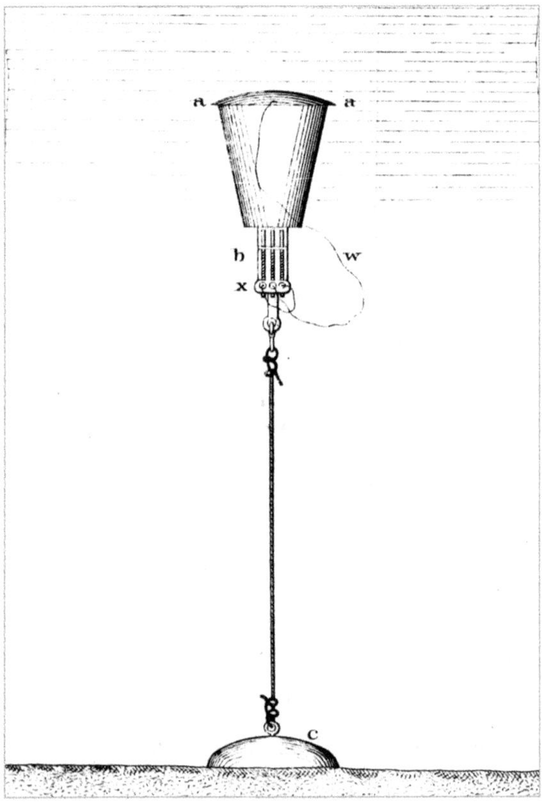

Above and opposite: Diagrams of the Fretwell-Singer lamppost-style torpedo. In W. R. King, *Torpedoes: Their Invention and Use from the First Application to the Art of War to the Present Time* (1866).

torpedo design resembled the top of a modern lamppost. Each torpedo contained between fifty and one hundred pounds of powder. It had a heavy iron cap on top. When a passing vessel hit the torpedo, the cap would be knocked off and its weight would pull the trigger pin that released the spring detonator.

Hundreds of these torpedoes were eventually built and installed. Dr. Fretwell personally installed these devices at places all the way from Mobile to North Carolina. He may well have installed more torpedoes at more places than anyone else in the Civil War. Because of his unique contribution and

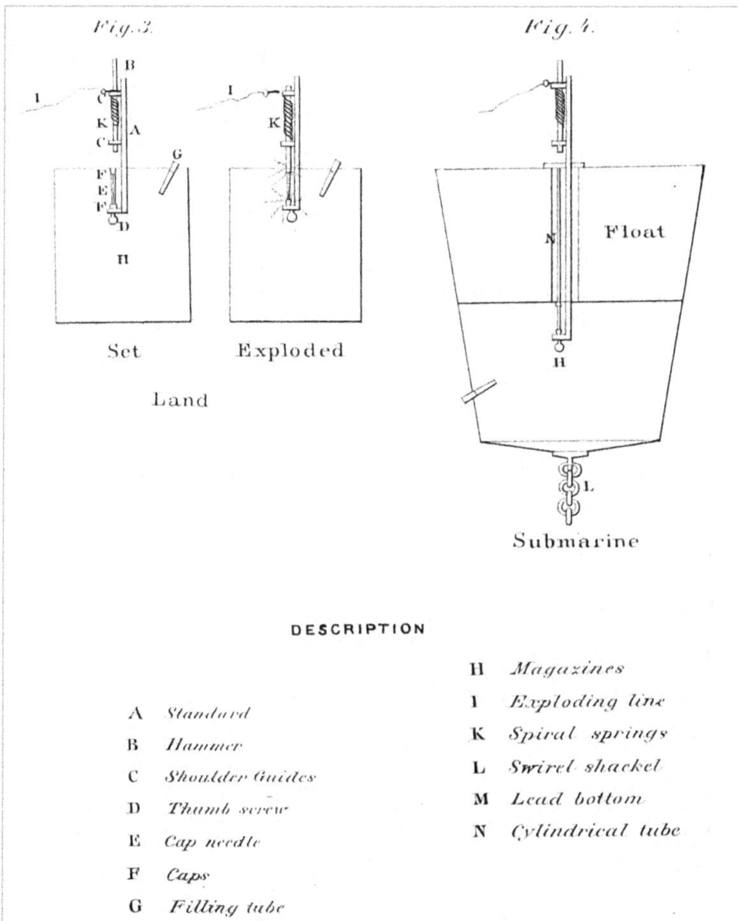

prominent status in the project, many sources both during and after the war referred to the group's torpedoes as "Fretwells" or "Fretwell-Singer torpedoes." In 1869, Lieutenant Commander John Sanford Barnes, the author of *Submarine Warfare*, the first book dedicated to the use of torpedoes in warfare, called the lamppost-style torpedo, "the most successful torpedo used by the rebels during the war."[167]

Many of the men Singer and Fretwell recruited for their project had special skills that would be useful. James Jones, for example, was a jeweler from Kentucky. His services would come in handy in creating and assembling the more intricate parts of the trigger mechanisms. The oldest recruit was fifty-nine-year-old William Longnecker, who ran the Lavaca livery stable. The youngest was twenty-seven-year-old John D. Braman, a local merchant. David Bradbury, a fifty-one-year-old contractor, would assume a central management role in Texas as the Singer torpedo operation expanded across the Confederacy.[168]

Perhaps the most interesting addition to the Singer team was Benjamin Augustus Whitney. "Gus" Whitney was a thirty-seven-year-old merchant who owned part of a shipping business and auction house. Born in Massachusetts, Gus came from the same family that produced Eli Whitney Jr., who was famous for his role in inventing the cotton gin. It is a remarkable coincidence that Whitney and Singer, both related to famous inventors, ended up in tiny Lavaca, Texas (population of 562 in 1860), where they then combined their talents to make major contributions to military science.[169]

The group of secret service operatives that Singer assembled would eventually swell to include more than thirty men. The group would usually be referred to as the "Singer Secret Service Corps," but occasionally received more colorful names like the "Singer Submarine Corps." Mark K. Ragan, who has done a remarkable job of chronicling this group and its activities, wrote an excellent article about the Singer Corps for a Civil War publication. The editors of the magazine could not resist summarizing the subject of Ragan's article on the cover as "the Texas gang that liked to blow stuff up."[170]

Things started moving very quickly for this Texas gang after the successful Buffalo Bayou demonstration. Working round the clock, they produced the first set of torpedoes ordered by Shea and Magruder within a month. In late January or early February 1863, the first Singer torpedoes were installed near the entrance to Matagorda Bay. Others were placed in a channel, Pass Lavaca, which led directly to that city. Protecting their homes with their own work was undoubtedly a deeply satisfying accomplishment for the entire Singer organization. Although Matagorda Bay was now secure, the first strategically important city to be protected was Galveston. Caleb G. Forshey, the engineer who had been instrumental in developing General Magruder's plan of attack at Galveston, got the distinction of directing where to place the first six torpedoes Magruder ordered for the entrance to the city's harbor.[171]

Even before installation of the Texas torpedoes was complete, plans were being made to essentially franchise the Singer torpedo business around the Confederacy. The utility of torpedoes seemed to have been confirmed as a general proposition when USS *Cairo* was sunk in Mississippi on December 12, 1862, by what some believed at the time was an electrically detonated mine. (The theory of electric detonation of the *Cairo* mine has now been proved incorrect).[172]

Unlike some of the mines produced on the East Coast, Singer's mines were never electrically triggered. Compared to electrically detonated mines, Singer torpedoes had the advantage that they did not require a wire to shore or operators to detonate them. They were also relatively cheap and could be produced and installed in larger fields. By March 1863, there were a host of Singer operatives fanning out east of the Mississippi River and pitching the group's products and services.

Under a law passed by the Confederate Congress on March 20, 1863, companies of engineers for special service were authorized. Secretary of War James Seddon quickly implemented the act by permitting Singer to form a company of twenty-five men for special torpedo service. Although the group was theoretically supposed to report to J. F. Gilmer of the Bureau of Engineers, in practice they operated very independently, signing separate contracts to supply torpedoes to local commanders at various places in Mississippi and Alabama.[173]

The terms of the contracts varied, but some of the contracts covered large numbers of torpedoes. In April 1863, for example, Gus Whitney and J. D. Braman signed a contract in Mobile as agents for "E. C. Singer & Co. of Lavaca, Texas," with General Simon B. Buckner. The contract called for the Singer team to produce and install one hundred torpedoes near Mobile. For this work, they were to receive $150 per torpedo. By July they had built all one hundred torpedoes and installed thirty-two.[174]

While Whitney and Braman were busy servicing the Mobile market, Dr. Fretwell was in Mississippi negotiating the installation of torpedoes on the Tallahatchie and Yazoo Rivers. Tasked with protecting the vital Confederate shipyard at Yazoo City, Captain Isaac Brown quickly agreed to Fretwell's proposal to install two torpedoes with a $20,000 bonus if the torpedoes destroyed a transport with troops on board. The bonus was reduced to $10,000 if the enemy vessel was a transport without troops on board. Brown later expanded the order to include fifty more torpedoes.[175]

The original inventor of these torpedoes, Edgar Singer, was at this point not actively involved in either building or installing them. Instead, he was spending a lot of time in marketing meetings in Richmond, Virginia. Some of the meetings were productive and others were merely frustrating. In between meetings with government officials, Singer drew up detailed written drawings and plans for his torpedo and applied for a patent. In May 1863, his initial request for a Confederate patent was denied because by this point there were several other torpedoes either deployed or in the development stage. Singer was told that he could obtain a patent for some unique mechanical elements in his torpedo, but not the entire device. Singer contested this decision and revised his application to narrow his claims. He would eventually receive a Confederate patent, but not until September 15, 1863.[176]

While in Richmond, Singer had a chance to meet with his nominal superior, Chief Engineer Jeremy Francis Gilmer. Unlike other Confederate officers who quickly signed purchase orders, Gilmer would not order any torpedoes to protect the Confederate capital without a formal study. He appointed a commission of three experienced engineers to study Singer's torpedo and instructed them to prepare a formal written report.

On July 14, 1863, the commission reported back on Singer's device. "One great advantage this torpedo possesses over many others," they noted, "is that its explosion does not depend upon the action or judgment of an individual, that it is safe from premature ignition, and at the same time is cheap and portable, while its position in river or harbor cannot readily be ascertained by an enemy's vessel." Gilmer could hardly have asked for a more enthusiastic endorsement. "We are so well satisfied with the merits of Mr. Singer's torpedo," the commission concluded, "that we recommend the Engineer Department to give it a thorough test, and, if practicable, to have some of them placed at an early day in some of the river approaches of Richmond."[177]

As the commission's report confirmed, Singer's torpedoes impressed everyone who took the time to study them. The design seemed simple and sound, and the mechanism ought to work. But did the torpedoes actually work or were they just clever toys? The answer to that question came on a muddy river in Mississippi in July 1863.

After the surrender of Vicksburg on July 4, 1863, Union forces turned their attention to the Confederate shipyard at Yazoo City. General U. S. Grant ordered his soldiers to board navy gunboats and head up the Yazoo River. His intent was to land sufficient troops to capture the city and shipyard before they could be further fortified. Captain Isaac Brown, in command of Confederate forces at the shipyard, knew that the Federal forces were approaching. He had signed a contract with John Fretwell to build and install fifty torpedoes, but the full number had not yet been constructed and installed. He urged Fretwell to hurry and deploy every completed torpedo he had in a frantic effort to stop the navy's approach. On the morning of July 13, as the Union gunboats steamed toward him, Brown went out and personally deployed two more "Fretwells," as he called the torpedoes, half a mile below his land battery.[178]

One of the Union vessels leading the Yazoo expedition was *Baron De Kalb*, an ironclad gunboat. As the Union force approached the city, Brown began setting fire to the remaining navy yard assets while he prepared to evacuate. Hoping to capture the Confederate guns intact, Union transports hurriedly approached the shore to land troops. To screen the army's landing attempt, the Federal gunboats steamed toward the city's fortifications with *De Kalb* in the lead. When *De Kalb* reached the lower end of the town, it suddenly struck a torpedo, causing it to sink in less than twenty minutes. To make matters worse, while *De Kalb* was going down, another torpedo exploded under its stern.[179]

Admiral David Porter was shocked by the loss of such a powerful vessel in such a short time, particularly to something unseen. Although the usual

"Admiral Porter's fleet at the mouth of the Yazoo [River],"
Harper's Pictorial History of the Civil War, vol. 2 (1894).

lookouts for torpedoes had been employed, the torpedoes that *De Kalb* struck were not visible because they floated well beneath the surface. "There was no sight of anything of the kind to be seen," he marveled. "This is some new invention of the enemy, which we will guard against hereafter," Porter vowed.[180]

Although he had been unsuccessful in protecting the shipyard, Captain Brown's investment in Fretwell's torpedoes had paid off even better than he could have hoped. His telegram to Confederate authorities describing the day's events was short and to the point. "Yazoo City has been abandoned to the enemy and with it the river." While admitting that he had been forced to abandon his guns, Brown noted that this cloud had a silver lining. "We have sunk, by torpedoes, in sight of Yazoo City, the ironclad *De Kalb*, of 13 guns."[181]

There was one unusual aspect of *De Kalbs* sinking that was probably unknown to those who witnessed it. *De Kalb* has occasionally been called "the Masonic Ironclad" because of the photograph below. Some modern Masons believe that it appears to show a Masonic symbol suspended between the

US Gunboat *Saint Louis* (later renamed *Baron de Kalb*), 1862. Matthew Brady. NAID 533123, Record Group 165, National Archives and Records Administration.

boat's two upper stacks. It is unclear why such a symbol would be so displayed, but there are a few possible explanations. Originally called *Saint Louis*, the city-class vessel was renamed in September 1862 to honor Revolutionary War hero John Baron De Kalb. There is some evidence that the original De Kalb was a Mason. There is also evidence that the vessel's captain, Lieutenant Commander John Grimes Walker, may have been a Mason. What is known for certain is that John Fretwell, who built and installed the torpedoes that sunk *De Kalb*, was the head of his Masonic lodge. In fact, the Singer group he helped lead was so dominated by Masons that some have described their later famous product, the submarine *H. L. Hunley*, as a "Masonic Secret Weapon." The author is all too aware that the long march of history inevitably tends to produce interesting and unexpected results. But it seems highly ironic that a devoted Mason using a device made by Masons was instrumental in destroying what may well have been the one and only Masonic ironclad.[182]

CHAPTER 6

SUBMARINES AND SECRETS

While the Singer group's torpedo business was rapidly expanding, there were others exploring more exotic options to even the odds for the Confederacy. The first originated in New Orleans. Baxter Watson and James McClintock were in the steam gauge business. Because of their experience working with pressurized vessels, they were a natural fit to attempt to build a submarine. Working with New Orleans attorney Horace L. Hunley, these men designed and constructed *Pioneer*, a prototype three-man underwater craft, in early 1862. Although preliminary trials of this first submarine were promising, the impending capture of New Orleans forced Hunley and his team to scuttle *Pioneer* and continue the project only after moving to Mobile, a safer location.[183]

Horace L. Hunley (1823–63). NH 48969, US Naval History and Heritage Command.

In Mobile, the Hunley group gave serious consideration to modifying *Pioneer*'s design to transform it into a submarine that would be propelled by an electric or steam engine. When these more exotic approaches proved impractical, McClintock and Watson built *American Diver* (also known as the *Pioneer II*) at the Park & Lyons machine shop in Mobile. Today, the location of that shop on Water Street is memorialized by a marker that calls it "one of the more important sites in the history of naval warfare." This is no exaggeration. The Park & Lyons shop is to undersea warfare what the Wright brothers' bicycle shop was to aviation.[184]

Much larger and more ambitious than the original *Pioneer*, the five-man *American Diver* submarine ended up suffering a host of operational problems. The biggest problem was its inability to generate sufficient speed to get into position to launch an effective attack. In February 1863, after less than a month of trials, the vessel was in the process of being towed to a position off Fort

Park & Lyons machine shop building, Mobile, Alabama (circa 1960). NH 53543, US Naval History and Heritage Command.

Morgan when it encountered stormy conditions and foundered. Although no crew members were lost, the total loss of the boat under these conditions meant that the team had to start from scratch to build a new vessel. At this point, the Hunley group was running out of options. The Confederate officials monitoring their work had become skeptical of the project and would provide no financial support. Even though Horace Hunley had been a wealthy man at the outset of the war, after financing two lost submarines, he was now running low on funds.[185]

It is at this point that the Singer group from Texas enters the submarine picture. Shortly after the loss of *American Diver*, Edgar Singer and John Fretwell arrived in Mobile to set up what would turn out to be their largest and most successful torpedo manufacturing facility. Much of the metal fabrication work would be accomplished at the same Park & Lyons machine shop where the Hunley group had their headquarters. Sharing the same workplace, it soon became clear that the two groups were compatible and had broadly similar approaches to their work. The Singer group was experienced with building watertight torpedoes; the Hunley group had experience building submarines that could be used to deploy those same torpedoes as weapons. Combining these two teams made perfect sense. An agreement was soon reached to absorb Hunley and his two associates into the Singer group and jointly construct a new and improved submarine.[186]

The partners estimated that their new submarine would cost about $15,000 to build. Hunley's capital commitment was set at $5,000, the same as Edgar Singer. The remaining $5,000 investment was split three ways between Singer operatives Robert W. Dunn, Gus Whitney, and John D. Braman. After this partnership was formed, the new submarine was effectively owned two-thirds by Texans, who showed their commitment by putting some of their torpedo profits to work funding the new venture. The new partnership also represented a unique combination in another way. Since Horace L. Hunley was a brother Mason like the Singer group, one member of a modern Masonic lodge has called the new group's famous submarine a "Masonic Secret Weapon."[187]

With financing in place, construction soon began on the new submarine under the direction of James McClintock. Called the "Fish Boat" by some observers, the new forty-foot-long submarine's hull was built out of wrought iron boiler plate. It was powered by a hand-cranked propeller worked by a crew of seven men and one pilot. There were ballast compartments forward and aft. The boat had two hatchways on top, with the forward hatch having a hole with a glass bullseye to provide some limited visibility for the pilot.[188]

Long after the war, Singer described the way the submarine was intended to function:

> The *Hunley*'s speed did not exceed four knots. She could remain submerged for an hour or so without any great inconvenience to her crew, although no means were provided for procuring fresh air after the hatch was closed. The plan of attack was to dive beneath an enemy's ship, hauling the torpedo after her; the bomb's triggers, or sensitive primers, would thus press against the ship's bottom, exploding the charge and inevitably sinking the ship. The *Hunley* used the Singer torpedoes exclusively.[189]

H. L. *Hunley* submarine as depicted by R. G. Skerrett (1902), NH 999, US Naval History and Heritage Command.

As much as they believed in the project, the Texans who went into partnership with Hunley in 1863 knew that they were making a risky investment. As the new submarine progressed and prepared for sea trials, they must have wondered whether it would turn out to be yet another dead end. No submarine, afloat or sunk, had ever managed to accomplish anything important. Would this new version be any different?

While the Singer group was expanding to include the Hunley team and building the third version of their submarine, there was yet another independent group making plans to use bold new undersea inventions to attack the enemy. Not long after the beginning of 1863, Ebenezer Allen and Robert Creuzbaur found themselves in Richmond with nothing but a set of plans for a vessel, *Avenger*, that would never be built. It seemed like they had hit a dead end. Although it was a clever concept, *Avenger* would never avenge anything. Creuzbaur grew discouraged and impatient and began making plans to return to Texas. At least in Texas, he reasoned, there were people who still appreciated his talents as a cartographer and engineer.

Although the *Avenger* project seemed to be either dead or on hold, Allen still hoped to achieve military (and economic) success with other schemes. Just as a jockey is always looking for the next horse to ride, Allen began looking around Richmond for another client to promote. He soon found the answer to his prayers in a St. Louis inventor known as C. Williams, who had many ideas for innovative nautical projects.

One of the mysteries that has long puzzled researchers in this field involves determining the identity of "C. Williams." This mystery now seems to have been resolved. Based on entries in the St. Louis city directories for the relevant period, the author believes that it is likely that C. Williams was Charles Williams, an accomplished St. Louis machinist. Williams had served as chief machinist for the Pacific Railroad and is memorialized in a local history as "having run the first engine west of the Mississippi going toward the Pacific" in 1852.[190]

Although Missouri was a border state, Williams viewed himself as a true patriot for the Southern cause. He had written to the governors of South Carolina and Mississippi in November 1860, even before those states seceded, offering to share his ideas for improvements to guns and projectiles. Neither of these governors took Williams up on his offer. The spring of 1863 found the inventor in Richmond trying to get someone—anyone—interested in his unique underwater weapon designs.[191]

Allen took one look at Williams's portfolio of inventions and designs and immediately saw their potential. Some of the designs seemed more practical than Creuzbaur's plans. Allen also saw their potential to be used in defense of his home state of Texas. Like Creuzbaur, Williams had bold ideas for new torpedoes. Unlike Creuzbaur, Williams planned to use submarine vehicles carrying divers to deploy his torpedoes. Instead of triggering the torpedoes by running into enemy ships, his torpedoes were designed to have timers and explode automatically after a set period of time.

Williams was not the first inventor to come up with the idea of deploying divers from a submerged vehicle to plant explosives. Charles Babbage, the English polymath who is often credited with inventing the digital programmable computer, published his idea for a "Submarine Apparatus for the Explosion of Vessels" in an 1855 London newspaper. Babbage's version was more of an inverted diving bell than a submarine vessel that carried divers. Whether Williams saw Babbage's concept before inventing his own apparatus is unknown.[192]

The projects that Allen represented all tended to have bold and imaginative names. It is likely that *Sea King* and *Avenger*, the names assigned to Creuzbaur's vessel designs, were due to his influence. Not long after he became involved in representing Williams and his submarine apparatus design, his new client's imaginative vessel was given the name *Triton*. Allen and Williams probably chose this name based on a sea god in Greek mythology who had the upper torso of a man and the tail of a fish. It was an appropriate name for a submarine project topped by exterior divers. The Triton name's popularity in maritime

"Submarine apparatus for the explosion of vessels proposed by Mr. [Charles] Babbage." *Illustrated London News*, June 23, 1855.

circles is further evidenced by its frequent use in the US Navy to this day. The name would become even more well known in 1960 when the submarine USS *Triton* accomplished a completely submerged circumnavigation of the earth. A portion of that famous vessel is now displayed in a Manhattan national historical park.[193]

Probably because of his difficulties getting the *Avenger* project past the navy's entrenched bureaucracy, Allen elected to go a different direction in promoting the *Triton* project. He first secured the cooperation of well-connected Virginia state senator Alexander J. Marshall, who wrote directly to James Seddon, the Confederate secretary of war, in April 1863, announcing the formation of the Triton Company. This new company, Marshall assured Seddon, would operate in the "utmost secrecy" and was designed to serve as a one-stop platform to research and develop various underwater projects to threaten enemy warships. Marshall disclosed to Seddon that the company's present owners included Ebenezer Allen of Texas, former Virginia Congressman Jeremiah Morton, and C. Williams of Missouri. Seddon promptly referred the Triton letter to the Engineer Department, which then characteristically began reviewing the proposal's merits at a glacial pace.[194]

While Allen and Williams were waiting for the government to respond to their Triton proposal, July 1863 found the expanded Singer group extremely busy on a number of fronts. A large number of torpedoes had been ordered and were being installed in the waters of Mississippi and Alabama. In Virginia, the chief engineer ordered torpedoes to be placed in the James River. The *De Kalb* sinking on July 13 furnished proof of concept for Singer's torpedoes. But it was the last day of July that turned out to be particularly significant for military history.

On the morning of July 31, 1863, an old coal barge was towed out and anchored in the Mobile River. As with Singer's Texas torpedo demonstration for General Magruder, officers of the Confederate Army and Navy jockeyed for position to enable them to closely observe the highly anticipated event. When the appointed time came, the crewmen crawled through the hatches of the new Hunley-Singer submarine and the strange contraption moved slowly out into the river, towing behind it a powder-filled floating torpedo. The submarine gradually dipped below the surface with only a trail of bubbles marking its position. After the torpedo was dragged forward and struck the side of the barge, a huge explosion occurred. A few minutes later, the submarine surfaced safely on the far side of the site where the destroyed barge had been.[195]

The experiment proved that, given the right conditions, the submarine could be a successful weapon. But Mobile was not the best place to test this concept. As the loss of *American Diver* established, navigators at Mobile struggled even to get a submarine out to a position where it could launch an attack against enemy blockaders. In addition, the waters where the blockaders were usually located were shallow, making it difficult for any submarine to maneuver safely under a heavy Union gunboat.

Unlike Mobile, Charleston seemed to be the ideal place to test the new submarine. A message was sent to General P. G. T. Beauregard, who immediately telegraphed an order to send it to him to use against the Union fleet: "Please expedite transportation of Whitney's submarine boat from Mobile here. It is much needed."[196] By referring to the craft as "Whitney's submarine boat," Beauregard suggested that the Texan was then viewed as being in charge of making arrangements for the vessel.[197]

By August 12, 1863, the rail cars on which the submarine was mounted had rolled into Charleston. Although Beauregard was eager to see the submarine in action, it would be some time before the submarine was ready to confront the enemy. To motivate the submarine's team, Beauregard's chief of staff sent Whitney a note informing him that Charleston merchants had put up a bounty of $100,000 for sinking the ironclad *New Ironsides* and that other merchants were expected to add to the reward.[198]

While the Hunley team was in Charleston optimistically contemplating submarine rewards, other teams with marine projects were experiencing mixed results. Charles Williams was in Richmond trying to get his own *Triton* submarine project off the ground. By this time, Robert Creuzbaur, Allen's other inventor client, had reluctantly given up on his *Avenger* project and was making plans to return to Texas. Although Creuzbaur continued to refine his torpedo designs, and even received a patent for a "wooden sole shoe" in August, his omission from the list of *Triton* owners confirms that he did not have any material role in this new project.[199]

In the summer of 1863, Creuzbaur obtained an introductory letter to General John B. Magruder from one of the general's old friends. Creuzbaur, the letter stated, "is the inventor of a floating torpedo to destroy vessels." Although the invention worked and gave every indication that it could be extremely useful, "the Secretary of the Navy appears to be disinclined to give the inventor any just or liberal facilities to test his invention."[200] Impressed by his friend's endorsement and Creuzbaur's qualifications, Magruder tendered him the position of assistant engineer. Creuzbaur accepted and began closing his operations in Virginia.

While Creuzbaur was moving his base of operations to Texas, Williams was continuing to refine his design for the Triton Submarine Company vessel that he called a "submarine apparatus." There is evidence that he submitted drawings of the apparatus to the Confederate patent office, which accepted it and placed it in the office's secret archives. Whether this amounted to a "secret patent," as some have suggested, is unclear. But it is clear that Williams was making serious progress on a number of fronts in his quest to design a practical and effective way to deliver large numbers of torpedoes to enemy warships.[201]

By this point, there were so many secret service groups operating in different places with similar projects that it was difficult to keep track of them all. Hoping to create an organizational structure that would avoid confusion, the Confederate Engineering Bureau decided to formalize assignments and divide up territories among the groups. On August 20, 1863, Lieutenant Colonel Alfred L. Rives, acting chief of the Engineer Bureau, wrote Lieutenant General E. Kirby Smith, commander of the Trans-Mississippi Department, informing him that a specially designated list of men was now assigned to his department. Although the men would appear on paper as enlisted in an engineer company, they were actually assigned "on the special service of destroying the enemy's property by torpedoes and similar inventions."[202]

The teams so designated for special service had no specific titles. Some later accounts have labeled them "Bands of Destructionists," a colorful and largely accurate title.[203] The designation of the Trans-Mississippi destructionists did not mention the Triton Company or Senator Marshall by name. Instead, the list identified seven men by name: John P. Kirk, Charles (presumably Caleb) Littlepage, John Silure, Robert Creuzbaur, E. Allen, W. D. Miller, and C. Williams. Most of these men were either Texans or (like Williams) members of the Allen group. John P. Kirk was yet another Austin inventor who remained close friends with Creuzbaur and Littlepage before, during, and after the war.[204]

There was an important reason that men involved in secret service projects like submarines and torpedoes needed to be formally assigned to an engineer company. If they were captured or caught in the act of deploying torpedoes, the men needed to be able to credibly claim that they were enlisted in a formally established branch of military service. This status might make all the difference between being treated as prisoners of war or being executed as spies or terrorists.

The notice to E. Kirby Smith about the secret service team assigned to his command provided that the team members would be entitled to the value of "fifty percent of the property destroyed by their new inventions, and all the arms and munitions captured by them by the use of torpedoes or of similar devices." Spelling this out gave the men involved in this dangerous service a powerful incentive to succeed. It also provided a defined formula that would eliminate controversy about the nature of a reward if they were successful.[205]

On the day following the letter to Kirby Smith, Rives sent a similar letter covering different agents to General Joseph E. Johnston, who commanded the Confederate Department of the West. That department covered a vast area extending from the Mississippi River on the west to Virginia, the Carolinas, and Florida on the east. Johnston was assigned a team of nine special service agents on identical terms to those furnished to Kirby Smith. The men assigned were E. C. Singer, J. D. Braman, R. W. Dunn, B. A. Whitney, D. Bradbury, James Jones, C. E. Tracy, J. B. Fretwell, and L. C. Hirschburger. Almost all these men were Texans and members of the Singer group.[206]

After the assignments of August 20–21, it seemed settled that the Allen group would be working west of the Mississippi while the Singer group would be working east of the river. This simple arrangement would later be modified and complicated when Chief Engineer Rives sent General Kirby Smith an addendum letting him know that E. C. Singer, R. W. Dunn, J. R. Fretwell and

F. M. Tucker would also be joining the group working west of the river in the Trans-Mississippi. Despite its potential for confusion, this change made sense given the Singer group's still active torpedo manufacturing and installation operation in and around Lavaca.[207]

August 1863 started out as a good month for the secret service groups. They now had formal geographic assignments with specified rewards. Torpedo sales were brisk. Even Robert Creuzbaur, who was on his way to Texas to look for a new place to work, was awarded three Confederate patents in the same month, the last being a patent for his torpedo. There were two events late in the month, however, that eventually cast all the positive events of early August into a negative light.[208]

General Beauregard grew impatient with the lack of serious progress by the crew of the Charleston submarine (still called the "fish boat" by many observers). He ordered that it be confiscated and turned over to a crew from the Confederate Navy. While most of the other Singer operatives moved on to torpedo operations in Richmond or Mobile, Gus Whitney stayed behind to monitor the submarine's activities. It is unclear whether he stayed on in some formal capacity, such as liaising between the navy and the submarine builders, or just remained in Charleston to monitor the Singer group's majority ownership position in the venture. By this time, the strain of endless trials was wearing on the submarine's crew. The late nights and strenuous activity also affected the support team ashore. In late August, Gus Whitney unexpectedly died of what Singer later described as "pneumonia contracted while experimenting with the boat."[209]

Whitney's sudden death was just the first of two August tragedies to strike the Charleston submarine project. The second involved the vessel itself. At around midnight on August 29, the submarine was moored at Fort Johnson with its crew on board. As usual, it took some time at the dock to load the submarine and prepare for the evening mission. There are conflicting stories regarding exactly what happened, but somehow water, possibly from a passing ship's wake, ended up pouring over into the hatchways and filling the boat.

The submarine quickly sank, and five members of the crew drowned because they were unable to escape from the tight enclosed space of the vessel.[210]

After the tragedy, Horace Hunley reminded General Beauregard of his partial ownership claim to the vessel and assured him that if he would only allow Hunley to raise the submarine and bring an experienced crew from Mobile, the boat could still achieve its original objective. Although skeptical, Beauregard agreed to Hunley's proposal. It took weeks to recover the vessel, clean out the bodies and debris, and get it back into position to go out on missions. It is interesting to note that in his request to Beauregard, Horace Hunley referred to the vessel he wished to recover as "the torpedo boat the *Hunley*." This is at odds with later reports suggesting that this renaming did not occur until after its owner's death.[211]

While the submarine salvage operation was in process, September turned out to be a relatively quiet month for the Singer and Allen secret service groups. On September 21, 1863, Creuzbaur finally reached Texas and reported to General Magruder. He found the general to be in an excellent mood and generally receptive to his unconventional ideas.[212]

As Creuzbaur soon learned, Magruder's mood had been markedly improved by a recent military success. On September 8, 1863, a large Union armada appeared suddenly off the entrance to Sabine Pass and attempted to pass the Confederate fort. The Confederate garrison at that fort (Fort Griffin) consisted of fewer than fifty men under the command of a former Irish saloonkeeper, Lieutenant Richard W. "Dick" Dowling. At the conclusion of the forty-five-minute Battle of Sabine Pass, Dowling and his men disabled the two leading gunboats and drove away the Union invasion force.[213]

The almost miraculous result of the Battle of Sabine Pass confirmed Magruder's view that large enemy warships could be destroyed, or at least kept at bay, by carefully positioned artillery. Because of his experience with Singer's torpedoes earlier in the year, he was also receptive to Creuzbaur's more unconventional schemes to add them as part of an even more creative defense strategy.

When Creuzbaur returned to Texas, he did not have any drawings or designs with him. This lack of materials was because, as later events would confirm, the engineer had wisely avoided bringing anything with him that might fall into enemy hands while crossing the Mississippi River. Magruder granted the engineer's request to use his friend C. V. Littlepage to help draw up some plans for the general to review. On the official service records, Creuzbaur's assignment was formally described as "duty for special services in constructing torpedoes and other infernal machines."[214]

Remarkably, even the Confederates planning to deploy them in Texas formally referred to their floating torpedoes as "infernal machines." Over on the East Coast, Confederates were planning a more active delivery system—torpedo boats—to bring the infernal machines into contact with their enemy.

CHAPTER 7

TORPEDO BOAT MANIA

Beginning in 1863 and extending throughout the remainder of the war, both Union and Confederate military planners experimented with the concept of building smaller and faster armored vessels that could maneuver into position to explode powerful torpedoes close to the hulls of enemy warships. Called "torpedo boats," these vessels were, for obvious reasons, prominent on the wish list of every Confederate commander defending a blockaded coastal city. In some ways, these attack crafts may be viewed as the forerunners of the American Motor Torpedo Boats ("PT Boats") that would provide valuable service in World War II.[215]

Although seemingly simple in design, torpedo boats proved unexpectedly difficult to construct in practice. In part, this was due to their lack of standardization. A time-honored tradition in maritime military construction is to build a series of similar if not identical vessels with subsequent ships referred to as part of the class named after the first constructed vessel. Thus, the United States Navy had "*Unadilla*-class" or "*Cairo*-class" gunboats, both named after the first member of their respective classes. This was more than a convenient form of reference. Finding a pattern that worked and then producing subsequent vessels on the maritime equivalent of an assembly line was an established way to standardize naval construction and enhance production efficiency. Constantly tinkering with designs and making every vessel a unique object from scratch was typically not part of a recipe for maritime success.

Although Confederate naval forces were the first to effectively employ torpedo boats, they tended to be experimental in nature and never really matured into a standardized class of design and construction. To be fair, differences in torpedo boat designs were often a function of the limited availability of resources (engines, iron, and anthracite coal, among others). A relatively large number of torpedo boats ended up being built at various times all around the Confederacy (including Texas), but never played any significant role in lifting the Union blockade. Despite tantalizing evidence that they might have been effective if properly used, they were never deployed in significant numbers.

At the end of the war, there would be at least three torpedo boat projects underway in Texas. But Confederate torpedo boats really got their start in the middle of the war on the East Coast. In the summer of 1863, a Confederate engineer named Francis D. Lee supervised construction of the first-ever torpedo boat near Charleston. The *Torch*, as Lee named it, mounted three spar torpedoes, each with fifty pounds of powder. Although *Torch* did not succeed in delivering any of its three torpedoes to enemy ships during its August 1863 missions, subsequent torpedo boat attacks supported the military case for such vessels.[216]

Lee's plan to build a torpedo boat like *Torch* had been in progress well before its 1863 missions. On October 13, 1862, General Beauregard had sent Lee to his superiors with a letter expressing his preference for Lee's torpedo boat schemes over attempts to build more large ironclad vessels. According to Beauregard, torpedo boats like Lee's *Torch* could be built for less than a third of the cost of an ironclad warship and would take one-third of the time to construct.[217]

An unrelated attack in October 1863 made Beauregard even more convinced that torpedo boats were the best—and possibly the only—way to effectively defend Confederate harbors. On an early October evening, the torpedo boat *David* steamed out of Charleston Harbor and approached the Union ironclad *New Ironsides*. *David* was to become famous as the first "torpedo boat" to directly attack an enemy vessel. Although its long cylindrical shape was similar to a submarine, it was actually a semi-submersible torpedo ram. As this description implies, *David* did not totally submerge; it was a low-relief surface vessel that had much of its machinery protected below the waterline to give enemy vessels less of a target.[218]

Unlike Horace Hunley's submarine, which at this point was still towing a torpedo, *David*'s plan of attack depended on a fourteen-foot piece of boiler tube projecting from its bow ending in a spar torpedo containing close to one hundred pounds of powder. The plan was to ram an enemy ship, triggering the explosion of the deadly torpedo. On October 5, 1863, *David*'s captain, Lieutenant William T. Glassell, managed to achieve his objective of ramming the ironclad *New Ironsides*. The problem was that the resulting torpedo explosion threw up a column of water that came splashing down through

Painting by unidentified artist depicting torpedo boat *David* at Charleston, South Carolina, in 1863. NH 54432, US Naval History and Heritage Command.

David's smokestack and extinguished the boat's boiler fire. Glassell gave the order to abandon ship, and he and his fireman floated off, later to be captured. Two other members of *David*'s crew ultimately managed to reboard the vessel, relight *David*'s fire, and then steer the damaged boat back into port.[219]

In 1970, a small booklet was published with a subtitle crediting *David* with making "the first successful torpedo boat attack in naval warfare."[220] In truth, the *David*'s mission was both a success and a failure. It was a success in the sense that it demonstrated that a small boat showing little surface area above the waterline could avoid detection and effectively employ a spar torpedo against a larger vessel. But how effective was the attack? As later became clear, *New Ironsides* did suffer some damage from the torpedo attack, although the extent of that damage remains both uncertain and controversial. The attack was a failure in that, unlike the Singer torpedo that sank *De Kalb*, *New Ironsides* did not sink. It remained a part of the Union blockade. The biggest failure of *David*'s attack was that the captured Confederate crewmen were found to have detailed diagrams of the torpedo boat in their possession. These were promptly forwarded up the Union Navy's chain of command, providing valuable information about this new mode of attack and suggesting ways to defend against it.[221]

Not an official Confederate vessel, *David* is generally believed to have been designed and built by St. Julien Ravenel, a Charleston physician and agricultural chemist. Although the Singer group was not directly involved with this torpedo boat, the near success of the attack was a significant development to everyone involved in designing small attack crafts. The fact that *David* was able to come so close to severely damaging its target emboldened Confederate officials who hoped to find a relatively simple and low-cost strategy to oppose enemy ironclads and blockaders. It also encouraged private groups to fund construction of torpedo boat privateers and explore efforts to secure rewards. All around the Confederacy, including Texas, military and private planners went to work evaluating how they could best adapt the new torpedo boat strategy to their own needs and waters.[222]

On November 14, 1863, a little over a month after *David*'s famous attack, General Beauregard issued a remarkable strategic analysis. With no stated recipient, the communication was included in the *Official Records of the Union and Confederate Navies* simply as "Remarks of General Beauregard, C.S. Army, relative to ironclad gunboats." Noting that previous Confederate ironclads were too slow and had too deep a draft to be useful, he observed that the enemy's ironclads were essentially invulnerable above the water except at very short range. The solution, he suggested, was to attack them below water using a swift, shot-proof torpedo boat that carried Francis D. Lee's spar torpedoes. With just one of those vessels, Beauregard believed the blockade could be lifted at Charleston. "Half a dozen of these steamers would raise the blockade of our Atlantic and Gulf coasts and enable us to recover the navigation of the Mississippi River."[223]

Because of Beauregard's enthusiastic endorsement and his prior experience with torpedo boats, Francis Lee was handed the assignment of attempting to coordinate their construction at coastal ports across the Confederacy. Chief Engineer Gilmer was generally supportive of the torpedo boat plan and thought it made particular sense at places with blockading fleets located close to shore. What he did not think made sense was Lee's initial plan to

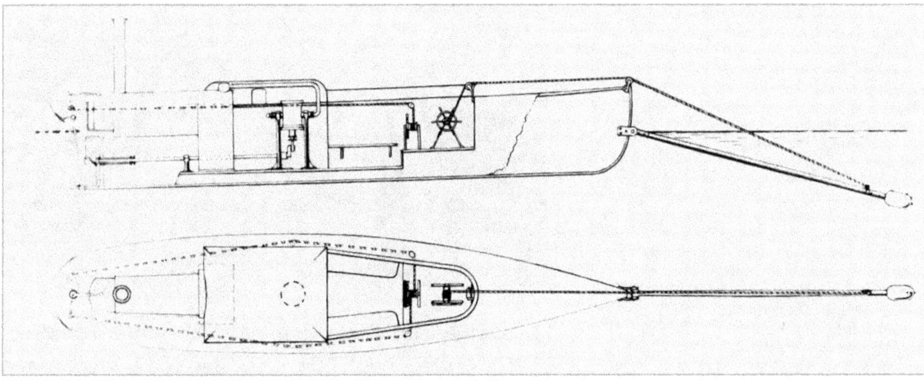

Drawing of Confederate torpedo boat *Squib*, which attacked USS *Minnesota* off Newport News, Virginia. NH 108833, US Naval History and Heritage Command.

build all of the torpedo boats at Charleston and then ship them across the South on railroads. "Will there be no difficulties in the transportation of boats from Charleston to Wilmington, Mobile, etc.?," Gilmer asked. "Would it not be more convenient and economical to build the boats at the harbors in which they are to be used?"[224] Gilmer would win this particular fight. Torpedo boats would eventually be built in various places around the Confederacy, including Texas. None of them, however, would achieve the level of success that Beauregard predicted.

David was not the only Confederate torpedo boat to achieve some measure of success. Following *David*'s famous mission, Confederate authorities on the East Coast authorized the construction of four similar vessels. *Squib*, the first completed boat, was not as semi-submersible as *David* had been. *Squib* was

Lieutenant (Later Commander) Hunter Davidson, CSN (1826–1913). NH 50688, US Naval History and Heritage Command.

described as thirty-five to forty feet in length with a six-foot beam. Covered with boiler iron, *Squib* had a small double-cylinder steam engine. The small size and engine made the torpedo boat relatively fast. Another key difference from *David* was that *Squib*'s spar torpedo was designed to be electrically fired.[225]

On the night of April 9, 1864, Lieutenant Hunter Davidson skillfully maneuvered *Squib* through the Federal blockaders at Hampton Roads in Virginia and exploded his torpedo against the hull of USS *Minnesota*. As with *David*'s encounter with *New Ironsides*, the true extent of the damage *Squib* inflicted on *Minnesota* is unclear. What is clear is that the target ship that Davidson attacked was not so badly damaged that it sank. Although the torpedo boat had once again shown promise, it had not proved to be the ship killer its designers had intended.[226]

Although *Squib* was intended to be the first of four members of a *Squib*-class of torpedo boats, the subsequent vessels would differ in size and key details, making the reference to a "*Squib*-class" essentially meaningless. The primary thing these four vessels would have in common is that none of them proved to be very effective.[227] Perhaps for this reason, subsequent torpedo boats would not follow either the *David* or *Squib* models except in general terms. Usually, their design would be tailored to fit the existing elements of whatever vessel was being altered to transform it into a torpedo boat. This was particularly true of the much larger torpedo boats that would be constructed in Texas in 1865. In the hands of people like the Singer operatives or Robert Creuzbaur, the Texas torpedo boats would morph into something quite unique.

CHAPTER 8

MISSING MAIL AND MYSTERIES

As *David* was attacking *New Ironsides* in October 1863, James Jones of the Singer group was in the process of completing and installing more than seventy-five torpedoes in the waters around Richmond. In his few off hours, Jones learned that Confederate secret service founder Bernard Janin Sage was about to leave Richmond to head to destinations farther south, including Texas. Deciding that the opportunity was too good to pass up, on October 13, 1863, Jones wrote what he believed at the time to be a secure letter to his associates back in Texas. He gleefully described a test of the Singer torpedo he had recently conducted for the War Department in Virginia:

> I set a machine in the James River and let a schooner float over it, and it was one of the prettiest sights I ever saw. It was a perfect success. It raised the schooner about 10 feet in the air, and when she came down there was nothing left but pieces.[228]

Jones was not the only temporary guest in Richmond who would write a letter for Sage to carry home to Texas. Although not involved in the installation of torpedoes, inventor Charles Williams and attorney Ebenezer Allen were also in Richmond, anxiously awaiting word from the government engineers about their design for the former's "submarine apparatus." The original design for the *Triton* submarine that Williams had drawn up involved a craft propelled by oars. Although this might work for short distances, it clearly would not be suitable for the long distances that would be required to get from many Confederate ports to the Union blockaders lurking offshore.

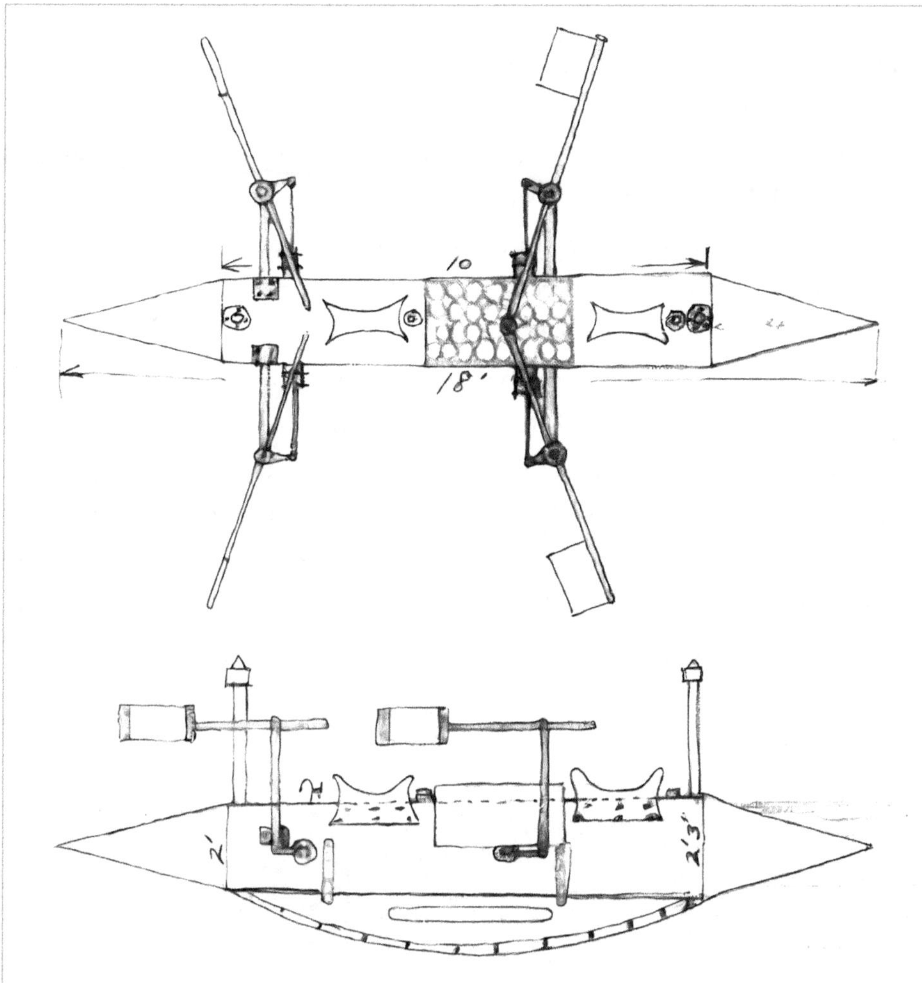

Triton submarine apparatus designed by C. Williams labeled "two operators and four torpedoes," top view and side view. Based on attachment to letter from Williams to J. F. Gilmer, October 27, 1863, Record Group 109, National Archives and Records Administration.

Williams's *Triton* design was a radical departure both from the *Hunley* submarine and semi-submersible vessels like torpedo boats. Instead of a pilot located inside the vessel, *Triton* would be steered by one or more divers seated in chairs on its deck. Instead of carrying a single spar torpedo, *Triton* would carry multiple torpedoes secured to the topside of its hull. Instead of detonating the torpedoes by contact or pulling a lanyard, *Triton*'s torpedoes would be triggered by a clockwork mechanism. Virtually every aspect of *Triton* was a unique feature that set it apart from other Civil War vessel designs.

Williams knew at least generally about the submarine *H. L. Hunley* and its design. He did not believe that such a vessel would solve the Confederacy's fundamental problem. Unlike Horace Hunley, Williams did not believe that the best way to attack blockaders was to use either a floating or spar torpedo. He believed that the most reliable way to cause torpedoes to damage enemy ships, particularly ironclads, was to stealthily approach underwater and then deploy divers who would physically attach torpedoes to their unprotected undersides. Rather than explode the torpedoes on contact, Williams planned to use "horological [clockwork] torpedoes" of his own design that would explode only after a set period of time, giving the Confederate vessel and its divers time to escape. In this way, a single Confederate submarine vessel might succeed in sinking multiple enemy vessels on a single mission.

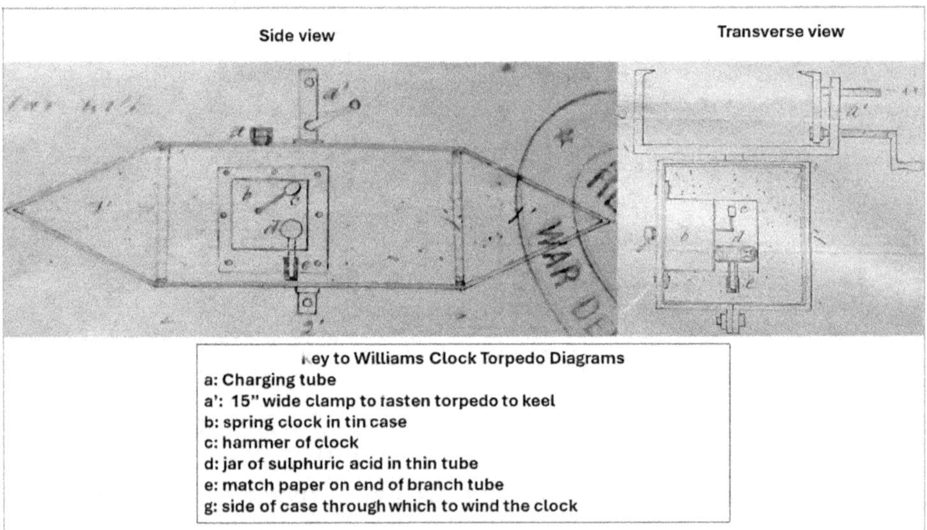

Drawing of "Clock Torpedo" by C. Williams labeled "Inside view of one side and Transverse section," with author's letter key. Attachment to letter from Williams to J. F. Gilmer, October 27, 1863, Record Group 109, National Archives and Records Administration.

On October 14, 1863, Ebenezer Allen wrote his own letter to an associate in Texas proclaiming the merits of Williams's designs. Allen noted that they had succeeded in getting capital of $50,000 raised for the project and said, "Just at present things look very well if they don't blow out." He advised his Texas contact:

> We have concluded to propose that you attempt to procure the construction of the apparatus . . . or the submarine boat—the latter I think preferable with the improvement added, for the Texas coast, one or more might be started; and with that view enclose a rough sketch of some of the main points which we shall adopt in the construction on this side of the river not going into details as you will understand and adopt them as well as ourselves . . . You could hardly start anything of more promise and less difficulty if properly planned and conducted and you had better start on one or more with as little delay as possible, for attention is being rapidly turned in that direction and it is bound to be the next great revolution in naval warfare and that in a near future.[229]

Although Allen clearly wrote this letter with an optimistic tone, he never had a chance to sign it. Instead, to this letter was attached a remarkable postscript:

> P.S.S., Oct. 16. I open this to communicate the melancholy and shocking intelligence of the decease of Colonel Allen who died suddenly of heart disease yesterday morning. He will be buried with marine honors tomorrow or next day. Break the news gently to his family.
>
> In haste Yours
>
> C.W. [original was apparently signed by Charles Williams]
>
> X. Our business was staked so that I shall be able to go ahead with it I think.[230]

Attached to this strange letter was a drawing of the larger version of Williams's design. This was likely the drawing that had been supplied to the Confederate Patent Department for the patent later issued to Williams for a "submarine apparatus" on October 25, 1863.[231]

On the day following Allen's death, Williams added the mysterious "P.S.S." postscript, signed the letter, and then gave it to Sage to be bundled with the Jones letter and delivered to Texas. Unfortunately for Williams, his letter would never reach his intended recipient. Before discussing where the letter actually ended end up, it is worth pausing briefly to examine the series of strange events surrounding the death of the letter's original author.

On the morning of October 15, 1863, before Ebenezer Allen could sign the letter quoted above, he met a group of men for a late breakfast at the Gem Saloon, which was located under his boarding house. It seemed to the restaurant staff to have been a cordial event. According to later reports, wine

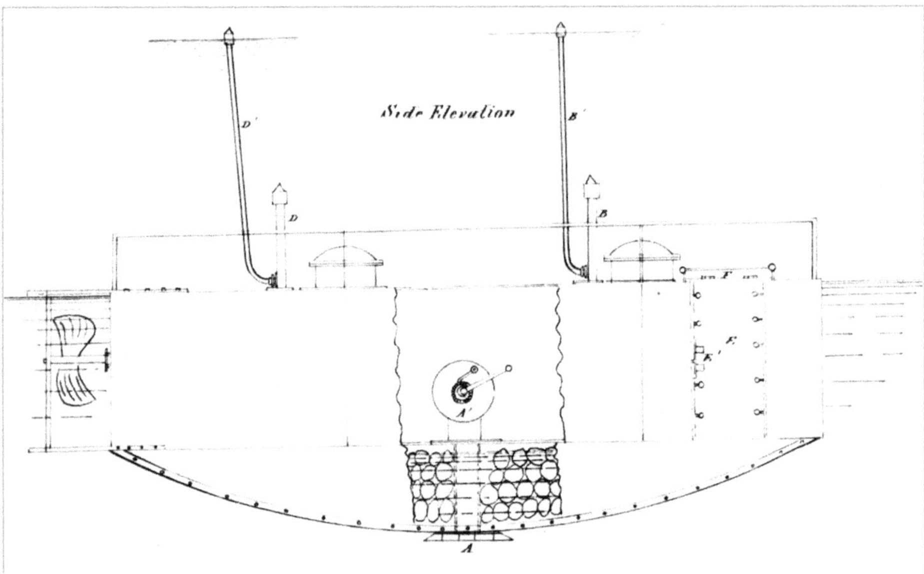

"Side Elevation" of Triton submarine apparatus drawn by C. Williams, forwarded in letter from Charles P. Stone to Adjutant General, November 27, 1863. File No. G487, Record Group 94, National Archives and Records Administration]

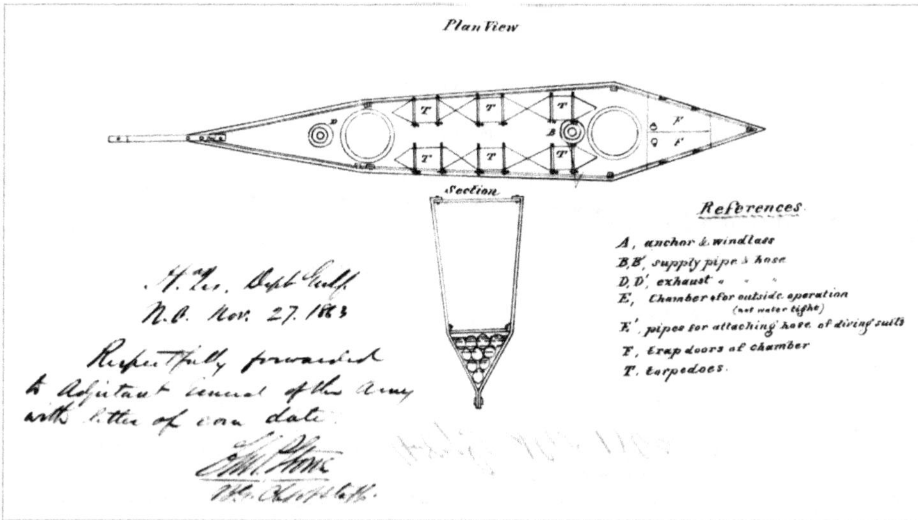

"Plan" and "Section" views of *Triton* submarine apparatus designed by C. Williams, forwarded in letter from Charles P. Stone to Adjutant General, November 27, 1863. File No. G487, Record Group 94, National Archives and Records Administration.

GREAT EXCITEMENT!

HURRAH FOR THE GEM SALOON, ON 12TH STREET.

All those who may be in want of a good. cool JULEP, SHERRY COBBLER or PUNCH of any kind, should call on TRUEHEART, at the Gem Saloon, 12th street, between Main and Cary, where all things to comfort the inner man can be found in great abundance. je 8—6t*

Advertisement for the Gem Saloon. *Richmond Dispatch*, June 8, 1860.

had been called for and passed around. The other guests at this breakfast have never been identified. After his guests left, Allen stayed at the table. All seemed to be fine. In a short time, however, one of the waiters noticed that Allen was beginning to turn blue. The restaurant patron who had seemed just a short time before to be in perfect health now seemed to be dying. By the time the saloon's proprietor reached him, Allen was dead.[232]

The *Richmond Examiner*'s October 16 account of what was headlined as a "Sudden and Mysterious Death," referred to the victim as Colonel Allen (a courtesy title). The article said that Allen appeared to be about forty years of age (he was actually fifty-nine) and "had the appearance of a speculator." The report noted that a Dr. Slack, who conveniently happened to be in the house, pronounced the death to be "the result of a disease of the heart." There was apparently no inquest and no autopsy.[233]

Allen, like the members of the Singer Secret Service group, was a Mason. The Richmond newspaper later reported that since Allen was a Mason, Masonic Lodge 10 had taken charge of his body and would see it properly laid to rest in Hollywood Cemetery. Despite diligent investigation, Allen H. Mesch, Ebenezer Allen's biographer, was unable to locate any record of his actual burial location.[234]

Although Mesch appears to have been unaware of the above-quoted submarine apparatus letter when he wrote Allen's biography, he quite understandably found the newspaper's account of Allen's sudden death the next day "perplexing" and believed that its circumstances left many unanswered questions. He published a chart weighing the available historical evidence to see whether it favored a heart attack, as the original physician apparently suggested, or a targeted assassination. Although Mesch finally concluded that the balance of evidence favored a natural cause of death, he noted that "another researcher might interpret the data differently and make a case for his murder."[235]

Although the present author cannot conclude that Allen was definitely murdered, the circumstances of his sudden death after breakfast are certainly mysterious, particularly given the submarine apparatus letter that was waiting to be signed in his hotel room. The fact that Allen had been actively raising money for a project that potentially threatened the destruction of many Union warships and was sending word that very day to begin construction of one or more of the secret vessels in Texas certainly adds to the circumstantial evidence that Allen may indeed have been murdered by unknown operatives.

Based on the symptoms exhibited, it is at least plausible that Union secret agents took the opportunity of conveniently disposing of Allen at breakfast with a poison like cyanide or arsenic. To add additional mystery to the mix, Mesch noted in his biography that Allen's wife contended long after the war that her husband was always a "Union man," raising the surprising possibility that Confederate spies might conceivably have believed Allen to be a double agent and murdered him to end that threat.[236]

Historians will probably never know the true cause of Ebenezer Allen's death, but the fact that it took place on the exact date the submarine apparatus letter was to be sent is certainly a remarkable coincidence. What makes the October 15 date even more interesting is that yet another letter was signed that same day. On the day that Allen died, Major General Jeremy F. Gilmer, the commander of the Engineering Office, Department of South Carolina, Georgia, and Florida, finally wrote a letter to Confederate Secretary of War Seddon noting that he had reviewed the submarine apparatus approach proposed by the Triton group and believed that "it must fail in practice."[237]

Gilmer thought the propulsion system was too weak, the air pumps badly designed, and questioned how the torpedoes could possibly be attached to an enemy vessel. He also said that the materials for armoring the boat could not be obtained in the Confederacy. In Gilmer's opinion, there were many obvious flaws with the vessel's design, and he did not recommend furnishing any materials for construction of the boat or even allowing work on it to take place in government facilities. Coming on the heels of Allen's sudden death, Gilmer's rejection of the *Triton* design must have come as a devastating blow to Williams, who had gone ahead and promptly forwarded Allen's letter to Sage in the hopes of getting it delivered to Texas and expediting completion of the project.[238]

The *Triton* was not the only submarine project facing a major setback on October 15, 1863. On the same day that Allen was having his last breakfast in the Gem Saloon, another tragedy was taking place in Charleston. With *Hunley* commander George E. Dixon temporarily absent on an assignment, Horace Hunley decided to take the raised and refurbished submarine out for a practice dive. It was an ordinary test dive that the submarine had successfully accomplished many times in the past. Approaching within a short distance of the receiving ship *Indian Chief*, the submarine closed its hatches and submerged. Watchers onboard the *Chief* witnessed a trail of bubbles proceeding in their direction and then turned, expecting to see the submarine come up. Unfortunately, *Hunley* never surfaced.[239]

Later reconstructions of the event suggest that Horace Hunley made a fundamental mistake in managing the forward ballast tank. As water from the forward tank began filling the vessel, Thomas Parks, whose Mobile machine shop had been the site where the submarine was constructed, worked feverishly in the rear to empty the back tank. His efforts were not enough. The submarine filled with water and the entire crew perished.[240]

In the wake of this tragedy, General Beauregard, usually a firm supporter of creative weapons, quickly washed his hands of the project. He concluded that the submarine "is more dangerous to those who use it than the enemy."[241] Some observers began referring to the unlucky vessel as the "peripatetic coffin." It would be two months before the coffin vessel was raised, cleaned out, and readied for renewed service under the direction of Lieutenant George E. Dixon. It is impressive that Dixon somehow managed to overcome all the obstacles and get the unlucky and dangerous project back on track. Perhaps the most remarkable achievement during this time was Dixon's success in securing a new crew of volunteers, each of whom had been informed of the dismal fate that befell their predecessors.[242]

While Dixon was attempting to get the *Hunley* raised and back into service in Charleston, in Richmond, Charles Williams was still struggling to revive the Confederate government's interest in his *Triton* project. On October 25, 1863, ten days after Allen's mysterious death, Williams finally was awarded a patent for his "submarine apparatus." This was likely the same apparatus that Chief Engineer Gilmer had recently rejected. The news must have been bittersweet; Williams now had a patent for something that nobody in authority seemed to be interested in building.[243]

On October 27, just twelve days after Allen's death, Williams responded to Gilmer's rejection in a letter he signed simply as "the Inventor." Williams probably used this signature not so much to hide his identity, but because he feared that Confederate officials were unaware of his role and had been operating under the assumption that Allen and Alexander J. Marshall had been heading up the *Triton* project. In his "Inventor" letter, Williams attempted to address some of the concerns Gilmer had expressed.

Williams started by warning that Marshall had inappropriately changed some things in his original description of the *Triton* submarine apparatus. He believed that these unapproved additions had led Gilmer to fundamentally misunderstand the manner in which the apparatus was intended to function. Gilmer's concerns about the air flow, for example, would have been entirely eliminated if Gilmer had known that the *Triton* sub's design included the ability to compress air into onboard air chambers before the vessel submerged.[244]

Williams also responded to Gilmer's comment that "the arrangements for attaching the boat to a ship for attaching a torpedo to the side or bottom are not explained." To Williams, this was the greatest strength of his design. The *Triton* submarine had an anchor in the center that could be deployed and adjusted using a windlass. As Williams noted, the vessel would simply anchor under an enemy vessel's keel and then be ratcheted up until the diver could reach the keel. From this position, the diver could either clamp a torpedo to the vessel or use a "sucker" to attach it. If both these attachment mechanisms failed, the diver would have some line and an anchor in reach that would enable him to simply float the torpedo up from the bottom and deploy it immediately adjacent to the keel.[245]

Finally, Williams refuted Gilmer's comment that the air pump was "liable to get out of order, and should this occur when the boat is submerged, it involves the loss of boat and crew." He pointed out that even before the boat submerged, enough air would be compressed on board to sustain the crew during the expected mission duration. Even if some problem developed, the ballast could be quickly dumped, causing the craft to immediately surface. Williams also pointed out that the floating air hoses of adjustable length (acting essentially as large snorkels) provided an easy way of bringing extra air in and out of the vessel. As Williams viewed it, the combination of all these features made the *Triton* apparatus "almost absolutely safe."[246]

Although Williams wrote his "Inventor" letter to Gilmer twelve days after *Hunley* had been lost for the second time, it is unlikely that the inventor knew about this terrible development. Instead, believing that a connection to that higher profile vessel might help his case, Williams spent a good deal of his letter discussing how his ideas could be used to improve operation of the *Hunley*. Although Williams continued to believe that his design possessed many advantages over the submarine at Charleston, he suggested that if the navy was not confident enough to build *Triton*, it should at least try some of *Triton*'s design concepts on *Hunley* to make it work more effectively.[247]

As far as Williams was concerned, the most important defect with *Hunley* was that it lacked the ability to deploy divers outside the vessel. This was crucial because without outside operators, the only way to deploy a torpedo while submerged was to either ram or tow it into an enemy vessel's hull. *Hunley* was limited to a single torpedo per mission, and it was challenging even to get that into the optimal position for an effective attack. If *Hunley* could be modified so it could anchor below the target vessel, as Williams favored, a diver on top could physically attach the torpedo to the most vulnerable part of the keel and, using a clockwork mechanism, might even proceed to attach torpedoes to multiple vessels before escaping. Instead of a single torpedo on a spar, Williams estimated that a boat like *Hunley* could potentially carry eight to ten torpedoes mounted on the hull's exterior.[248]

Another of *Triton*'s alleged design improvements over *Hunley* was an external compass. Williams was correct in his identification of this as area where improvement was needed. Writing after the war, James McClintock identified two major problems with *H. L. Hunley*, the famous vessel that he had helped construct. The first was its relative lack of speed, which he eventually proposed to address with the addition of an ammonia gas engine. The second major difficulty concerned underwater navigation, which in 1864, depended purely on dead reckoning with the aid of a compass. McClintock admitted that the compass inside *Hunley* acted unreliably and sluggishly, undoubtedly due to its placement inside an iron hull.[249]

Williams told Gilmer that his outside diver design provided the ideal solution for *Hunley*'s compass problem. As he explained to Gilmer, "an outside compass should be placed in front of the outside operator who acts as pilot, elevated from the deck to the proper height and the covering, raising and lowering will be controlled by this operator or pilot; the signals being given by a certain number of taps upon certain places of the deck with a small iron rod." To help Gilmer understand how the diver and compass operated, Williams attached a drawing of the pilot diver sitting on an outside chair. The exterior compass is depicted near his outstretched hand.[250]

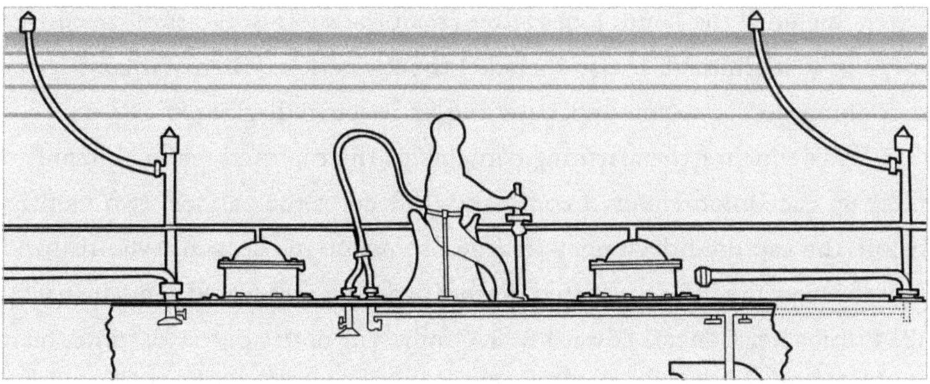

Drawing by Andrew W. Hall of top of *Triton* submarine apparatus with exterior diver based on drawing by C. Williams, attachment to J. F. Gilmer, October 27, 1863. Record Group 109, National Archives and Records Administration.

Although no substantive response to Williams's "Inventor" letter has been located, his suggestions for improving *Hunley* apparently were furnished to the Charleston submarine's operating team. There is no evidence, however, that any of the suggestions offered by Williams were seriously considered. *Hunley*'s commander, George Dixon, was undoubtedly too fully occupied readying the submarine for its final mission and never had the opportunity even to experiment with any of the modifications Williams proposed.[251]

Williams must have realized that the disrespectful tone of his letter to Gilmer meant that it would not change any minds at the Engineer Bureau. He had probably resigned himself to the fact that all his hopes now lay in the letter he had signed for Allen and sent to Texas. In Texas, he believed, there might still be people willing or desperate enough to take a chance and bring his visions to reality. What Williams did not know was that his letter and drawings would never reach their target recipient in Texas.

There was just something about the waters of the Mississippi River that seemed determined to undermine—no pun intended—the efforts of the Confederate secret service, In November 1863, Union soldiers from the Sixth Michigan Infantry Regiment captured a shipment of Confederate mail that carriers were attempting to ferry across the Mississippi River near Tunica Bend. Much of the intercepted mail was destined for Texas. The captured letters included the James Jones letter about the successful test of the Singer torpedo at Richmond. It also included the mysterious Allen-Williams letter describing the submarine apparatus and its attached diagram.[252]

It took time for the alarming contents of the captured mail shipment to filter up the Union chain of command. Indeed, it took almost two months before the captured documents reached someone in the army who realized that the navy might be interested in what had been discovered. On January 18, 1864, Brigadier General Edward R. S. Canby sent notice of the alarming mail to the Union secretary of the Navy. In addition to the letter from Jones about torpedoes, Canby forwarded what he described as a "diagram of a proposed

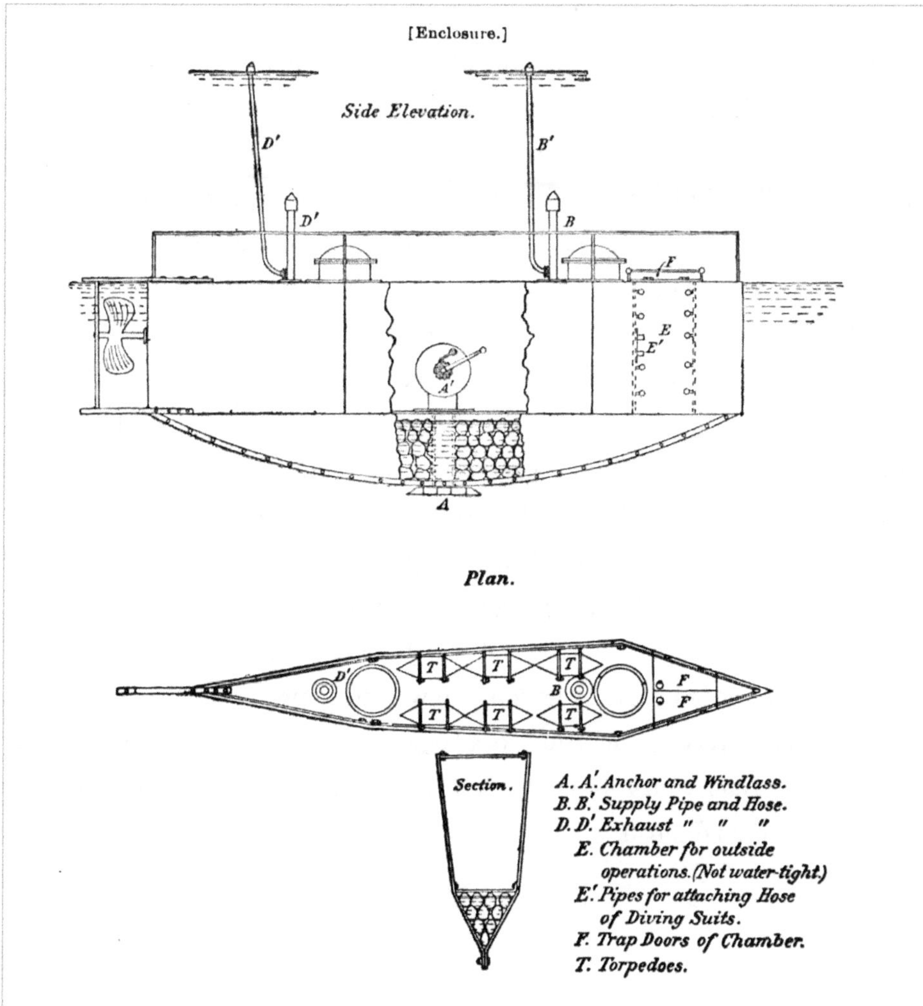

Captured drawing of *Triton* submarine apparatus designed by C. Williams as depicted in volume 9 of the *Official Records of the Union and Confederate Navies* (1899).

submarine torpedo vessel, suggested to be used on the coast of Texas." Although the drawing attached by Canby made its way into the published version of the *Official Records of the Union and Confederate Navies*, the mysterious cover letter from Allen and Williams that accompanied the drawing did not.[253]

Despite Gilmer's dismissal of the *Triton* plan, the Charleston Confederates were far from giving up on the idea of attacking enemy vessels with torpedoes. As Gilmer and Williams were corresponding, *H. L. Hunley* was once again in the process of being raised and made ready for service. In addition, the engineers still had high hopes for a potential fleet of torpedo boats like *David*.

In addition to designing *Torch*, the first Confederate torpedo boat, Francis D. Lee made one other important contribution to the military story that was unfolding at Charleston. As his *Torch* design reflected, Lee had always favored spar torpedoes over those like *Hunley*'s that merely floated or were dragged. While *H. L. Hunley* was being prepared for the course of service that would culminate in its final mission, Lee convinced General Beauregard to insist on one important modification. Instead of towing a torpedo behind it, as it had done in every trial so far, *Hunley* would now mount a spar torpedo and attack an enemy vessel by ramming it below the waterline. Lee claimed later that he personally superintended the installation of a fifty-pound torpedo on *Hunley*'s newly added spar. Although Lee was quite proud that his suggestion had been taken, recent scientific work suggests that the explosion of the spar torpedo near *Hunley* may have been at least one of the things that eventually contributed to its demise.[254]

CHAPTER 9

STOPPING THE FEDERALS IN TEXAS

Shortly after the Battle of Sabine Pass, General Magruder's engineers decided to strengthen the fortification that Dick Dowling and his Confederate garrison had defended so effectively. Fort Griffin had resisted the fire of gunboats, but it certainly looked like a fort that would be vulnerable to a more determined force of enemy infantry. The engineers knew that there were no more available soldiers or larger guns that could be sent to Sabine Pass. Reviewing his options, Chief Engineer Valery Sulakowski decided that torpedoes used as land mines might be the most effective available force multiplier.

On October 5, 1863, Sulakowski ordered that Fort Griffin be surrounded by a covered way and a five-foot-high abatis of sharpened stakes made from mesquite trees. Sulakowski also directed that a strip of sod be laid six feet wide. Under that sod, thirteen-inch artillery shells were to be buried spaced forty feet apart. On the fort's southwest side, its most vulnerable side because of the absence of guns, there would be a double line of buried torpedoes. These explosives were to be joined by a trip wire extending about four inches off the ground. Although part of Sulakowski's defense plan was later implemented, it is unclear whether any of these dangerous mines were ever installed.[255]

Although the Confederate victory at Sabine Pass had temporarily derailed Union plans to invade Texas, General Magruder knew that it was only a matter of time before the Northerners got back on track and returned in force. His opponent, Major General Nathaniel P. Banks, had been instructed by Abraham Lincoln that it was imperative to raise the United States flag in Texas at the earliest possible opportunity because of diplomatic problems involving Mexico. After bitter defeats at Galveston and Sabine Pass, however, Banks decided to launch a different plan of attack from a different direction. This time, the invasion would start as far down the Texas coast as possible.

On October 26, 1863, General Banks set sail for the Rio Grande with an expedition of six thousand men. The plan for this western expedition was to land at Brazos Santiago, a village on Brazos Island near the entrance to the Rio Grande. After a very rough passage, Banks finally stepped ashore at Brazos Island on November 1, 1863. His landing was unopposed. Banks wasted no time in informing Lincoln and his other superiors that his latest plan had been a complete success. Belatedly, the Union flag had finally been planted on sandy Texas soil.[256]

The Rio Grande expedition started off well for the Federals. After wading ashore and raising the flag, Banks returned to New Orleans at the beginning of December. General Napoleon J. T. Dana then took charge of the expedition and began putting Banks's plans into action. The Union strategy involved marching up the Texas coast, primarily along a series of long barrier islands, capturing coastal cities like Corpus Christi and Indianola along the way. Staying close to the water would enable the Union army to have constant access to naval supplies as well as protection from the heavy artillery pieces mounted on the navy's gunboats. General Magruder didn't need to look at a map to see where his enemy was headed. At the end of the long march up the beaches would be Houston and Galveston, the most strategically important cities in Texas.

If he hoped to maintain a meaningful Confederate presence in Texas, Magruder had to find ways to either delay or defeat this seemingly unstoppable invasion force. None of the deception tactics that had served him so well on the Virginia peninsula would help him on the narrow Texas beaches. To stop the advancing troops, he would have to depend on fortifications, primarily relying on those that already existed at the strategic points where bays and rivers emptied into the Gulf of Mexico.

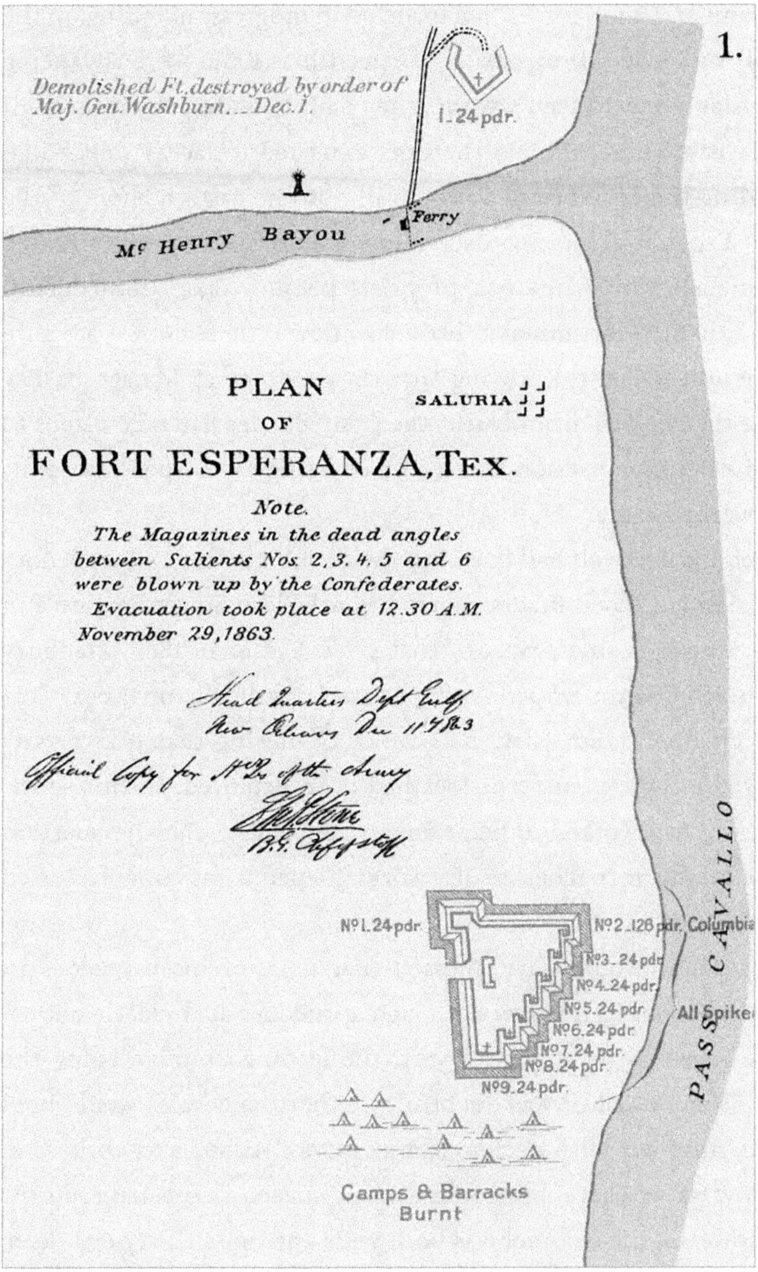

Detail from "Plan of Fort Esperanza, Tex." on Pass Cavallo. Plate 26(1), *Atlas to the Official Records of the Union and Confederate Armies* (1892).

By late November, Union forces had made good progress marching up the coast. They had succeeded in capturing Corpus Christi and were advancing up Matagorda Island toward Pass Cavallo, the channel leading from the Gulf into Matagorda Bay. There, the Northerners expected to face a substantial obstacle. Guarding the entrance of Pass Cavallo on the eastern shore of the island was Fort Esperanza. The Spanish word "Esperanza" is often translated as "hope" in English. This name is appropriate because Texas Confederates certainly hoped that the fort might at least slow down the relentless advance of their enemy up the coast. Knowing that the entrance to Matagorda Bay was likely to be the site of a major battle, the Confederates had taken steps to strengthen the defensive position there, in part using the torpedo weapons developed in nearby Lavaca.

While Singer and Fretwell had been busy with submarines and torpedoes east of the Mississippi, David Bradbury had been the lead Singer operative in charge of the torpedo business west of that river. Earlier in 1863, Bradbury had placed eighteen floating torpedoes in the Pass Cavallo channel near Fort Esperanza. So far, the Union Navy had avoided entering that pass or any Texas waters where they knew torpedoes had been deployed. In this sense, the devices clearly had worked to deter enemy movement. But the question remained: Would the torpedoes really work if enemy movements tested them?[257]

If asked, Bradbury would have guessed that none of his torpedoes in Matagorda Bay were still effective. Although torpedoes had clearly shown their explosive power in freshwater rivers, the leading example being the sinking of the *Baron De Kalb*, it was doubtful whether the devices would hold up very long in an open saltwater environment. Torpedoes worked best in relatively shallow water where they could densely cover an expected route. At Pass Cavallo, however, the channel was both wide and up to thirty feet deep. To make matters worse, the tidal currents coming in and out were very strong. The constant daily movements of the torpedoes eventually caused some of them to break loose and drift. There was also the problem that in such an environment, marine organisms like shellfish tended to accumulate on the springs and, over time, became concretions that would prevent the torpedoes from detonating.[258]

Bradbury would later admit that "I made up my mind when I put them there that it was doubtful if they ever did any good." Less than nine months later, he would warn his army's commanders that "the length of time they have been in makes them useless now."[259] Bradbury's assumption was correct. Although there would be one remarkable example of success at Mobile, Confederate torpedo success throughout the war was rare where a torpedo field remained unrefreshed for a substantial length of time in an open saltwater environment.

If there was reason to doubt the water defenses at Pass Cavallo, there was even greater reason for concern about the viability of the land defenses at Fort Esperanza. This vulnerability was not due to an insufficient number of guns. The fort mounted eight twenty-four-pounders and one one hundred-twenty-eight-pounder Columbiad. The problem was that Fort Esperanza's design was intended to repel ships in the channel—not a concentrated force of infantry like the one that was approaching up the coast. Esperanza had a triangular design, with all but one of its guns positioned to fire at targets sailing up through the pass. The Union infantry force now marching toward the fort from the south would be approaching from the southwest side. Unfortunately for the fort's garrison, that side had very little direct artillery protection.[260]

To make matters worse, there was a significant disparity in the numbers between attackers and defenders. On November 24, 1863, Colonel William R. Bradfute, who was in command of the Confederate garrison at Fort Esperanza, sent an urgent request for reinforcements to his superiors. He estimated the enemy's approaching forces to be ten to twelve thousand and noted that his own force consisted of only five hundred men. Despite the odds, Bradfute vowed that he would "make the best fight possible under the circumstances."[261]

In his request for reinforcements, Bradfute did not mention one, potentially large, recent addition to his defenses. When it became obvious that the fort was facing the potential threat of an attack by land, Colonel Bradfute contacted

David Bradbury and directed him to bring every available torpedo to the fort. At Bradfute's request, Bradbury brought twenty-four torpedoes to the fort and planted them in the ditches in front of the fort's walls. They were installed in such a way that they could be manually exploded by pulling lanyards from inside the fort.[262]

The torpedo field deployed at Fort Esperanza was probably one of the largest torpedo fields installed on land during the entire Civil War. It was capable of doing enormous damage to the large number of unsuspecting Union soldiers approaching the fort. At first, things went as planned. After briefly skirmishing with Union forces in the outer trenches, the heavily outnumbered Confederates withdrew into their fort and manned their guns. The Union troops, many of whom had extensive siege experience from operations conducted at Vicksburg, began creating field fortifications and gun positions on November 28, 1863. They then commenced a heavy and steady bombardment the following day. The Union infantry's artillery firing was supplemented by supporting fire from Federal gunboats in the rear.[263]

Outnumbered and outgunned, on the night of November 29, 1863, Colonel Bradfute ordered his Confederate garrison to evacuate the fort. He was justly concerned that the enemy was about to circumvent his position and block his line of escape to the mainland. The evacuation and retreat began around 10:00 p.m. Shortly after midnight, the last remaining Confederates exploded one of the powder magazines and set fire to the structures in the fort's interior. The Union forces soon realized what was happening and rushed into the fort, saving much of the unexploded powder and capturing intact a large quantity of rations and equipment.[264]

When day dawned on November 30, the Federals were delighted to discover that they had captured one of the most extensive fortifications remaining in Texas while suffering relatively light casualties in the process. Later that morning, they also made another, far less pleasant, discovery. A captain of engineers named J. T. Baker was surveying the edges of the captured works when he noticed some long straight lines in the soil covered with dead grass.

Digging beneath one of these lines, he discovered that it covered a wooden channel through which ran a lanyard made out of raw hide. Tracing the line to its end he observed that it terminated at an unexploded torpedo, which was buried in a ditch outside the fort's walls. He soon discovered other such lines and buried explosives.[265]

Baker carefully cut the lines and disarmed sixteen torpedoes that he was able to locate. Baker noted that thirteen of the devices appeared to be land torpedoes. Each of these torpedoes was a cylindrical metal vessel containing thirty-five to forty pounds of what Baker described as "fine diamond-grained powder." There were three torpedoes, however, of a different shape. Baker assumed (correctly) that these other models had originally been intended for "submarine defence" since they had an attached air chamber. After the war, Baker was asked to write a report about the torpedoes he uncovered at Fort Esperanza and how they operated. He not only described them but drew detailed schematics of both types (land and marine) that he examined. These drawings are some of the best remaining depictions of Civil War torpedoes.[266]

As it turned out, Baker was only able to locate and disarm a fraction of the torpedoes that the Confederates had installed at Fort Esperanza. It would take months to locate and neutralize the remainder. The hunt for unexploded torpedoes was complicated by the fact that the Federals had no idea how many had originally been installed. At one point, frustrated Union officers forced Confederate prisoners to march back and forth in the ditches in an effort to expedite the search.[267]

Lieutenant Charles H. Chace of the Fourteenth Rhode Island Heavy Artillery, a Black regiment, was not impressed with the appearance of what his men dug up, calling it "something after the style of a milk pail or a milk can with a plunger fitted in the top." But no matter how much they complained, everyone stepped carefully around the outside of the fort's walls. "If a soldier stepped on the plunger of one of these torpedoes," he warned, "it would have meant certain death for him."[268]

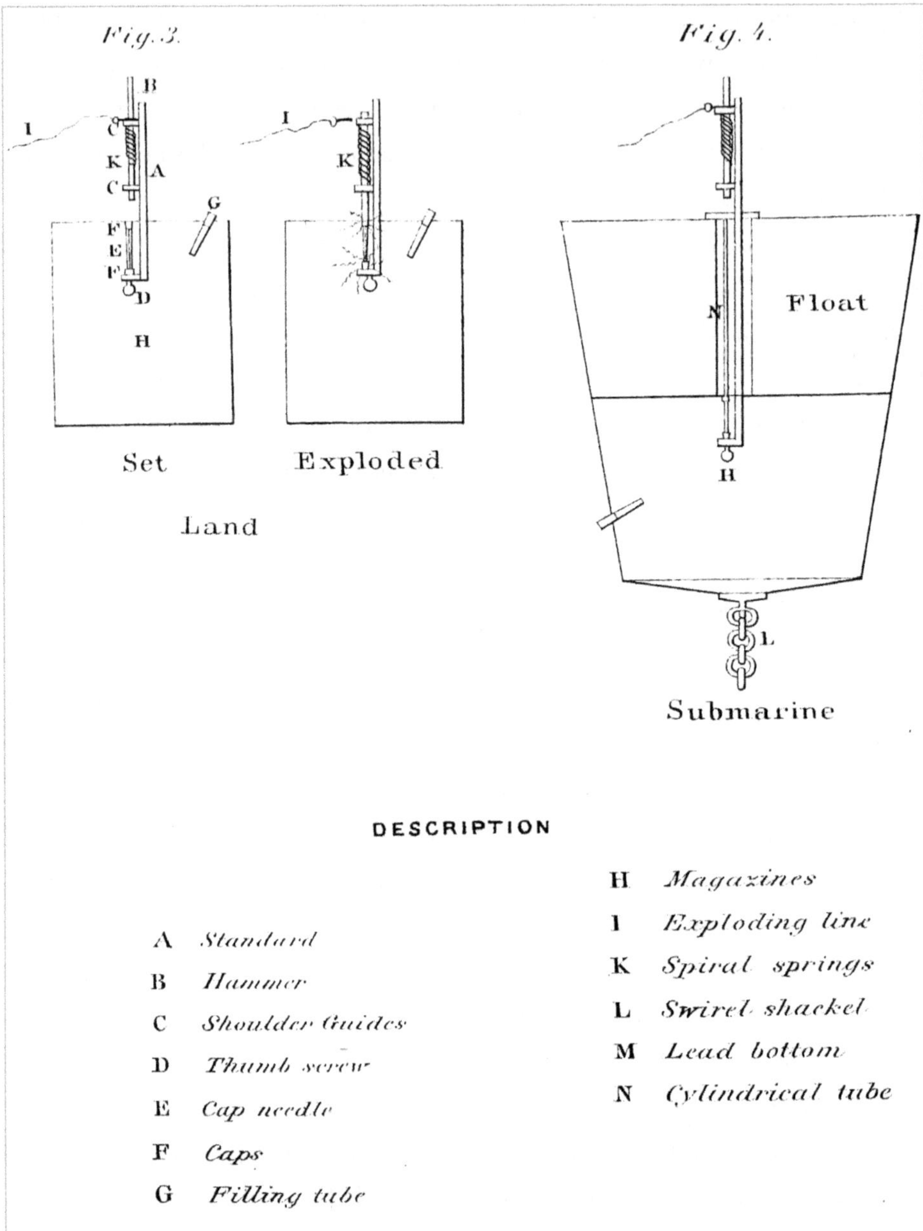

Drawings by Capt. J. T. Baker, engineer, of Singer land and submarine torpedoes recovered at Fort Esperanza, Texas. In W. R. King, *Torpedoes: Their Invention and Use* (1866), plate A.

Some of the Union soldiers who occupied the fort were surprised by the fact that it had been given up by the Rebels so easily. Noting that each torpedo was capable of killing at least fifty men, one soldier was astonished that the Confederates had not at least taken the opportunity to spill a substantial amount of enemy blood before suddenly evacuating what seemed to be a strong position.[269]

In addition to Baker's schematic drawings, a surviving map in the Texas State Library and Archives makes the torpedoes buried at Fort Esperanza some of the best documented explosives of the Civil War. Enos Reed, a private in the Thirty-Fourth Iowa Regiment, was part of the Union infantry force that anxiously watched the initial artillery bombardment of Fort Esperanza. Reed was familiar with forts and siege operations, having served under General Ulysses S. Grant's command at the siege of Vicksburg. He was also familiar with torpedoes, having been part of the Yazoo Pass operation during which the *De Kalb* was sunk. After the battle concluded, Reed drew a detailed map of Fort Esperanza and its surroundings. Reed drew dots just outside each parapet of the fort. As his map key helpfully notes, "The dots (.) represent the position of torpedoes that have been dug out since our troops occupied the fort." As he drew these dots, Reed must have thought himself lucky not to have encountered what they represented during the struggle that resulted in Union control of the fort.[270]

In the Civil War, the difference between life and death was sometimes as capricious as the flip of a coin. As David Bradbury, who planted the Esperanza torpedoes, later summarized, "if they had made an assault on us, they [the torpedoes] would have been very destructive, but as it was we lost them."[271] Because the Union chose to assault Fort Esperanza with only a heavy artillery bombardment and did not directly attack the ramparts, casualties were relatively light (two men killed and two wounded).[272] If the infantry had been ordered to charge the fortifications, a strategy that was almost certainly contemplated at the time given the great Union superiority in numbers,

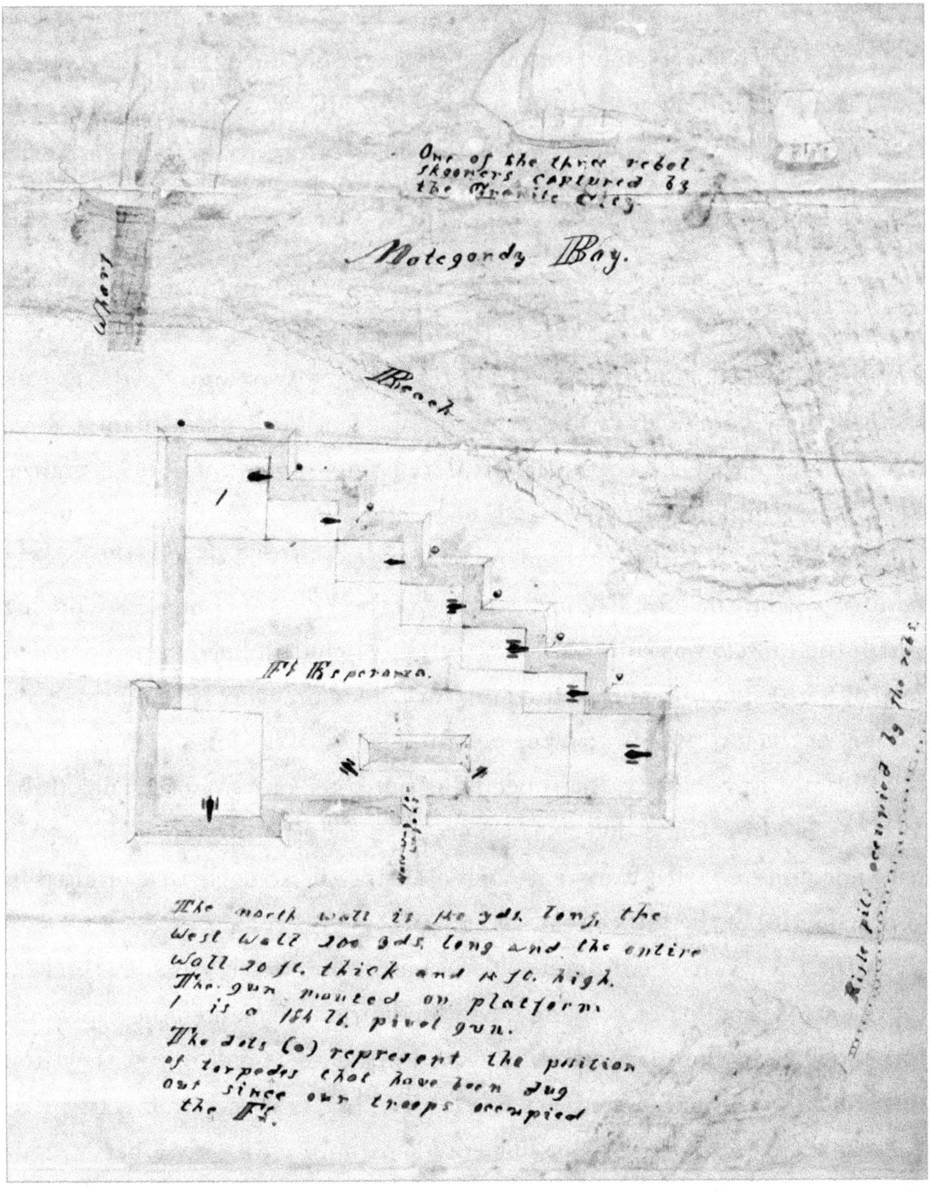

Detail from map of Fort Esperanza, Texas (south to the right), prepared by Prvt. Enos Reed of Co. K, 34th Iowa Regiment, 1863. Map No. 00014a, Texas State Library and Archives.

Confederate defenders would undoubtedly have pulled the lanyards and exploded the torpedoes. In that event, the resulting casualty numbers of this battle might well have been the most horrific of any Texas battle.

Although land mines were not put to the test at Fort Esperanza, Singer operatives soon found a surprising new land application for their torpedoes. The opportunity presented itself because of large Union armies marching throughout the South in 1863. Such armies required a constant flow of supplies, much of which had to come by rail. The Singer group experimented and found that it was relatively simple to transform one of their marine torpedoes into an explosive device that could be activated by a train rolling over a trigger mechanism. Such devices could be buried beneath the tracks in a single night and were much easier to install than the floating variety.

Although Singer had originally proposed the idea in August, the teams did not begin actively deploying rail torpedoes in serious numbers until October and November 1863. It is at that point that Union records begin reflecting an increasing number of sabotage reports involving trains. Because of the absence of accurate records, it is difficult to tell precisely how many trains were affected. It is also hard to determine which group's torpedoes were responsible for the damage to any particular train. Robert Dunn would later boast to General Magruder, however, that the Singer group blew up at least eight trains in Tennessee alone.[273]

Although the rail explosions made for good headlines, it is possible to overestimate the damage that these rail torpedoes caused. The engines and tracks were typically repaired within a few days. But the knowledge that such devices might be lurking unquestionably made trains run more slowly and cautiously. In addition, Union forces now had to be diverted from active combat operations to patrol railroad tracks behind Union lines.

Over time, these rail torpedoes would become a serious irritant to certain Union generals. Probably the most vocal on the subject was Major General William T. Sherman. He believed that the use of torpedoes to stop an enemy from advancing was perfectly proper. But once an advance had succeeded, he did not think it was fair for an enemy to use them behind the lines. In 1864, he wrote that "the use of torpedoes in blowing up our cars and the road after they are in our possession is simply malicious." He directed that "if torpedoes were found in the possession of an enemy to our rear, you may cause them to be put on the ground and tested by wagon-loads of prisoners, or, if need be, citizens implicated in their use."[274]

Rail torpedoes had their inherent limitations. One of the problems with the Singer rail torpedoes was that they were just as likely to blow up under a train carrying civilians as a train loaded with military cargo. Once set, they would explode whenever the pressure of the first portion of a train activated the trigger. Realizing this fact, Union railroad engineers soon responded by pushing unoccupied flat cars called "devils" ahead of them to explode any torpedoes that might be lurking in their path. Shortly before he left for Texas, Robert Creuzbaur heard about the Singer railroad torpedoes and contacted Confederate authorities to suggest an improvement. Instead of having a torpedo explode automatically, Creuzbaur proposed that it be triggered remotely using a pin attached to a line that could be pulled by an operator situated more than a hundred yards from the track.[275]

Creuzbaur's version of the rail torpedo would be buried next to a cross-tie with a hole through which a retracted rod could project. When the operator pulled the pin, a carriage spring would activate and send the rod up through the hole in the center of the track. When the rod struck the first approaching railroad car's axle, the force of the collision would then be used to propel a pin that would impact the buried explosive charge and ignite the torpedo. Using this new system, the operator could choose to let a passenger train go by and then pull the pin to activate the bomb as a freight train passed. He could also let the engine pushing a devil go by and then explode the device under the portion of the train most likely to be carrying troops or war matériel.[276]

While the Singer group had significant success destroying enemy trains and ships east of the Mississippi, that record of success did not extend to their home state. As it turned out, the torpedoes so carefully placed by Singer

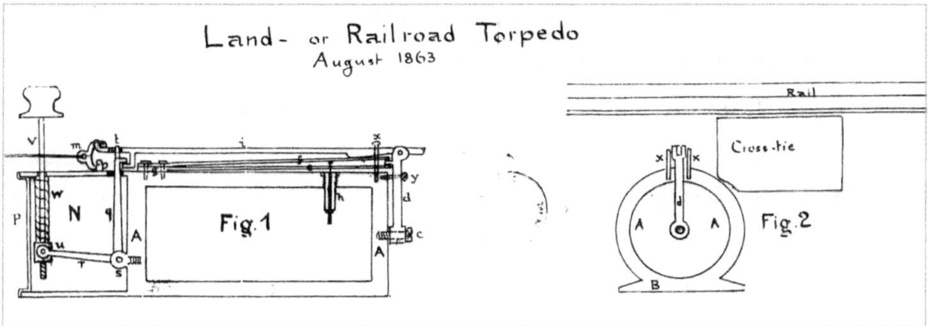

Diagram of proposed "Land or Railroad Torpedo" by Robert Creuzbaur, August 1863. Mines and Torpedoes-Charleston-Miscellaneous, Record Group 45, National Archives and Records Administration.

operatives in Texas waters ended up doing virtually no damage to the enemy. Two horses were wounded by torpedoes while crossing an oyster reef in the spring of 1864, but the soldiers riding them were not injured.[277] Although torpedoes were tremendously effective elsewhere in the South, not a single Union soldier, sailor, or vessel would become a victim of them in the Lone Star State. That did not mean, however, that there were no casualties.

There were exactly two torpedo casualties in Texas, and both were on the Confederate side. J. T. Banon, a conscripted soldier from Falls County, was part of a group carrying torpedoes to be installed at the east end of Galveston Island near Fort Point. The unlucky soldier happened to drop a torpedo in just such a way that it hit the trigger mechanism and detonated at his feet. The explosion severely mangled his body and set his clothes on fire. To put out the fire, he crawled into the water and almost drowned. When help finally reached him, his rescuers discovered that he had been severely wounded in the hand and leg. He had also been badly burned over much of his body. Worst of all, his leg had been crushed below the knee, which resulted in an amputation later that day.[278]

Banon's story was sad, but his gruesome injuries did not prove fatal. Ben C. Stuart, one of the great chroniclers of Galveston history, recalled the case of an even less fortunate individual who made the mistake of playing with a torpedo that had broken loose and drifted ashore on Galveston Island. Stuart did not mention the man's name, but he vividly remembered what had happened to him. "Like the boy with a watch, he proceeded to open it in order to see what was inside, when it exploded and tore him to pieces."[279]

As 1863 was drawing to a close, General James E. Slaughter wrote to General Magruder concerning the torpedoes protecting the entrance to Galveston Bay. Noting that parts of them were made of tin, Slaughter said he greatly feared that they "have oxidized and thereby [been] rendered worthless." Although Slaughter thought the torpedoes were now ineffective, he realized that there was at least a chance that some might still be functional. While suggesting that Magruder order all torpedoes to be replaced immediately, he recommended that they be placed at a slightly different location to avoid triggering any remaining torpedoes that might still be able to explode.[280]

CHAPTER 10

THE ROCKETS' RED GLARE IN TEXAS

Although Union forces had captured Fort Esperanza and the entrance to Matagorda Bay in November 1863, they were still a long way from their main objectives on the upper Texas coast. If the Federals were to reach Galveston and Houston, they would need to continue slogging their way up the Matagorda Peninsula and then cross several rivers. The remaining distance to Galveston was almost 150 miles. Union scouts reported that a Confederate fort was situated strategically at each of the intervening major river crossings. There were particularly strong defensive works near Caney Creek. As the Union had shown at Fort Esperanza, however, even strong fortifications could be overcome given the application of enough men and artillery. It helped, of course, that coastal forts also had also proven to be highly vulnerable to fire directed from large guns mounted on navy warships.[281]

As Union forces moved slowly but deliberately up the coast, Magruder chose to anchor his western line of defense along the Brazos River. His engineers were doing everything they could to strengthen the defenses in this area, but Magruder worried that it might not be enough. He needed some way to supplement his forces, preferably something the enemy would not be expecting. It was time for Prince John and his players to do some creative thinking.

As the Federals were reaching the end of Matagorda Island, Robert Creuzbaur proposed a radical new approach to defending the coastal route to Galveston. Ever since Union forces had landed at the Rio Grande, Creuzbaur and his associate Caleb V. Littlepage had been looking for creative ways to use their torpedoes to delay or prevent an infantry advance. Whatever they came up with had to be both portable and relatively easy to manufacture and deploy. John P. Kirk, a fellow Austin inventor, had suggested an idea that the group thought fit Magruder's needs perfectly. Repeating a name that Creuzbaur had used in the past, they called their new joint invention the "Torpedo Cannon."

The idea was in some ways a portable version of the Singer minefield that had been abandoned at Fort Esperanza. Torpedoes spaced at ten-yard intervals would be placed in a line about three feet above the top of an embankment or breastwork. They would then be positioned to focus their explosions at the enemy's projected line of advance. Creuzbaur projected that each finished torpedo would weigh about 118 pounds, which meant that a wagon carrying three thousand pounds could carry about twenty-four fully charged torpedoes. This should be enough, he estimated, to install a line of torpedoes about one-eighth of a mile long.[282]

The beauty of this device, Creuzbaur assured the general, was that it required very few defenders to operate such a battery. In fact, if Magruder wished them to do so, the engineers could even rig the weapon so that the enemy would literally trigger it themselves. In a variation of the lanyards used at Fort Esperanza, the line of explosives could be set to trigger when a stretched trip wire was breached, or a pitfall stepped upon. To maximize effectiveness, a few could even be strategically positioned on the sides to fire upon the enemy's flanks. Creuzbaur believed that this was the answer Magruder had been looking for:

> With these pieces as an auxiliary, managed by a properly organized corps, comparatively few men would suffice to defend a work against assault. The enemy could be held in check from evacuated works, and on a retreat, at every little rise (made artificial if wanting), the advances of an enemy could be checked, and great destruction inflicted upon him by their discharge.

After explaining his idea to Magruder's staff, Creuzbaur asked, in underlined letters: "<u>Will the General desire any of these for immediate purposes</u>?"[283]

Magruder referred Creuzbaur's drawings, which also included a potential marine application for the torpedo cannon, to the engineering department headquarters in Shreveport. Engineer Henry T. Douglas responded that the cannon sounded interesting, but he thought Creuzbaur's alternative of deploying it on a series of lightly armored boats was "entirely inadequate."[284] Although the weapon was not deployed on this occasion given the enemy's subsequent decision not to continue the advance up the Texas coast, Creuzbaur would continue to promote some version of his torpedo cannon for the remainder of the war.

Magruder's decision not to place all his eggs in Creuzbaur's torpedo cannon basket was probably due in large part to his increasing fascination with a different form of artillery: the rocket. As a creative artillerist, Magruder had long seen the potential utility of rockets. He had seen rockets used somewhat effectively in the Mexican-American War and had seen them used briefly but unsuccessfully during the 1862 Virginia campaign. Prince John still fostered a lingering hope that if properly deployed, rockets might be one of the keys that enabled him to defeat the enemy marching up the coast toward him.

In the fall of 1863, Magruder learned of the unique experience of Lieutenant George H. Schroeder, a German machinist who was at the time serving as an ordnance officer at Galveston. Schroeder would not have been anyone's choice for the key man around which to build a military unit. Prior to the war, he had been a Galveston machinist whose primary business involved making and repairing sewing machines.[285] Although Schroeder's engineering superior described him as "a most useful man," he noted that "he had the unhappy characteristic of not being able to get along with anyone and he believed he was a renowned genius." Because Schroeder was very gruff with officers, his record reflected that he had been transferred many times.[286]

Because of his reputation for being difficult to deal with, Schroeder eventually wound up under the command of Major Julius G. Kellersberger, a Swiss engineer who had become one of Magruder's most trusted subordinates. Kellersberger was willing to look behind Schroeder's rough manners because

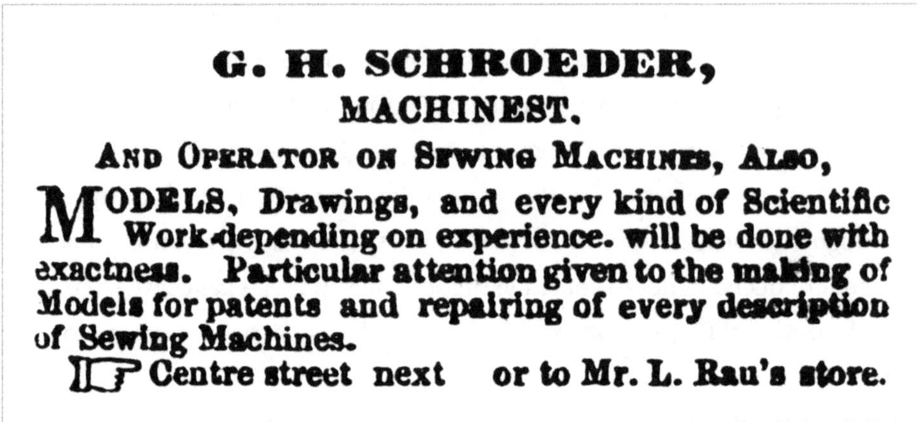

G. H. SCHROEDER,
MACHINEST.
AND OPERATOR ON SEWING MACHINES, ALSO,
MODELS, Drawings, and every kind of Scientific Work depending on experience. will be done with exactness. Particular attention given to the making of Models for patents and repairing of every description of Sewing Machines.
☞ Centre street next or to Mr. L. Rau's store.

Advertisement for G. H. Schroeder. In *The Civilian and Gazette* (Galveston), December 11, 1860.

he knew that under that façade, the man was talented and had the potential to be extremely useful.[287]

Schroeder had frequently boasted to Kellersberger that in the old country, he had served as a lieutenant in a dedicated rocket battery during the Hungarian War of Independence (1848–49). Kellersberger mentioned this experience to General Magruder, who was immediately interested in seeing how such a battery could be recreated in Texas. What intrigued Magruder was that not only did Schroeder seem to know how to fire rockets, he also claimed to know the "secrets of blending and construction" that would enable the Confederates to manufacture them.[288]

Magruder was so fascinated by Schroeder's claim and experience that he authorized Kellersberger to supply him with the materials to make a small test batch of rockets. This was exactly the procedure that Magruder had successfully followed with E. C. Singer and his torpedoes. Schroeder soon produced a three-foot rocket stand and a half dozen small rockets carrying six-pound grenades as their payload. These rockets were fired in Magruder's presence, and the general found the test results satisfactory enough to expand the experiment.[289]

Despite Magruder's enthusiasm for the project, there were still quite a large number of challenges that would need to be overcome before Schroeder's rockets were ready for active service. The first problem was how to manufacture the rocket propellant. The powder used to propel rockets at this time was not ordinary gunpowder; it had to have specific characteristics. It needed to burn quickly enough to generate adequate thrust while not burning so quickly that it exploded the rocket and stand when ignited. This was a problem because the Confederates lacked the necessary saltpeter (potassium nitrate), brimstone, and other materials that would be needed to power large war rockets. To overcome this obstacle, a search was soon underway for the necessary mineral deposits and chemicals.[290]

On December 1, 1863, Magruder issued a special order appointing Schroeder to the position of acting assistant ordnance officer "to take charge of the execution and construction of a rocket battery and the proper ammunition." Magruder decided to motivate his new rocket scientist through an unusual compensation arrangement. Not only would Schroeder receive the pay of a captain of cavalry, the machinist would also be entitled to an additional bonus of fifty dollars upon the completion of each rocket stand and one dollar for each completed rocket.[291] By December 10, nine days later, Schroeder submitted a requisition in Galveston for various anvils, lathes, forges, and machines. He signed this requisition in his capacity as the new "Superintendent of Rocket Factory."[292]

While Schroeder was setting up his rocket factory near Galveston and hunting for the needed materials, Magruder wasted no time in starting to assemble the force that would eventually—he hoped soon—carry and fire the rockets. In the same order that placed Schroeder in charge of the rocket factory, Captain John Sunderland Greer was appointed to command what would soon become known as "Greer's Rocket Battery, Texas Artillery." The forty-five-year-old Greer had experience that made him a good fit for his new assignment. He had been exposed to a wide variety of service in the infantry, cavalry, and artillery. He had also fought in the Mexican-American War, where he had suffered a wound to the forehead by a spent ball at the Battle of Palo Alto. Like Magruder, Greer had been involved in the famous campaign that marched inland and captured Mexico City. During that campaign Greer may well have witnessed the last American force to successfully employ rockets. It would now be his turn to lead such a force.[293]

On February 9, 1864, Greer reported to Magruder that he found his new command to suffer from a unique manpower problem. Greer had recently been notified by Schroeder that he would soon complete the initial six pieces of the rocket battery. The problem was that Greer had no men assigned to his battery. He requested that fifty men be temporarily assigned to the battery and thought that it might be best if they came from the cavalry or be well mounted so they could transport the rockets and associated equipment. He also thought it would be helpful if at least some of the men were mechanics.[294]

Although Greer was temporarily short of manpower, he managed to gather some men and found a way to begin to move the first elements of his battery to places like East Bernard and Columbus, where other units were being consolidated for service. Summer of 1864 found his battery still in no condition to fight. Not only did he not have any rockets, but he still did not have sufficient men to drill, let alone effectively service a battery. To help his cause, Greer placed an advertisement in a Houston newspaper on April 22, 1864, which announced that the rocket battery was "now fitting out for the western frontier." Greer claimed that this was a "new branch of the service" and was "one of the lightest and easiest ever introduced."[295] This cheery advertisement did Greer little good. By 1864, everyone in Texas who actually wanted to serve had been presented with ample opportunities to do so. Joining a mysterious "rocket battery," whatever that was, made little sense to the relatively few Texas men out there who were still potentially available for service.[296]

On June 9, 1864, Greer wrote Magruder a very discouraging status report about his battery. The fifty soldiers who had been temporarily loaned to him earlier had by now rejoined their original units and headed for Louisiana. He now had only two officers and twelve men. That was barely sufficient to take care of his unit's collection of mules and horses. Of the six hundred rockets he believed he needed before he could start for the field of battle, Greer counted only forty-three that he anticipated could potentially be fired at an enemy. Greer asked Magruder to temporarily assign him fifty more men, noting that he had optimistically taken the liberty of requisitioning forty horses and saddles for the new members of his battery.[297]

As it turned out, lack of horses and manpower was the least of Greer's problems. His fundamental problem involved the rockets that were now supposedly in the process of production at Schroeder's rocket factory. A rich saltpeter bed had been located in San Antonio, and Schroeder had moved his factory there to finish creating the remaining rockets. There were now about a thousand rocket tubes at the rocket factory that were waiting to be filled with something. Were they worth filling and completing?

Major Kellersberger was starting to have grave concerns about the future of the Texas rocket battery. He had been working at a foundry located not far away from the rocket factory and had in passing noticed some things about the assembly process that bothered him. Schroeder seemed uncertain about his rocket propellant formulas and kept changing them, sometimes in significant ways. Believing that consistency and precision must be critical to the quality

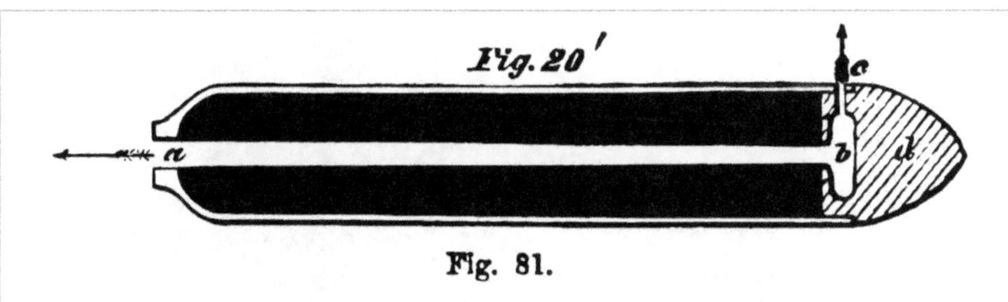

Diagram of filled Hale rocket tube. From Lt. Edward Simpson, *A Treatise on Ordnance and Naval Gunnery* (1862).

of rockets, Kellersberger called a halt to the assembly process until a quality control test for Schroeder's existing rockets could be conducted.[298]

In preparation for the test, Kellersberger and Schroeder selected a random sample of a dozen completed rockets to fire. The rocket test was designated to take place at a clear area located about 500 feet from a major road. Kellersberger mounted his horse and headed for a nearby elevated hedge area to better observe the action. Kellersberger gave the signal to proceed with the test and anxiously awaited its results. The first rocket went 100 feet in the right direction, landed by a tree, and then ricocheted into the ground just behind Kellersberger's terrified horse. Seeing his mount's reaction, the engineer then wisely chose to ride farther away to view the remainder of the test. Schroeder's second rocket hit the ground almost immediately and then made several zigzags, none of which was in the right direction. Not one of the test rockets went where it was intended to go. As Kellersberger had feared, the test was an unmitigated disaster. The only thing that the demonstration succeeded in producing was "a hellish smoke and a deafening noise, which, of course, put fear into man and beast alike."[299]

Getulius "Julius" Kellersberger (1821–1900). Image 068–2696, General Photograph Collection, University of Texas at San Antonio Libraries.

Needless to say, what Kellersberger had witnessed did not inspire confidence in the general's pet rocket project. At the test's conclusion, a large number of horses had broken loose and run away. So had some men who were being recruited to become prospective members of the rocket battery. After it was over, the only witness who was not terrified was Schroeder, who calmly informed Kellersberger that he was not surprised at all. In Schroeder's mind, this was all caused by his inability to secure the proper chemicals. Kellersberger angrily told Schroeder that he should have mentioned this problem earlier, well before he had built nearly a thousand rockets that might never be safely loaded and fired.[300]

Kellersberger mentioned the disastrous test results to General Magruder and anticipated that the general would follow his lead and put a hold on the rocket project unless the problems with the rockets could be resolved. Surprisingly, the general declined to cancel or delay the project. Why? There were probably several reasons for this decision. First, Magruder probably hoped that, through trial and error, Schroeder would eventually hit upon the right formula that would enable him to get his rockets to work.

Magruder's second reason for not putting the brakes on the rocket project may have had to do with the reaction of the horses. That horses tended to be scared by rockets would not have surprised Magruder, who had undoubtedly observed this same phenomenon in Mexico. Although this reaction appears to have surprised Kellersberger and his horse, it had long been observed that horses tended to be scared by rockets. In fact, this was one reason that European armies had increasingly come to utilize rockets as anti-cavalry weapons.

Magruder had every reason to believe that large Union forces arriving in Texas would eventually leave the coast and make their way inland. When they did so, Magruder was particularly concerned that the Northerners might come sweeping across the Texas plains with a host of cavalrymen. One of the reasons that Magruder felt so strongly about the utility of rockets was their potential effect on his enemy's cavalry horses. It is not surprising, then, that Magruder was unwilling to give up this potentially powerful defensive weapon on the basis of a single test that he had not personally observed.

Although Magruder may have had good reasons for continuing the rocket project, Kellersberger was convinced that there was yet another explanation that had nothing to do with the enemy; in fact, it had nothing to do with the war at all. Kellersberger suggested in his postwar memoirs that Magruder decided to proceed with the next scheduled rocket test because it was "just at the most beautiful season of the year and he had already invited many officers and ladies and a grand picnic had been planned."[301]

Based on the previous test, Kellersberger felt it best to avoid the picnic demonstration that Magruder had scheduled for the Fourth of July. As the day of the test approached, Kellersberger reported himself strangely and conveniently ill with such a headache that he had to excuse himself from attending. The picnic event attracted quite a crowd. A large number of men and women came long distances by wagon or on horseback to be part of the festivities. The fifty men newly assigned to the battery attended with their officers. Everyone eagerly awaited the unveiling of what some believed might be the Confederacy's next great weapon.[302]

Unlike the assembled spectators, Kellersberger expected nothing but danger from the rockets and sent his servant to unobtrusively attend the picnic test and report on the demonstration. Unfortunately, it turned out to be an even worse spectacle than the engineer had feared. As he later learned, "one rocket burst on its stand, one tore the stand down with it, and a hellish chaos broke forth. No horse could be held, and the picnic turned out to be a general flight to safety!"[303]

On the evening following the picnic test, Kellersberger received a sudden order dissolving Rocket Battery No. 1, which Magruder referred to as the "professor's army of Texas." In response, Kellersberger ordered "the professor" (Schroeder) to dispose of the remaining 1,200 rockets in the deepest part of the San Antonio River, where they could do no more damage to the general's friends, enemies, or their horses. As Kellersberger summed up the incident in his memoirs, "So goes the story of the first and last rocket battery in Texas."[304]

Although Kellersberger said in his memoirs that all of the remaining rockets had been thrown into the San Antonio River, there may have been at least one exception. A rocket described as a genuine Texas Confederate rocket of the Hale design appeared on eBay in 2017, where it purportedly sold for $1,275. The listing stated that the rocket was in good shape considering that it was then over 150 years old and had been stored for many years in an old barn. The author offers no opinion as to whether the auctioned rocket artifact was genuine. What the author will say is that based on his historical research, he would not wish to be anywhere near the object and would certainly urge that it be kept away from horses.[305]

CHAPTER 11

A NEW PHASE IN UNDERWATER WARFARE

While Magruder was experimenting with rockets down in Texas, the H. L. *Hunley* submarine, newly raised and restored after its second sinking, was preparing for its first and final combat mission at Charleston. On December 14, 1863, General Beauregard issued a special order appointing Lieutenant George E. Dixon of the Twenty-First Alabama Infantry regiment to command the vessel. His orders were to "proceed tonight to the mouth of the harbor, or as far as capacity of the vessel will allow." Once there, Dixon was directed to "sink and destroy any vessel of the enemy with which he can come in contact."[306] Although the wording of this order made it sound like action was imminent, in reality it would be over two months before *Hunley* actually came into contact with the enemy.

There were three main problems that *Hunley* would have to overcome before the submarine could make its attack. The first was that by early 1864, the *Hunley*'s advantage of surprise had evaporated. Union blockaders were on high alert about potential attacks coming from Charleston. It was bad enough that *David* had made its partially successful attack three months previously. Now, however, deserters were reporting that there was not only a steam-powered torpedo boat, but that the Confederates also possessed a fully submersible submarine that could attack blockaders from underwater.[307]

Admiral John A. Dahlgren warned all vessels in the Union fleet of this new threat and ordered precautions to be taken. The ironclads were instructed to put fenders on their sides and drop netting to keep enemy vessels from approaching. They were also advised to anchor in shallow water to prevent a submarine craft from passing beneath them. The combined effect of these precautions was to largely exclude Union ironclads from *Hunley*'s potential target set. Dahlgren knew that there was still risk, however. One of the reasons he advised anchoring in shallow water was so "there will be less difficulty in raising a vehicle if sunk."[308]

The second problem facing *Hunley* arose from the locations where its targets were now located. To get to enemy vessels that were less protected, *Hunley* had to travel a greater distance out to sea. In earlier exercises, the little submarine had been towed out to its initial starting position at the entrance to Charleston Harbor by the torpedo boat *David*. However, one evening in early January while *Hunley* was being towed, the vessels lost control of the submarine's torpedo, which came floating over and almost collided with *David*.[309]

As this experience demonstrated, swirling surface currents near the entrance to the harbor could be tricky and unpredictable. If the torpedo had drifted just a few feet farther, the mission would have been brought to an unexpected and explosive conclusion. That experience put an end to using another vessel to tow *Hunley*. It would now have to reach its target on its own. This was a problem because *Hunley* had very limited speed due to its hand-cranked propulsion system. It was extremely difficult to move it very far or very fast, particularly against the tide. Because of this constraint, Dixon and his first officer, William Alexander, secured permission to move *Hunley* to Breach Inlet, which was located near the northern tip of Sullivan's Island. The new base of operations provided a more convenient location, where the submarine stood a better chance of getting where it needed to go in a timely manner.[310]

The third challenge that Dixon and his crew faced involved the explosive device that *Hunley* planned to employ. From its earliest test in Mobile, *Hunley*'s primary mode of attack had always involved towing the torpedo behind the vessel on a rope. By going under an enemy vessel, the floating torpedo would eventually contact the target's hull and detonate. It was now apparent that the towed floating torpedo was a problem because *Hunley* could not control its position.

At approximately the same time as *Hunley* moved to its new base of operations, an important change was made to the sub's torpedo-delivery system. Instead of towing the torpedo behind it as a floating contact weapon, the torpedo would now be deployed near the end of a spar extending from the bow of the vessel. There is a great deal of controversy about the precise manner in which *Hunley*'s torpedo was mounted. One idea is that the torpedo was to be attached to a barbed spike that would be driven into the enemy's hull and detached. Then, the sub would simply back off to a safe distance and explode the torpedo remotely using a lanyard. Another idea is that the torpedo was fixed to the end of an adjustable spar and would simply explode on contact with the enemy's hull. Although several people would later claim credit for making this change, it was a logical development given *David*'s prior experience with a spar torpedo and the near disaster with *Hunley*'s floating version. However the torpedo was actually mounted, it seems clear that the torpedo itself was a version of the Singer torpedo.[311]

Having made their preparations as best they could, Dixon and his *Hunley* crew waited for a night with calm seas and tidal conditions that favored their plan of attack. As darkness fell on February 17, 1864, Dixon and his men left Breach Inlet and headed toward their rendezvous about three miles out to sea with USS *Housatonic*, a 1,240-ton sloop of war mounting eleven guns. *Housatonic*'s crew had been warned to watch out for attacks by small enemy boats. At about 8:45 p.m., two *Housatonic* officers observed something relatively small approaching them on their starboard side. One described it as a porpoise, another said it looked like a plank. What the object was, of course, was *Hunley* in the process of partially submerging before ramming its torpedo into *Housatonic*'s vulnerable starboard hull. Crewmen quickly started firing small arms at what they could see of the approaching vessel. Before the large guns on the warship could be depressed sufficiently to fire, the torpedo planted by *Hunley* exploded.[312]

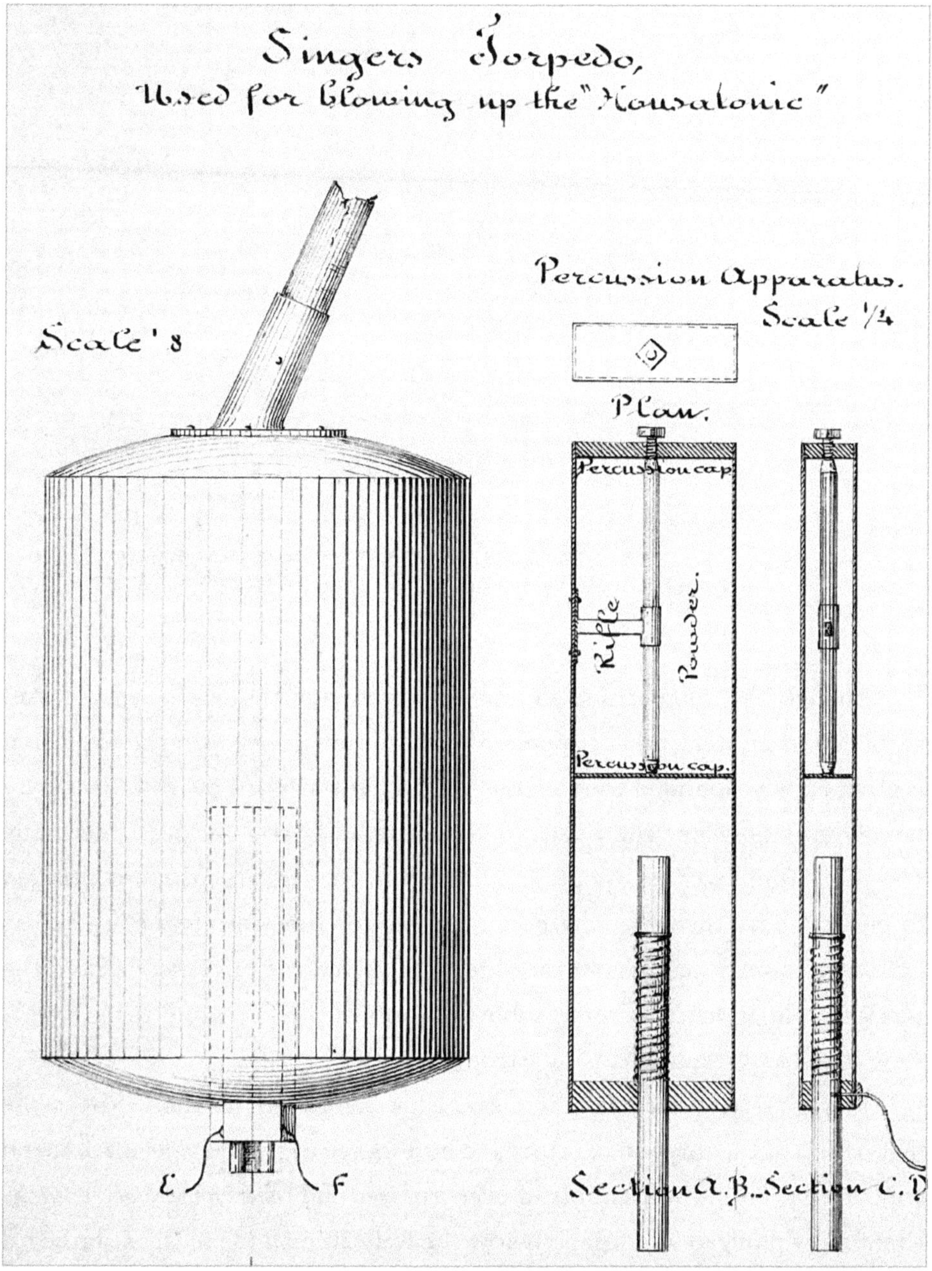

"Singer's Torpedo Used for Blowing up the *Housatonic*." Papers of General Quincy Adams Gillmore, Record Group 77, National Archives and Records Administration.

"Destruction of *Housatonic* by a Rebel Torpedo, Feb. 17, 1864."
Sketch by William Waud, LC-DIG-ppmsca-21443, Library of Congress.

Although the submarine's movements following the explosion are still shrouded in mystery, what happened to the Union vessel after the explosion is clear. Fatally wounded with a large hole in her starboard quarter, *Housatonic* rapidly took on water and began to sink. The water was not deep and many crewmen were saved by simply moving up in the rigging, which continued to project above the waters. Others managed to climb into two of the boats that were lowered just before the ship sank. Given the circumstances of the sudden night attack, it is remarkable that only two officers and three sailors were killed as a result of this catastrophic event.[313]

Although *Housatonic*'s fate is clear, what happened to *Hunley* after the detonation of the torpedo continues to be a source of endless speculation and controversy. From the accounts of eyewitnesses on board *Housatonic*, it seems that *Hunley* plunged its torpedo below the waterline on *Housatonic*'s starboard quarter. One witness described *Hunley* as backing up and being only forty or fifty feet away at the time of the explosion. This short distance has led some analysts to calculate the likely blast radius and conclude that the submarine may have been fatally injured by being too close to the blast.[314]

Others who have studied the event point to a mysterious "blue light" seen after the sinking both by Confederate observers ashore and Union survivors on *Housatonic*. There is much controversy about this reported light and its potential significance. If this light was indeed a lantern signal that *Hunley* had arranged in advance with troops on the shore, it suggests that *Hunley* survived the blast and that the submarine later sank and its crew perished in some other yet undetermined fashion.[315]

Union observers contended that *Hunley* must have been sucked into the hole made in *Housatonic* and destroyed. Salvage divers later claimed to have seen the submarine's wreck embedded where the sunken Union vessel's wreck was located. They were all mistaken. On May 3, 1995, novelist Clive Cussler and his organization discovered *Hunley* lying in forty feet of water about four miles off Sullivan's Island. Surprisingly, the small submarine was located seaward of the *Housatonic* wreck site. Amid the intense publicity accompanying the discovery, some noted the orientation of the bow pointed toward *Housatonic*'s wreck and suggested that the vessel may have been headed home to celebrate a great victory when some mysterious last disaster befell it.[316]

Although shore observers were unable to confirm what had happened to *Hunley*, Confederate sentries soon used their spyglasses to observe the rigging of sails jutting out of the water and reasoned that *Housatonic* must somehow have been sunk by Dixon and *Hunley*. It was unquestionably a remarkable achievement produced by such a small number of men in an experimental craft. But the failure of the vessel to return meant that Confederate authorities learned very little from the mission. They had no way of determining which parts of the attack had succeeded. More importantly, they had no way to ascertain what problems the vessel had encountered and, if they could be fixed, how to fix them. Although many in the Confederacy continued to believe that some form of submarine warfare could play an important role in their defense, it would be difficult to convince the military establishment to devote the resources it would take to build a fleet of *Hunley*-like vessels based on so little firm information.

CHAPTER 12

MORE FLOATING PAPERS AND SINKING GUNBOATS

It took time for the results of *Hunley*'s last mission to filter out. Ironically, the US Navy, whose ship was first to be sunk, was the first to realize what had happened. Even weeks after the *Hunley*'s crew had been lost, Confederate newspapers continued to report that its crew had somehow miraculously survived. Eventually, it became clear that the small crew of *Hunley* had indeed lost their lives in the process of sinking an enormous Union warship. *Hunley*'s first and last combat mission had succeeded, but the vessel did not return from that mission and had now cost the lives of almost three separate crews. To many, it seemed a high price to pay.

In the spring of 1864, the window that would mark the end of the Confederacy seemed to be closing fast. What could be done to help prop it open? Robert E. Lee and other officers were doing what they could with the Confederate armies. but it was unlikely to be enough. The increasingly famous Union General U. S. Grant commanded larger and better equipped armies and was planning a massive campaign aimed at the heart of the Confederacy in Virginia. To make matters worse, having captured or neutralized many of the key coastal Confederate cities, Union naval forces were now continuing to further penetrate Confederate waterways and were supplying critical logistical and artillery support to the army's overland campaigns.

With little in the way of uncommitted resources, what could the Confederacy do to avoid being overwhelmed on the naval front? There were basically four options. First, they could continue to place torpedoes both on land and sea at the likely avenues of approach. These were low cost and had already proved relatively effective on the rivers. Second, they could find ways to attack elements of the Union fleet with small surface vessels or semi-submersible vessels like the torpedo boats. A third approach was to build more large ironclad warships that could directly confront the Union fleet and its increasing component of armored vessels. The fourth approach was to continue to develop new warships like *Hunley* or even more exotic craft like the submarine apparatus proposed by Charles Williams in a last desperate effort to find some way to even the odds using the available but dwindling resources.

Although the Confederacy would eventually settle on a combination of all these approaches, it does not seem to have been a course arrived at by carefully weighing the cost and efficacy of the available options. Instead, 1864 would wind up being the year of the torpedo, primarily because it was the quickest and cheapest means of defending Southern waters while other more elaborate plans like submarines, torpedo boats, and ironclads were in the process of approval and construction. As it turned out, almost none of these larger and bolder plans would come to fruition before the end of the war.

Before reviewing what the Confederates actually did in 1864, a word about what they considered doing is necessary. As George Dixon was preparing *Hunley* for its fatal final mission in Charleston in February 1864, many letters were being written by key secret service operatives in Richmond and other Confederate cities east of the Mississippi. This sudden enthusiasm for writing was because Singer group member Robert Dunn had been ordered to travel to Texas to use his knowledge of torpedoes and submarines to help the Confederate cause. Knowing that Dunn was headed to the Southwest, many of his colleagues chose to trust Dunn to deliver their letters to recipients in Texas and other places west of the Mississippi. It would turn out that this trust was badly misplaced. All of these letters, a treasure trove for modern historians, ended up in Union hands and, eventually, Federal archives.

Edgar Singer gave Dunn a letter to his wife dated February 8, 1864, in which Singer said that he was "about to commence an enterprise that the government will watch with great interest as it promises the redemption of

New Orleans and the Mississippi River." Singer did not go into detail about his plans because of the chance that his letter might (as it eventually did) fall into enemy hands.[317]

Thomas E. Courtenay, an Irishman residing in St. Louis, gave Dunn a letter that reported on his progress in developing a "coal torpedo." As its name suggests, this weapon involved placing explosives in a casing that resembled coal. Courtenay's plan was to secretly add some of these into enemy coal bunkers and wait for them to explode in the boiler machinery that powered the Union gunboats. For this strategy to work, the coal torpedo needed to look and handle just like a regular piece of coal. So far, things were looking promising. "The castings," Courtenay boasted in his letter, "are so perfect that the most critical eye could not detect it."[318]

Dunn took both of these letters south with him to Mobile, where he encountered John D. Braman, another Singer operative. Knowing that Dunn was heading to Texas, Braman handed Dunn a letter to his wife dated March 3, 1864. In his letter, Braman told his wife about the interest he had purchased in the *Hunley* and its successful sinking of USS *Housatonic*. He also boasted that he had "got up the plan of an ironclad torpedo boat that all who saw it admitted was equal to the task of destroying any war ship now afloat."[319]

Dunn took Braman's letter and stuffed it in the pouch together with the Singer and Courtenay letters. He left Mobile about March 8 and headed west to Louisiana, where he waited about a week for an opportunity to cross the Mississippi River. On the night of March 16, he and two other men attempted to cross the big river in a small boat. Unexpectedly, they found themselves being chased by launches from a Union gunboat with crews who fired shots at them from swivel guns. In the course of escaping, Dunn inexplicably managed to lose his papers overboard, where they were ultimately recovered by a nearby Union patrol. It is unclear whether Dunn accidentally fumbled the bag overboard or was deliberately trying to sink the mail pouch to keep it out of enemy hands. The author confesses that he finds it difficult to believe that a torpedo installer would have difficulty figuring out how to sufficiently weight a bag so that it would sink. Whatever the cause, the author agrees with Mark Ragan, who called this case of floating papers "the greatest wartime blunder of the Confederate secret service."[320]

In addition to the three letters mentioned above, Dunn's recovered pouch included his formal orders to report to General E. Kirby Smith for torpedo engineering service and the July 1863 report of the Confederate Engineer Headquarters affirming the value and effectiveness of the Singer-Fretwell torpedo design. There was one final document in the floating pouch, however, that was even more sensitive and troublesome than any of the other letters or orders. Bernard J. Sage, one of the leaders of the Confederate secret service, had written a letter of introduction for Singer, Dunn, and Braman. It was addressed to Sage's "friends" at various places west of the Mississippi River. The letter named each friend and identified his location. The friends were requested to give the members of the Singer group "all necessary hospitality, aid and information." The Sage letter was nothing less than a road map to Confederate sympathizers and operatives in key cities.[321]

Admiral David Dixon Porter of the US Navy was understandably horrified by the materials that had floated into Union hands. On March 20, 1864, Porter issued a general order warning officers in his fleet about coal torpedoes and directing them to be extra vigilant in protecting the security of their coal supplies. "Guards will be placed over them at all times, and anyone found attempting to place any of these things [coal torpedoes] among the coal will be shot on the spot." He said the same fate would await any "persons who are caught planting torpedoes, or floating them down, or with any of these inventions in their possession." Porter named Dunn and other members of the Singer group and suggested "the sooner they are got rid of the better."[322]

On March 21, 1864, Porter followed up his "shoot on sight" order by attaching the "friends" list in Sage's letter of introduction to an order declaring all of the named individuals to be "rebels, engaged as agents for the Confederate government, employed for the purpose of furthering the views of said Government in destroying Union vessels by torpedoes and other inventions." Porter sent a copy of his order to Navy Secretary Gideon Welles together with a photograph of one of the named individuals. Porter hoped that these materials would be of help to detectives assigned to track the Confederate agents down. In the meantime, he told Welles, "I have given orders to commanders of vessels not to be very particular about the treatment of any of these desperadoes if caught—only summary punishment will be effective."[323]

Porter's decision to get detectives involved in the search for Confederate conspirators was at least partially successful. On March 21, 1864, Porter wrote to the Office of the Provost Marshal General in St. Louis and noted that the second page of Thomas Courtenay's letter about the coal torpedo mentioned a man named Clendenin, who was supposedly furnishing money for the coal torpedo project. Porter wanted this man arrested immediately and his home searched for incriminating papers. The man in question turned out to be William A. Clendenin, Courtenay's brother-in-law, who was promptly arrested along with his business partner. Despite the fact that Clendenin denied all knowledge of the plot, he was held in prison until January 1865 with only a brief period of release to move his family. Clendenin was not the only alleged conspirator. A Union agent in St. Louis reported that Courtenay had both a partner in Canada and connections with a merchant named McCartney in St. Louis.[324]

While Porter's detectives were expanding their search for Confederate conspirators, Robert Dunn was continuing to make his way to Texas to report to General Magruder. Dunn was apparently clueless that his papers had floated into the possession of Admiral Porter. He certainly did not know that Porter had effectively signed a death warrant for the Singer operatives if they were captured. Dunn simply proceeded to Houston, and on April 6, 1864, delivered a status report to Magruder bragging about the Singer group's achievements since they had left Texas. He observed that Singer torpedoes had been used to successfully sink *DeKalb* and *Housatonic* and claimed that the torpedoes had then been adapted on land to successfully blow up eight trains. "These successes," Dunn noted, "show conclusively the certainty of explosion of our torpedoes."[325]

While awaiting further orders from General Kirby Smith, to whom he had reported by letter, Dunn requested an appointment with General Magruder to discuss in greater detail the real project that had brought him to Texas. In Richmond, Dunn confided, the Singer group had presented a torpedo boat plan of their own to Confederate officials that would "enable us to operate with safety to our crews, and, at the same time, strike terror to the enemy." This torpedo boat plan was undoubtedly the exciting new project that Singer and Braman had both hinted at in the lost letters to their wives, which were now in Admiral Porter's hands.[326]

According to Dunn, the Confederate secretary of war had already authorized building of the Singer group's new torpedo boats at Selma, Alabama, and Wilmington, North Carolina. What made these new boats so special? Dunn described them as follows:

> [The boats would be] of the following dimensions vis. 160 feet long, 28-foot beam, and 11-foot hold with flat deck, carrying all their machinery below—to be iron sheathed and with no capacity for guns, and only showing 2 feet above water when ready for work. They [are] to be arranged with torpedoes, worked from below decks, and through tubes, forward, aft, and on both sides. It is believed by Engineers of the highest rank, after a full investigation of our plans, that these boats will be perfectly able to raise the blockade of all the harbors in the Confederacy.[327]

The plan that Dunn put before Magruder had little resemblance to the *David* or *Squib* torpedo boat designs that had seen action on the East Coast. Dunn's plan was much more ambitious. In some ways, it resembled Creuzbaur's discarded plans for *Avenger*.

While Generals Magruder and Kirby Smith were evaluating Dunn's torpedo boat plans and their potential applications in the Trans-Mississippi, Admiral Porter was in Louisiana leading a formidable naval force in the Red River Campaign. In fact, Porter's "shoot on sight" orders about torpedo agents had been issued on March 25–26 in Alexandria, where the fleet had rendezvoused with General Nathaniel Banks before the final push up the Red River. From Alexandria, the combined naval and army expedition continued up the river about fifty miles to Grand Ecore.[328]

On April 7, 1864, the navy left Grand Ecore and continued up the Red River toward Shreveport. Banks had left the preceding day, choosing to leave the river road and the navy's artillery support to march northwest along what was believed to be a shorter route. What this meant was that the army and navy were now on different lines of advance with only limited means of communication between them. Porter eventually found his way up the river to be blocked by the wreck of a steamer that the Confederates had sunk across a narrow section as an obstruction.[329]

With no way to advance up the river and with Banks and his army out of contact, Porter became concerned about the very real possibility that he might be abandoned, left unable to run his fleet through the gauntlet of enemy forces that he feared would soon line the riverbank leading back down the Red River to its junction with the Mississippi. These fears were soon realized when the ironclad *Osage* was attacked by a contingent of Confederate cavalry and small artillery pieces at Blair's Landing (also called Pleasant Hill Landing) on April 12, 1864.

The battle at Blair's Landing would be one of the strangest battles of the Civil War. Strapped to the transport *Blackhawk*, *Osage* had run aground attempting to make a turn above the landing. The stranded vessel was positioned so that its starboard broadside battery was facing the high riverbank about one hundred yards distant. Thomas O. Selfridge, an experienced captain, was in command of *Osage*. When the Confederates suddenly attacked, Selfridge moved *Blackhawk*'s crew to safety behind *Osage*'s armored casemate. This precaution saved many lives in the ensuing action. After later examining *Blackhawk*'s upper works, Admiral Porter would say that there was "not a place six inches square not penetrated by a bullet."[330]

When the Confederates attacked, *Osage* loaded its guns and soon began firing grapeshot and canister at every target that presented itself above the shelter of the bank. Confederate General Thomas "Tom" Green led his Texans in what was primarily a musketry attack on the stranded Federal vessels. This strange action between an ironclad and an infantry force lasted about an hour and a half. During this skirmish, Captain Selfridge made what may be the first combat use of a periscope in military history to help direct his fire at the Confederates. At one point, Green tried to rally his men on horseback. *Osage* responded by leveling an eleven-inch gun loaded with canister at him. The firing of this weapon at such close range decapitated Green. The loss of General Green, a famous San Jacinto veteran who had been a household name to Texans since the recapture of Galveston, was a heavy blow.[331]

USS *Osage* photographed on the Red River, Louisiana, circa March–May 1864. NH 49997, US Naval History and Heritage Command.

Following the battle of Blair's Landing, *Osage* managed to free itself from the mud and continued to meander with the remainder of the fleet downstream. This operation was extremely slow and difficult with vessels almost constantly running aground and having to be worked free. After overcoming numerous obstacles, by April 13, the navy had retreated back down the river as far as Grand Ecore, where they learned that Banks and his army were now in full retreat after a series of disastrous battles at Mansfield and Pleasant Hill.[332]

While Banks and Porter debated their next joint course of action at Grand Ecore, Singer operatives continued placing torpedoes in the shallow waters south of the town. Since the Union naval vessels could not avoid passing through this position on their way back down the Red River, this was an ideal application for torpedoes. In the movement south from Grand Ecore, Porter decided to send USS *Eastport* ahead to deal with enemy forces on the banks. He sent *Eastport* not only because it was his heaviest armored vessel, but also because he desperately needed to get it into deeper water as soon as possible. As *Eastport* steamed slowly and carefully down the river, it ran hard aground at seemingly every turn. Then at about 4:20 p.m. on April 15, the boat suddenly shuddered, and the forward hold began rapidly filling with water. Everyone aboard knew that something had gone badly wrong.[333]

When the pumps from *Eastport* and a neighboring boat were unable to clear the rising water, it became clear that the vessel must have struck one of the Confederate torpedoes. This torpedo explosion was unusual in that it initially went almost unnoticed. According to Porter's report the following day, "the damage was slight, and the shock only noticed by a few persons on board, and it was not for some time after they found water in her hold. She was five hours sinking, but we had no pumps that could save her."[334]

Captain Seth Ledyard Phelps, *Eastport*'s commander, described the event in more dramatic terms. According to Phelps, he knew almost immediately that he had struck a torpedo. His official report confirmed that at the time of the incident he was maneuvering very slowly over a shallow section of the river with his paddle wheels not turning. Suddenly, the vessel received a "severe shock forward," which caused the crewman monitoring the depth to be almost tossed overboard.[335]

When his vessel suffered its "severe shock," Phelps immediately suspected that *Eastport* had struck a submerged torpedo. His small boats had already disabled torpedoes in the vicinity, and he knew they were a constant threat. He quickly ruled out the possibility that he had struck a snag. *Eastport* had been only recently put in service and had an extremely strong bottom. Phelps believed that no ordinary snag could have been responsible for the volume of water that suddenly started filling *Eastport*'s forward hold. In addition, the vessel did not stop moving forward after the shock. The only explanation for what the ship experienced was that it had struck an enemy torpedo. After *Eastport* was later raised, the damage survey confirmed that a torpedo had been responsible for its initial sinking.[336]

Civil War Gunboat *Eastport*, Thornton Barrette folder, Inland River Photographs Collection, Cincinnati and Hamilton County Public Library, Cincinnati, Ohio.

To prepare his boat for rescue, Phelps quickly went to work moving his guns and heavy machinery over to barges. With the help of other pumping vessels and a huge amount of labor from his crew, Phelps finally managed to lighten *Eastport* just enough that it could be raised off the bottom and towed down the river. The carpenters from several ships worked day and night to confine and stop the leaks while the vessel continued to ground every few miles as it limped painfully down the rapidly falling river. By April 26, Phelps was forced to admit that his crew was "was worn out by labor beyond its power of endurance" and that the ship could not be moved any further toward secure Union lines. After removing anything and everything that might be valuable to the enemy if salvaged, Phelps and Porter prepared to blow up the ship with fifty barrels of powder.[337]

An attempt to destroy the boat using a galvanic (electric) detonator failed, and the explosion had to instead be triggered by lighting conventional fuses

Lieutenant Commander Seth Ledyard Phelps, USN. *Officers of the Army and Navy (Regular) Who Served in the Civil War* (1892).

and trails of powder. Because this manual lighting procedure required close proximity, the planned explosion of *Eastport* almost did more damage than the original torpedo encounter. As Porter recalled, "so careful were the two pyrotechnists in charge of the explosion [Phelps and Porter] to see that the powder all exploded, that we came very near going up with the vessel. Phelps was in a boat near the bow, and I was in a boat but a very short distance off, and great pieces of the hull fell all around us."[338]

As it turned out, the destruction of *Eastport* was not as complete as Porter and Phelps had planned. On June 23, 1865, over a year after *Eastport* was blown up, the side-wheel steamer *Ed. F. Dix* struck *Eastport*'s wreck and sank virtually on top of it. At the time of its sinking, *Ed. F. Dix* was steaming up the Red River laden with government stores and supplies and US cavalry units destined for service in northwestern Louisiana and the eastern part of Texas. Thus, the torpedo that sank *Eastport* indirectly led to the sinking of yet a second boat.[339]

The fact that a Texas torpedo had sent the heaviest ironclad in the western Union fleet to the bottom of the Red River did not take long to get back to Confederate commanders in the Trans-Mississippi. If there were any doubts about the Singer torpedoes and their effectiveness, those doubts had now been dramatically erased. Instead of pondering whether the weapons were effective, the question now was how many Singer torpedoes could be produced and how fast they could be installed at key locations across the South.

After the Red River Campaign sputtered to a halt, there was very little mystery about the Union's next major target in the Gulf of Mexico. Capturing Mobile and Alabama had long stood out as important military and political objectives. Before the war, the city of Mobile had been the second largest cotton port in the South after New Orleans. After the capture of the Crescent City in 1862, Mobile had become the most important Confederate port on the Gulf Coast and the second largest Southern city by population after Richmond. It was also a key rail junction and a haven for blockade runners.[340]

To get to the city, Union naval forces would first have to fight their way into Mobile Bay. Entering the bay would undoubtedly be a difficult and dangerous operation. There was a good reason why Mobile had not been attacked earlier in the war. By 1863, many military observers considered the military complex surrounding Mobile to be virtually impregnable. The reason was that there were two enormous masonry fortifications guarding the entrance to Mobile Bay. Fort Morgan, the largest, had many heavy guns within almost point-blank range of the narrow channel that a large warship would need to follow

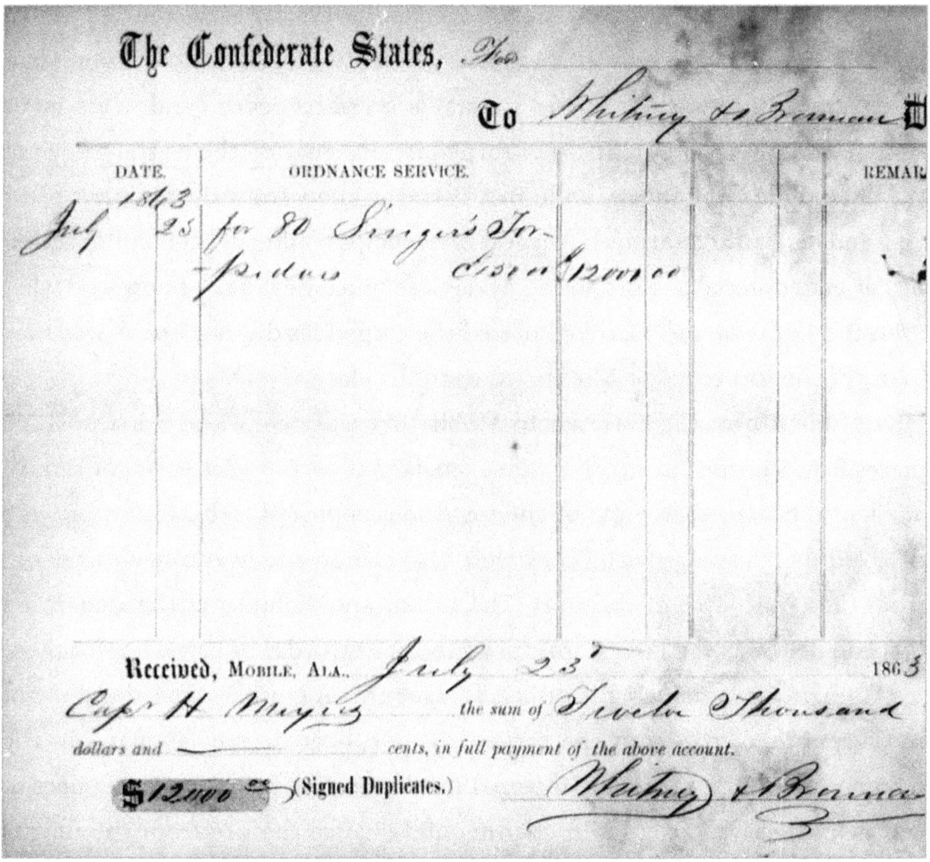

The Confederate States,

To Whitney & Braman

DATE.		ORDNANCE SERVICE.		REMAR
1863 July	23	for 80 Singer's Torpedoes	$12000 00	

Received, Mobile, Ala., July 23 1863

Capt H Myers the sum of Twelve Thousand dollars and —— cents, in full payment of the above account.

$12000 00 (Signed Duplicates.) Whitney & Braman

Purchase order for 80 Singer torpedoes at Mobile, July 23, 1863. Confederate citizens file for Whitney and Braman, Record Group 109, National Archives and Records Administration.

to enter the bay. The Federals also knew that the edges of the channel were protected by torpedoes.[341]

Singer operatives had signed a contract on April 17, 1863, to construct and install one hundred torpedoes at Mobile. They proceeded promptly to fill this order. Singer operatives placed additional torpedoes near the entrance to Mobile Bay; by the middle of 1864, the total number of installed torpedoes was approaching two hundred.[342]

In planning his famous entry into Mobile Bay in the summer of 1864, Admiral Farragut was neither surprised nor intimidated by the presence of Confederate torpedoes. By now, torpedoes were an expected feature of virtually every major Southern waterway. Federal blockaders off Mobile had carefully monitored their enemy's installation of torpedoes and made maps showing a large triangular field of torpedoes obstructing the western edge of the channel leading into Mobile Bay. Farragut knew from the sinkings of *De Kalb* and *Eastport* that even the biggest of his ships could be taken out of action if they encountered one of the deadly devices. What he did not know, and what even the Confederates who had placed the torpedoes did not know, was how many of the torpedoes at Mobile were still in place and able to function. The environment near the entrance to Mobile Bay was one of the worst possible places for torpedoes to survive. Some small boat parties that Farragut sent in at night reported that some of the torpedoes appeared to be absent or were disabled by marine growth. They were also able to cut away a few torpedoes from the outer layer of defenses. The extent and viability of the remaining torpedo field was the largest unknown factor as the day of battle approached.

As Farragut launched his attack at dawn on August 5, 1864, he did not initially intend to "damn the torpedoes" and float over what many in the navy regarded as a carpet of "infernal machines." He planned for his fleet to proceed directly up the main channel and chance the fire from the nearby Confederate fort. His assault would be led by four ironclads, followed by his fourteen remaining ships lashed together to provide more protection. The plan went astray quickly. At about 7:30 a.m., as the first ironclads passed the

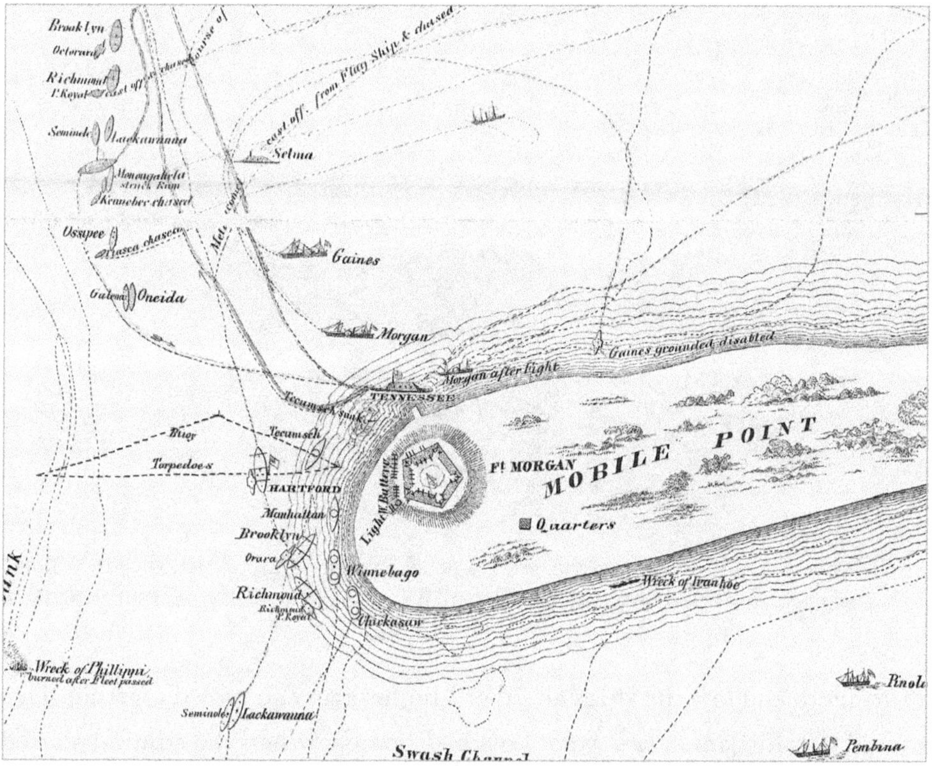

Detail from "Chart Showing the Entrance of Rear Admiral Farragut into Mobile Bay, 5th of August, 1864," and the triangular field of torpedoes. Lithograph by Hatch & Co. (1864), LC No. G3972.M6S5, Library of Congress.

fort, USS *Tecumseh* inexplicably veered to the west and entered the edge of the torpedo field. Suddenly, the great ironclad struck a Singer torpedo. It abruptly rose out of the water and nosed under, its propeller still spinning wildly as the stern submerged. Some witnesses said it took only half a minute for the ship to go under. Only twenty-one men out of the one hundred forty-one aboard survived. Maritime historian Milton F. Perry accurately characterizes this as, without question, "the most completely disabling blow struck by torpedoes during the entire war."[343]

Farragut, who had positioned himself in the rigging of his flagship to observe the battle and give instructions, watched the shocking destruction

"Destruction of the Monitor *Tecumseh* by a Rebel Torpedo in Mobile Bay, August 5, 1864." Line engraving based on a sketch by Robert Weir in *Harper's Weekly*, September 10, 1864.

of *Tecumseh* and saw the ships ahead of him hesitate and crowd together. This caused a traffic jam at the worst possible location. When the admiral started to direct the following ships to move left to avoid a collision, he was reminded of the presence of the torpedo field in that direction. It is at this point that Farragut may have uttered some version (there are many) of his famous order "Damn the torpedoes!" followed by the instruction to go full speed ahead. Having just seen his leading ironclad sunk by a powerful torpedo, Farragut's order to direct most of his fleet directly over the torpedo field was one of the boldest decisions in the history of naval warfare. It turned out to be the correct call, although nervous Union sailors reported afterward that they had distinctly heard the snapping of torpedo triggers without explosions as the ships plowed their way through the field.[344]

Farragut's entry into Mobile Bay made two things clear. As Singer operatives had long suspected, it was difficult to install an effective and long-lasting field of torpedoes in a tidal saltwater environment like the entrance to a bay.

Portrait of Rear Admiral David G. Farragut, circa 1864.
LC No. B813–1561 A. Library of Congress.

But as the sinking of *Tecumseh* also dramatically illustrated, it only took one functioning torpedo to sink one of the most powerful ships afloat. As the number of active Confederate ports continued to shrink, the Union Navy would now be operating largely on inland waterways. In the more restricted environments of rivers and bays, where rows of torpedoes could be anchored to obstruct narrow channels, Confederate torpedoes were still a potent weapon.

Farragut's successful entry into Mobile Bay made Confederate officials even more interested in practical strategies that would enable the South to counter the Union fleet. The answer did not seem to lie in large ironclad vessels, one of which, CSS *Tennessee*, had been captured at the conclusion of the Battle of Mobile Bay. Instead, Confederate generals were becoming increasingly convinced that armored torpedo boats might prove to be the one and only great equalizer that would enable them to overcome the powerful Union gunboats blockading their ports.

The main problem with torpedo boats was that the resources to build them were hard to come by in much of the Confederacy. One solution seemed to be to build either the boats or their primary components abroad and then find a way to smuggle them back into the Confederacy. On April 16, 1864, orders were placed in England for twelve engines and boilers to equip torpedo boats. As described, the boats under construction were small, being only forty to fifty feet in length with a five–six-foot beam. These smaller torpedo boats were more along the lines of *David* and *Squib* than the larger boats then under consideration in Texas.[345]

On July 18, 1864, Confederate Secretary of the Navy Stephen R. Mallory instructed purchasing agent J. D. Bulloch to construct six torpedo boats in England as soon as possible. These boats were intended to carry from five to seven men for no more than twenty-four hours. The key objective was that they needed to be capable of going at least ten miles an hour with all on board. The spar torpedo would be made of copper or iron and able to contain between forty and one hundred pounds of powder.[346]

Since the torpedo boats were intended to be "miniature swift steamers," they must "be strongly built, of good iron and as light as may be consistent with strength, and particularly strong forward, as they may sometimes run into a vessel." Mallory even provided a rough diagram of the boats to aid in their construction. If it was not possible to send the completed boats over, Mallory said they could be sent over in sections. Because the navy was "destitute of mechanics," however, Mallory requested that the boats be sent as complete as possible.[347]

In accordance with his instructions, Bulloch soon placed orders for six lightly armored boats to be produced near London. On September 16, 1864, Bulloch reported that he had placed orders for six additional steel torpedo

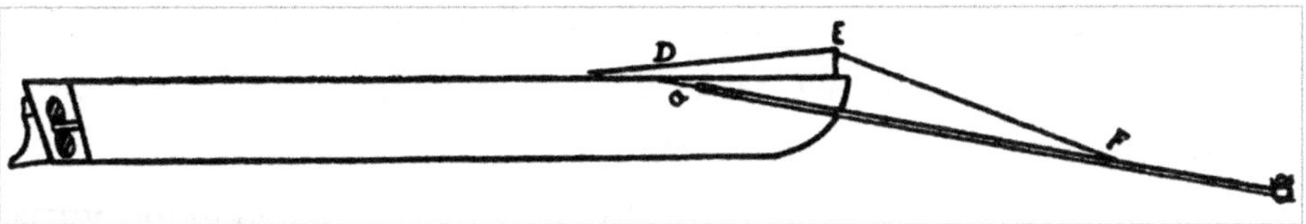

Sketch of torpedo boat sent with July 18, 1864, letter from S. R. Mallory to J. D. Bulloch, *Official Records of the Union and Confederate Navies in the War of the Rebellion*, series 2, vol. 2.

boats with builders near Liverpool. At least six of the steel boats were later built and shipped out. Some of these boats were tested on the Thames and some may even have been shipped back to the Confederacy as deck cargo on blockade runners. Although none of these boats made any important contribution to the war effort, the engine for one of these boats did find its way through the blockade to Texas near the end of the war.[348]

On November 18, 1864, Gabriel J. Rains, the superintendent of the Torpedo Bureau, prepared a candid status report for the Confederate secretary of war concerning operations under his direction. Rains confessed that notwithstanding a few scattered successes like the sinking of *Tecumseh*, his experience with Singer torpedoes led him "to doubt their efficiency in salt water where barnacles and young oysters abound." Rains noted that he had recently sent John Fretwell to North Carolina to employ his Singer torpedoes in the river systems of that state. As it turned out, this assignment would be one of the engineer's best decisions.[349]

One of the key Union objectives in North Carolina was severing the Weldon Railroad that ran between Richmond and Wilmington. Cutting this important Confederate supply line would isolate the blockade running operation at Wilmington and materially hamper the South's war effort. Union naval planners decided that the best way to accomplish this task was to send gunboats up the Roanoke River and destroy the Weldon Railroad bridge near Rainbow Bluff. On December 9, 1864, the 974-ton side-wheel gunboat *Otsego* entered the Roanoke and steamed up to its intended place of anchorage for the night, near Jamesville, North Carolina. As the anchor was being deployed, a torpedo exploded under *Otsego*'s port side. Shortly thereafter an additional torpedo exploded under its forward pivot gun. *Otsego* sank in about three minutes, leaving its spar deck about three feet underwater.[350]

Commander W. H. Macomb, who commanded *Otsego*, noted in his official report that he had ordered spars and nets rigged ahead of his vessel to catch floating torpedoes and keep them at a distance. Singer operative Fretwell had so skillfully installed his torpedoes, however, that they were not easily seen or exploded from the surface. Macomb concluded that it was just bad luck that he had somehow "stopped directly on top of a line of these infernal machines."[351]

Macomb was fortunate to report that none of his crew had been killed as a result of the torpedo explosions that had sunk his boat. But the string of disasters on the Roanoke River was not yet complete. The next morning, Macomb was attempting to salvage what could be recovered from the wreck of *Otsego*. He sent the tug *Bezely* up to get some men and an officer who were working at the site of the wreck. As *Bezely* got within a few yards of the wreck, yet another torpedo exploded and *Bezely* sank alongside *Otsego*, killing two members of the tug's crew.[352]

"Wreck of the *Otsego*, and the Explosion of the Tug *Bezely* in the Roanoke River." *Harper's Weekly*, January 21, 1865.

After the disaster, a small launch was sent up the river to gather information about the area. It soon returned with belated warnings from enslaved people that the river was full of torpedoes, there being as many as forty at one place. This was undoubtedly an exaggeration, but Macomb prudently determined not to risk any additional vessels to find out. Unfamiliar with Singer torpedoes, Macomb examined some of the recovered torpedoes, reporting that they "are made on some new plan with an air chamber." As opposed to other torpedoes he had encountered earlier in the war, the Singer-Fretwell version looked "very sure" and "everyone we picked up was in good condition."[353]

Although Superintendent Rains continued to have his doubts about the value of the Singer torpedo in a pure saltwater environment, the Roanoke River sinkings confirmed their value when properly installed in a river setting. Torpedoes would continue to demonstrate their value through the end of the war. Ironically, some of the last successful torpedo operations would occur once again in the waters around Mobile and involve a vessel that was all too familiar to Texans.

Although Farragut's bold movement in August 1864 had led to the capture of the forts at the entrance to Mobile Bay, the Confederates continued to hold the city of Mobile itself well into 1865. The approaches to the city were solidly protected by fortifications on the east of Mobile Bay, including Spanish Fort and Fort Blakely. As its name suggests, Fort Blakely was located near the mouth of the Blakely River. In late March, the Union Navy attempted to provide support to the army's efforts to capture these forts and advance on the city of Mobile. Anticipating that a Union naval force would be employed, Singer operatives had planted extensive fields of torpedoes in the rivers and waters surrounding these positions.

USS *Milwaukee*, a double-turreted ironclad monitor launched in 1864, proceeded up the Blakely River on March 28, 1865, to shell a Confederate transport. The vessel was returning to its original position when the captain felt a sharp shock near his aft turret, about forty feet from his stern. Although the stern sunk in three minutes, the forward compartment did not fill with water for more than an hour, giving the crew a chance to escape without any serious casualties.[354]

As if to confirm that torpedo disasters now had to come in multiples, on the following day, Captain William M. Gamble stopped his single turreted monitor, USS *Osage*, near the entrance to the Blakely River. As Gamble was preparing to release his anchor, a torpedo exploded under the bow and the vessel sank in about five minutes. Four men were killed and eight more were wounded in the incident. Gamble chalked the sinking up to bad luck. He believed that an errant Confederate torpedo must have come loose and drifted into him since the area where he was sunk had been thoroughly dragged to make sure that it was safe. It is ironic that a torpedo planted by Texans at Mobile caused the end of *Osage*, the same vessel that had fired the shot that killed Texan General Tom Green during the Red River Campaign.[355]

As the experience of the tug *Bezely* proved in North Carolina, it was always dangerous to approach the wrecks of vessels sunk by torpedoes. Where there is one torpedo, there is always the risk that there may be more. But when ships with large guns were sunk in shallow waters, commanders were always tempted to make some effort to salvage the guns and other critical machinery. On April 1, 1865, the sternwheeler USS *Rodolph* was sent up to

USS *Milwaukee*, photographed by T. Lilienthal in the Mississippi River area circa 1864–65. NH 510, US Naval History and Heritage Command.

"The Siege of Mobile—Wreck of the *Osage* and the Monitor *Milwaukee*."
Harper's Weekly, April 29, 1865.

the wreck of the *Milwaukee* towing a barge loaded with equipment needed for the salvage operation for that vessel. Suddenly, a torpedo exploded directly under *Rodolph*'s bow. The explosion came all the way up through the gun deck, making a hole that the captain judged to be at least ten feet in diameter. The ship sank quickly, with the gun deck soon submerged under more than five feet of water. *Rodolph* experienced casualties of one man killed, eleven wounded, and three missing.[356]

The three gunboats sunk by Singer torpedoes near Mobile may have been the last three significant torpedo casualties of the war. The sinking of these vessels so suddenly in such close proximity to one another had a profound effect on the naval officers who witnessed these events. It was disconcerting for every captain to realize that one moment he could be sailing along with not an enemy in sight and suddenly an unexpected explosion could send his ship to the bottom in a matter of minutes. This vulnerability would eventually lead to enormous changes in military science and fundamental revisions to the world's naval tactics.

"Destruction of the Tin-Clad No. 48 [USS *Rodolph*], April 1, 1865."
Harper's Weekly, April 29, 1865.

In 1878, Admiral David Dixon Porter wrote an article titled "Torpedo Warfare" for the *North American Review*. Porter had a unique perspective on this subject. Throughout the war, Porter commanded ships that encountered torpedoes. He had even narrowly escaped from a burning ship that had suffered an explosion probably caused by a coal torpedo. It was Porter who had been the naval officer to first ring the alarm bell about such infernal devices when the papers of the inventors came into his possession in 1864. He had then issued "shoot on sight" orders for the people who spread such devices and sent detectives out to deal harshly with their potential conspirators.

All in all, Porter probably had more understanding of the realities of Civil War torpedo warfare than anyone in the world. His thoughts on the subject just thirteen years after the war ended are particularly illuminating. The existence of torpedoes, Porter believed, had fundamentally changed the experience of serving in the navy. "Persons unacquainted with a sea-life are apt to imagine it a fine thing to be a naval officer, roaming around the world

Rear Admiral David Dixon Porter (1813–91).
LC-USZ62–113173, Library of Congress.

in a noble ship, with all sail set slow and aloft, and doubtless it is a privilege to serve one's country in so honorable a calling; but this is only the rose-colored view of the matter, and there are very many incidents in the profession which would be extremely distasteful to a landsman—among them the liability to being blown to atoms when skimming over the bosom of a summer sea."[357]

Porter said that those who dismissed the importance of torpedoes deserved "little credit for judgment." He admitted that "when I hear a naval officer speak contemptuously of the torpedo, saying that it can be of no great use in time of war, I set him down as one whose opinion is of no consequence on that or any other professional subject, for he has either benefited nothing by experience or never had any experience by which to benefit."[358]

Porter's experience had made him a reluctant but firm believer in the power of torpedoes. He observed that once the Confederates protected their inland strongholds in 1864 with fields of submarine torpedoes, these positions became "almost insurmountable" from a naval standpoint. He noted that Confederate General Beauregard had once said that he preferred one of his pet torpedoes at Charleston to five ten-inch guns, and added that "well he might, since our ironclads were impervious to the latter, and entirely vulnerable to the former."[359]

In the end, Porter concluded that the Confederate torpedo had demonstrated its viability because of the devastating effect that it could achieve with so little cost. "Who does not remember the fate of the gallant [Captain Tunis] Craven and his officers and men, when fearlessly advancing in the *Tecumseh* to the attack on Mobile, how the ship encountered a hundred-pound torpedo, and in thirty seconds after the explosion went to the bottom, leaving but a few survivors to tell the story? Here was a vessel, costing over a million dollars, destroyed by a small torpedo which cost less than one hundred."[360]

What had started as a simple experiment in a barrel of water behind E. C. Singer's Lavaca home would end up as one of the most devastating weapons of the Civil War. In terms of results, 1864 would be the year of the torpedo. Surveying the tumultuous events of the previous year, on January 23, 1865, The *Houston Tri-Weekly Telegraph* estimated that "torpedoes have, in proportion to numbers laid down, been twice as effective as shells." If torpedoes were regularly replaced with fresh ones, the newspaper declared, "we believe it might be utterly impossible for the enemy to penetrate the country." The paper went on to recite the long and growing list of enemy ships that had been sunk by torpedoes and noted that many of the most important losses had been caused "by a well-known Texas company [the Singer group], some of whom have been employed on our coast for the last two years."[361]

Although the unnamed company had been successful in the past, the newspaper predicted that even greater success could be expected from its members in the future. "The same firm submitted to the War Department at

Richmond eighteen months ago, a plan of an invulnerable iron clad torpedo boat." Noting that some of these boats were under construction elsewhere, the newspaper said that it would not be astonished if some of them arrived soon on the Gulf Coast.[362]

This report was part of a disinformation campaign. The journalist who wrote these words probably knew that at least two and possibly three of these torpedo boats were then actively under construction near Houston. As the calendar turned the page to 1865, the question was whether these game-changing vessels could be completed and deployed before the Confederacy was forced to surrender. As it turned out, this would be a race against time that would run all too close.

CHAPTER 13

TEXAS TORPEDO BOATS

As the Houston newspaper was preparing its readers for stories about the imminent exploits of "invulnerable torpedo boats" along the Gulf Coast in 1865, reality was quite different. The journey of Texas torpedo boats from concept to reality had been quite a tortuous one, and it was not at all likely that the journey would successfully reach any destination.

To refresh the reader's memory, Robert Dunn had reported in Houston in April 1864 (minus his floating papers) with the intention of creating a large torpedo boat near Galveston that would challenge the Union blockade and confirm Southern supremacy. By the end of May, Dunn had received orders from General Kirby Smith to build two such boats, with one of these boats to be constructed under the direct supervision of David Bradbury.[363]

When Dunn was ordered to produce two large torpedo boats, he was taking on a task that the Confederate Navy had already dismissed as virtually impossible to complete. Lieutenant Jonathan H. Carter, who was in command of the naval defenses of western Louisiana, had been asked about the prospect of building a torpedo boat in March 1864 and had quickly declared it "impracticable." "[S]uch a vessel as the plan and specifications call for cannot be built within fifteen months or two years, if at all, and at a cost of not less than one million of dollars." Carter sent a naval constructor to Houston who confirmed his pessimistic assessment that the necessary labor and materials simply could not be obtained. He then met with the usually optimistic General Magruder, who agreed with Carter that because of the lack of iron for armor and machinery "no iron clad can be built in Texas."[364]

If Magruder and Carter were correct in their assessment of the difficulties of building one torpedo boat, Dunn's task of simultaneously building two such vessels seemed ludicrous. The task was made even harder when Dunn was suddenly pulled away from the project in June and sent to deploy torpedoes in southwestern Louisiana. Here, however, Dunn made a valuable discovery that helped speed up his work.

On May 6, 1864, a small force of Confederates with four cannons surprised and captured two Union gunboats at Calcasieu Pass, a narrow inlet in Louisiana that connects Calcasieu Lake with the Gulf of Mexico. The two captured gunboats were USS *Wave* and USS *Granite City*. By coincidence, the Confederate artillery force that proved decisive in this capture was a battery of German immigrants from Fayette County under the command of Captain Edmund Creuzbaur. Captain Creuzbaur had recently attempted to resign his command, and it was only a matter of luck that his resignation was still pending without action at the time of the battle. Of interest to our story, Edmund was inventor Robert Creuzbaur's brother.[365]

While Dunn was in Louisiana, he learned that the Confederates were then in the process of converting the two armored gunboats to blockade runners by stripping the boats of heavy materials in order to increase their speed. For service as blockade runners, the boats' iron armor and other heavy machinery were considered unnecessary. But this armor and some of the machinery could be easily adapted for use on a torpedo boat. As soon as Dunn heard about this situation, he put in a request for the surplus materials.[366]

On June 21, 1864, a special order was issued that gave all the iron taken off the *Wave* to Dunn for "torpedo service." To help him get the iron back to Houston, another order in July directed the Marine Department to provide Dunn with all necessary "transportation of negroes, tools, materials etc. engaged in the manufacture of torpedo boats." By this point, orders and agreements were referring to Dunn as the "Chief of Torpedo Service" and David Bradbury as "Chief Constructor" of torpedo boats.[367]

While Dunn was away in Louisiana on torpedo duty, Bradbury kept the project going by negotiating an agreement with Galveston merchant Hiram Close to provide iron work for the torpedo boats. This was a critical step. H. Close & Sons was the first and oldest iron foundry in Galveston, having started business in 1844. It was also the largest foundry, taking up an entire city block. When Dunn approached him about the torpedo boat project, Close was in the process of casting projectiles for the guns protecting Galveston and, unlike many other businesses on the island, still had a steady stream of work.[368] Bradbury reported to Magruder's staff that Close had reluctantly agreed to manufacture all of the boilers and machinery necessary for the construction of the torpedo boats but insisted on being formally ordered to perform the work in order to avoid interference with any other branch of the government.[369]

Although it is difficult to determine their source, rumors soon began to circulate in the Union Navy that Confederate torpedo boats were under construction in the Trans-Mississippi. On June 25, 1864, Admiral Porter confidently declared: "The rebels are fitting out at Shreveport four torpedo boats. They will be ready in two months." He then directed that the mouth of the Red River be obstructed with a chain and a nearby gunboat. With that protection, he suggested, "no torpedo boats can get out." It is uncertain how Porter obtained his information, but it is interesting to note that he did not yet seem to be aware of the two boats then under construction near Houston. It would only be a matter of time, however, before such projects were discovered by spies or revealed by deserters.[370]

The end of June also saw Edgar Singer's temporary return to Texas. He was accompanied by John Braman, who soon became closely involved in the construction of one of the two Texas torpedo boats. On August 14, 1864, Singer sent a status report to the Adjutant General's Office regarding his operatives and their various assignments. In making his report, Singer disclosed that he and three of his company were in Houston working on a torpedo boat project. He described the boat then in progress as follows: "The following is her dimensions: length of 114 ft, breadth of beam 14 ft with sponsons of 2 ft making overall 18 ft draught . . . double flued boilers 24 ft long with 2 direct acting oscillating engines 12x16 in., diameter of propeller 6 ft with 10 ½ ft pitch to make 120 turns per minute."[371] If Singer's dimensions and almost scribbled notes are correct, this boat was significantly smaller than the boat that Dunn had originally proposed to Magruder (one hundred sixty feet long with a twenty-eight-foot beam).

Very little is known about the course of Texas torpedo boat construction activity over the course of the next several months. One of the boats was apparently being built at Captain Thomas Chubb's shipyard on Goose Creek (called Tyber Creek in some communications at the time). Captain David Bradbury was supervising construction of that boat. The other was being constructed at a site called Lubbock's Mill, which was located closer to Houston on Buffalo Bayou. From the special orders that were issued, it appears that Chubb was helping Bradbury supervise construction of the boat at his yard and Singer operative John D. Braman was supervising construction of the Lubbock's Mill boat.[372]

While the Singer group's two torpedo boats were being constructed, Robert Creuzbaur was beginning to work on his own, entirely separate, project. Although details are scanty, Creuzbaur's project apparently involved a number of smaller armored boats mounting a large number of torpedoes. It is possible that these boats were being modified to deliver torpedoes with floats like the *Avenger* design. It is also possible that the torpedoes were to be exploded in a line, as his modified torpedo cannon design called for.

Whatever Creuzbaur's secret plans might have been, they seemed to require a lot of boats and torpedoes. On August 19, 1864, Julius Kellersberger, the chief engineer for Texas, submitted a special requisition for forty sheets of flat iron. The iron was described as "needed immediately for Capt. Creuzbaur's torpedoes."[373] Shortly afterward, Kellersberger approved Creuzbaur's request for arms "to be used from boats at night in case of meeting with hostile boats while operating with torpedoes."[374]

At some point near the end of 1864, the relationship between iron supplier Hiram Close and the various torpedo boat builders began to sour. Deadlines for constructing critical machinery were not being met and some began to question whether Close might be deliberately delaying his support for the project. By December, the engineering department in Shreveport was growing impatient about the lack of progress on the boats. In fact, the engineers became so concerned that they began preparations to impress Close's foundry and take over operations. They also questioned whether it might be necessary to seize Captain Chubb's shipyard in order to speed up the construction of the boat there.[375]

Given the concerns that had been expressed by the engineers, General John G. Walker, who had taken over General Magruder's position in Houston, made a personal visit to the Goose Creek yard to check on construction progress. On December 2, he reported back to the engineers that "the work on the hull is progressing very satisfactorily at Capt. Chubb's shipyard under the management of Capt. Bradbury, a most excellent man." Noting that Chubb himself was deeply devoted to the Confederate cause, Walker admitted that "without his assistance in furnishing spikes, iron, lumber and other material the work on the boat must have long ago come to an end." He saw no reason to impress the Goose Creek facility and believed the team of workers there was productive.[376]

Thomas Chubb, who would eventually become the central figure in constructing the Goose Creek boat, was undoubtedly one of the most interesting characters in Civil War Galveston. Born in Massachusetts in 1811, he left home at about the age of seven and went into service in the US Navy. He tried a wide variety of commercial endeavors, including managing a theater and traveling with a circus, before returning to the navy as a coxswain. When the Texas Revolution broke out, Chubb sailed down with a cargo of arms and powder that some reports claim helped Texans win their independence.[377]

When the Civil War broke out, Chubb placed himself and his schooner, the *Royal Yacht*, at the service of the Confederacy. On November 7, 1861, a Union raiding party captured Chubb and his crew and left his vessel in flames. After a few months of imprisonment at Fort Lafayette in New York, he was exchanged and returned to Galveston in the spring of 1862, where he promptly issued a warning that the Yankees were "moving Heaven and Earth for our subjugation." Upon his return, Chubb was placed in charge of the small vessels in the harbor and assumed the courtesy title of "Commodore." In addition to his duties in the harbor, Chubb also served as superintendent of naval works at his shipyard near the mouth of Goose Creek. It was in this connection that he came to be the passionate leader of the 1864 project to build a torpedo boat that might even the score with his enemies.[378]

Although Chubb impressed General Walker as someone who would see his end of the torpedo boat project successfully through to completion, Walker expressed much less confidence in Hiram Close and his foundry:

> In regard to the engine and machinery: while in Galveston I had an interview with Mr. Close, the owner of the foundry and after much artful dodging on his part to escape doing the work at all, I extracted a promise from him that he would go to work at once upon the shaft which is necessary to have at once, and as soon as that is completed to commence work on the engine. His good faith, however, is more than doubtful and he will avoid doing this work if possible. The truth is the Government owe[s] him something like two hundred thousand dollars and he is not anxious to increase the debt or to compromise himself with the Yankees by working for our government.[379]

Even though Walker discouraged the engineers from going through with the formal procedure to impress the Hiram Close foundry, he soon demonstrated that he was serious about improving its performance. When Close failed to comply with his promised schedule, Walker had him placed under arrest for a few days in order to motivate him and convince him to reorder his priorities.[380]

One thing that may have permitted General Walker to act so firmly with Close was that a new source for an engine had been located. In his letter of December 2, Walker noted that he had recently learned that there were two locomotive engines at Columbus formerly belonging to a railroad company owned by an alien (Northern citizen). He sent Dunn to go examine them and determine their condition, noting that "the gentlemen think they will answer [their] purpose well and by their use we will save at least two months in completing the boat." After receiving a favorable report from Dunn on December 20, 1864, General Walker issued a special order impressing one of the locomotives and fixtures and directing that the material be turned over to Robert Dunn for use on his torpedo boat project.[381]

As the end of 1864 approached, the Goose Creek torpedo boat project was reaching an important but complicated milestone. The original agreement with Captain Chub provided that he would be paid a total of $80,000 for constructing the boat. Since this secret project was an off-the-books arrangement, however, the contract had not gone through the normal approval process. The agreement with Chubb originally specified that he would be paid a partial completion payment of $40,000 when the work was half completed. Being short of funds, however, the engineers in Shreveport tried to substitute a new payment arrangement by which Chubb would be paid the appraised value of the boat only if and when it was completed. Thus, the important question of how and when to pay Chubb remained unresolved.[382]

On December 29, General Walker directed the attention of the Shreveport engineers to the payment provision of the agreement with Chubb and said that more than half the work on the torpedo boat had now been completed. Either the government needed to set aside the contract and force Chubb to accept the appraised value at the end or a large progress payment needed to be made. Walker expressed his opinion that it would be unwise to set aside the contract since the rapidly depreciating Confederate currency meant that the appraised value might be substantially higher than the originally agreed-upon contract price. It also seemed unfair to Chubb to leave him without any compensation at this critical stage in the work. Walker closed his letter by noting that "if the boat is ever completed and put in successful operation, it will be due to the patriotic energy of Mr. Chubb, who seems devoted heart and soul to the completion of the work."[383]

Although wanting to see the torpedo boat completed as soon as possible, there was considerable doubt at the engineering headquarters in Shreveport about the best way to handle Chubb's compensation. Captain William A. Freret of General Kirby Smith's engineering staff responded to General Walker's letter with a frank admission that the engineering department found itself "nearly destitute of funds" and asked for Chubb's indulgence in receiving payments.[384]

Later in January, the engineers managed to scrape together enough funds to provide Chubb with two payments of $20,000 each, with the stipulation that these amounts would be applied either against the contract price of $80,000 or the appraised value, whichever the final form of contract required. The failure to place the torpedo boat in service before the war ended would eventually moot the necessity of any final accounting settlement.[385]

While Chubb and the engineers were debating the way that he would be compensated for building the Goose Creek torpedo boat, the Union naval forces blockading the entrance to Galveston Bay were getting their first reports about the strange new vessel. On January 2, 1865, two deserters from the Confederate Army rowed out to the Federal blockade. When questioned about the ships in the port, the men mentioned that a 140-foot-long torpedo boat, which was said to be armored with railroad iron, was being built at Goose Creek.[386]

Although the extent of progress on the boat at the Lubbock's Mill site near Houston is difficult to ascertain, there clearly was some ongoing activity at that site also. On February 9, 1865, Freret submitted a special requisition for four thousand dollars. The stated purpose for this payment was "for building one torpedo boat near Houston, Texas." The payment was requested "in specie," suggesting that Houston suppliers and contractors were now prudently hedging their bets on Confederate currency and the war's outcome.[387]

By the end of January, the time to begin putting the iron armor on the Goose Creek torpedo boat was approaching. This step in the construction raised a complicated issue because the completed vessel might be too heavy to get out of Goose Creek and into deeper water. On February 21, General Walker ordered Chubb to dredge out the creek's entrance to a depth of five feet nine inches and to move the vessel to a shipyard at Lynchburg, where the depth of water would be sufficient to accommodate the vessel with all of its armament and machinery. Lynchburg was located across the San Jacinto River from the famous battlefield. Water depth was not the only reason for moving the boat. Walker admitted to Chubb that he wished to "save it from being shut up in Tyber [Goose] Creek, where it might be lost in case the enemy should get into the bay."[388]

Demonstrating his continued belief in the project's merits, on February 21, 1865, Walker urged Chubb to "hasten forward the work as rapidly as possible." If possible, he wanted work to be conducted in two shifts so construction of the torpedo boat could be continued night and day until completed. "The importance of this cannot be overestimated," he stressed. "I feel assured you and Capt. Bradbury will spare nothing in meeting my expectations and the expectations of the country."[389]

Leaving Chubb in the process of moving his torpedo boat to Lynchburg, it is now time to examine whether there might have been a functioning submarine in Texas waters at the end of the war. In a book filled with mysterious and enigmatic subjects, this may be the hardest and most controversial subject to address because of the limited nature of the evidence.

Although building a submarine had been under discussion in Texas since early in the war, the first concrete reference to launching such a project seems to have come in 1863. On November 15, 1863, Henry S. Lubbock (brother of the

Texas governor) wrote a memorandum to some prominent Texas businessmen, including William J. Hutchins. This document reports that Henry S. Lubbock had recently met a man named Walker, who had been "ordered to build a submarine propeller for offensive purposes against the enemy."[390]

Lubbock said that the plan was "one that has been successfully tried in England, France and America," and he was confident it would serve their purpose. The reference to those three countries may be because they were all builders of ironclad warships. What Lubbock actually meant by the term "submarine propeller" is, of course, very uncertain. Lubbock said that he had been appointed the superintendent "to commence operation immediately." The only obstacle left, as Captain Lubbock saw it, was getting state approval for the project and freeing up sufficient time to focus entirely on it. If Lubbock's project ever went forward, there seems to be no preserved record of it.[391]

The next portion of the Texas submarine story starts with a casual conversation in 1865 between two strangers on a long Texas journey. As it turned out, one of them was a Union spy. Mordecai Peebles Hunnicutt, who always signed his name "M. P. Hunnicutt" for understandable reasons, was a colorful character and an excellent espionage agent. Although he was born in Clinton County, Ohio, in 1827, Hunnicutt had spent a good part of his early life in Prince George County, Virginia, not too far from Richmond. Hunnicutt moved back to Ohio before the age of twenty-one and served in an Ohio regiment during the Mexican-American War. He was later captured as part of one of William Walker's filibustering expeditions in Central America and was subsequently reported to have somehow worked his way into the position of pastry chef in the Costa Rican presidential palace. At some point during his wide-ranging pre–Civil War career, Hunnicutt had served as a detective and acquired valuable experience as an investigator.[392]

In November 1862, Hunnicutt joined the Seventy-Third Ohio Regiment. By the spring of 1863, it became clear that because of his age (thirty-six), travel background, and detective skills, the newly promoted Sergeant

Hunnicutt was an excellent candidate for intelligence gathering operations. The Army of the Potomac needed someone reliable who could travel through Confederate lines and send back confidential reports and Hunnicutt fit the bill. Hunnicutt was sent south to Richmond on two occasions and sent back valuable reports about the Confederate Army and their positions. Of interest to our story, Hunnicutt may have been in Richmond on the day that Ebenezer Allen died under mysterious circumstances. Like every good spy, Hunnicutt was particularly adept at getting people to talk. His sources for one report, for example, included the colonel of a Mississippi regiment and an adjutant general on General A. P. Hill's staff.[393]

Hunnicutt's cover story while traveling behind enemy lines in Virginia was that he was a deserter from the Union army. He even joined a Tennessee regiment to add credibility to his story. Eventually, however, people around Richmond began paying too much attention to Hunnicutt and started asking unwanted questions. It was time to move on. On September 19, 1864, Hunnicutt wrote a letter to Major General Edward R. S. Canby requesting the opportunity to continue doing the same type of intelligence gathering work in Louisiana and Texas, where he was not known. Saying that "I have facilities that few people have for procuring information," Hunnicutt attached a strong letter of support from Colonel George H. Sharpe, his former commander and handler. Sharpe stated that Hunnicutt had satisfactorily handled "work of the most confidential and delicate nature" and noted that the only reason he had been let go was that he had become "known to the authorities on the other side."[394]

Canby wasted no time in accepting Hunnicutt into his service. On December 17, 1864, Hunnicutt signed a receipt in New Orleans for five hundred dollars in Confederate money "to be used on special service." Shortly thereafter, he departed on what would turn out to be a two-month journey through Confederate territories west of the Mississippi River. He traveled from Little Rock to Shreveport and then headed to Marshall, Texas, on his way to Austin.[395]

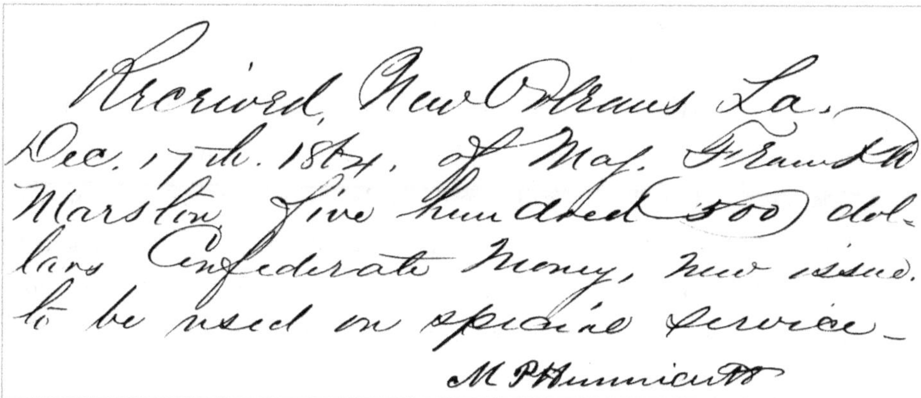
Received, New Orleans La., Dec. 17th. 1864. of Maj. Frank H. Marston Five hundred (500) dollars Confederate money, new issue. to be used on special service –

M P Hunnicutt

Receipt for Confederate currency signed by M. P. Hunnicutt before his scouting mission to Texas, December 17, 1864. Letters Received by the Adjutant General's Office, National Archives and Records Administration

On the stage from Marshall, Hunnicutt encountered Singer operative and former Lavaca jeweler James Jones. In the course of casual conversation during their long journey, Jones told Hunnicutt that he had been part of a torpedo secret service group back east and was now in the process of relocating so that he could construct a boat designed to destroy the USS *Tennessee*, the former Confederate ironclad that had been captured at Mobile Bay. He encouraged Hunnicutt to invest $5,000 in the new venture. Amazed that a man purporting to be a secret service operative would be so open about his work, Hunnicut said he would carefully consider the proposition and urged Jones to share additional details.[396]

Jones was apparently as talkative as he was indiscreet. As Jones described the project to Hunnicutt, there were at least four of the secret boats in progress at Shreveport and one at Houston. If this was all that was reported, it would be safe to assume that Jones was simply referring to the torpedo boats that were then either planned or (in the case of Houston) already under construction. The problem is that the boats that Jones described to Hunnicutt were not torpedo boats. Instead, the boats that Jones outlined were something quite different.[397]

According to Hunnicutt's later account of the conversation:

> The boat is forty feet long, 48 inches deep, and 40 inches wide, built entirely of iron, and shaped similar to a steam boiler. The ends are sharp pointed. On the sides are two iron flanges (called fins), for the purpose of raising or lowering the boat in the water. The boat is propelled at the rate of 4 miles an hour by means of a crank, worked by two men. The wheel is on the propeller principle. The boat is usually worked 7 feet under water and has four dead lights for the purpose of steering or taking observations. Each boat carries two torpedoes, one at the bow, attached to a pole 20 feet long; one on the stern, fastened on a plank 10 or 12 feet long.[398]

The vessel that Jones described to Hunnicutt was obviously a submarine like *Hunley*—not a torpedo boat like the one then under construction at Lynchburg. Jones boasted that it had air arrangements sufficient to support four men at work and four men at rest for a period of two to three hours. Unlike *Hunley*, which mounted only a single spar torpedo, Jones said the new design featured both a forward and rear torpedo that could be exploded when they struck the hull of a target vessel. The torpedoes were made of sheet iron and were said to resemble butter churns. But these churns each carried forty pounds of explosive powder.[399]

It is difficult to know what to make of this strange account. Was there ever really a functioning submarine like *Hunley* near Houston? Although possible, it seems unlikely. No other reports of such a vessel have been found. It is clear, however, that the details about the new submarine clearly came from someone intimately familiar with *Hunley*.

Why did Hunnicutt come away from the conversation with the impression that a functioning submarine existed? Hunnicutt's report was not written up until March, well after his February encounter with Jones. Jones may have boasted about *Hunley* and his desire to build another one in a fashion that confused Hunnicutt. The fact that he was attempting to get Hunnicutt to invest may also have played a part by leading Jones to suggest that the new submarine was more of a present reality than an idle pipe dream. In the end, the possibility of a functional Confederate submarine near Houston seems to be destined for the file of mysteries that will probably never be solved.

Although there is little evidence about a hypothetical Houston submarine, it is possible from some tantalizing details in the records to confirm that by the spring of 1865, construction on the torpedo boat at Lynchburg was approaching the finish line. A special order dated March 24 issued ten pounds of candles to Bradbury for use on the boat. (It is unclear whether the candles were to be used for inside finishing work on the vessel or whether they were intended to serve as part of the initial stores for the new vessel's crew to employ during missions.)[400]

Three days after Bradbury obtained his candles, seven German deserters from Cook's Heavy Artillery regiment rowed out to the Federal blockaders. The deserters knew little about torpedo boats other than that they had heard one was being constructed on the San Jacinto River near Lynchburg. When questioned further, one man claimed that he had seen such a vessel floating in the main channel at Galveston. According to his testimony, "It was shaped like a box, with square corners, and was quite low in the water." He could not tell whether the strange vessel was covered with iron. If this account is accurate, it is the only account that has been located establishing that the torpedo boat was completed to the point that it was afloat and undergoing some form of sea trials.[401]

Another indication that the torpedo boat was nearly finished was the Confederate Navy's sudden interest in getting involved. Major General Magruder had been placed back in command of the Department of Texas on March 31, 1865. In a letter from Trans-Mississippi Headquarters in Shreveport dated April 10, Magruder was notified that Lieutenant John L. Phillips from Alabama had been assigned by the navy to command the new torpedo boat. Phillips was a good choice. He had been in charge of a force of artillery on CSS *Arkansas* when it boldly steamed through the Federal fleet in 1862. He had also commanded CSS *Webb* on the Red River. He had the right experience for the job. The question now was whether larger events in the course of the war would make his new torpedo boat command irrelevant.[402]

On April 9, 1865, as the Lynchburg torpedo boat was being readied for its new commander, Robert E. Lee surrendered his army at Appomattox Court House in Virginia. Generals Magruder and Kirby Smith both issued fiery statements declaring that they would continue the fight, but it seemed increasingly likely that the end of the war was now in sight. This was confirmed when Joseph E. Johnston surrendered his Army of Tennessee on the same terms a couple of weeks later. Despite these discouraging developments, Magruder continued to operate as though the torpedo boats would be completed and soon directed at the enemy. On April 25, Magruder issued an order providing that Phillips would be temporarily assigned to the defenses of Galveston while the last few details were sorted out on his new vessel.[403]

Some of the last few nagging details involved obtaining sufficient coal to fire the boilers and completing the torpedoes with which the vessel would be equipped. Dunn and Bradbury were both now scurrying around to find the final materials they needed. On April 28, Dunn notified Magruder that a blockade runner had recently brought in 200 tons of coal. Magruder quickly ordered that a portion of it be diverted for use in the torpedo boat. On the next day, Dunn submitted a request that Magruder allow him to telegraph the engineering department in Shreveport seeking permission to buy copper to make the boat's torpedoes. The record of telegrams sent shows a simple notation from General Magruder: "Let this be sent."[404]

In the same letter that notified Magruder about the blockade runner's cargo of coal, Dunn informed the general that it also included an engine and a boiler that would be perfect to complete the second torpedo boat on "short notice." It is likely that this spare engine was one of the torpedo boat engines that Secretary Mallory had secretly ordered from England for use on the East Coast. Magruder was uncertain whether he could legally seize this engine but decided to go through the motions of doing so. On April 30, Magruder issued an order declaring that despite the obstacles, the torpedo boat at Lubbock's Mill "will be constructed to completion." By this point, the Marine Department was being supervised by Henry S. Lubbock, the former governor's brother. Magruder instructed Lubbock to afford Braman "all the assistance in his power to facilitate the work" and ordered that "as the early completion of this boat is desired, Capt. Lubbock will put upon the work as many mechanics as possible."[405]

While Dunn and Bradbury were approaching the finish line, a third torpedo boat project may have been in the process of coming together. In the same order that General Magruder issued to Lubbock to expedite the work at Lubbock's Mill, Magruder authorized the purchase of a cutter formerly owned by Mr. J. Hancock of Galveston. This vessel was "to be used by Capt. Cruesbar [Creuzbaur] for special service." What Creuzbaur intended to do with this small vessel remains a mystery, but it may well have been a variation on a strategy that had been successfully employed by Union naval forces in a famous action the year before.[406]

On the night of October 27–28, 1864, Lieutenant William B. Cushing of the US Navy used a steam-powered launch with a spar torpedo to make a daring raid up the Roanoke River in North Carolina. There, he attacked the Confederate ironclad *Albemarle* and detonated his torpedo. The explosion caused *Albemarle* to sink. During the operation, Cushing towed a small cutter behind him, which he used as a guard boat to keep the enemy from interfering with his plans.

There is good reason to believe that Creuzbaur may have been part of a secret operation in the spring of 1865 seeking to copy Cushing's successful tactic from the year before. In the summer of 1864, the engineer in charge of the foundry at Houston was ordered to supply Creuzbaur with all materials and labor that would assist "in constructing torpedoes and shields for protection of the crews."[407] A month later, Creuzbaur requested ordnance and stores "to be used from boats at night." From the brief descriptions, it appears that Creuzbaur intended to create a small fleet of armored boats that would swarm out and attack the Union blockaders with torpedoes.[408]

Because of a shortage of materials and the priority of other projects, it had taken more than six months for Creuzbaur to get his small boat project off the ground. In the early months of 1865, however, Creuzbaur finally began assembling the elements of his plan. On March 4, 1865, a special order was issued directing Captain Lubbock to give Robert Creuzbaur all the materials and tools needed for an unspecified "special service." Three weeks later, Lubbock was ordered to procure an unspecified number of launches that Creuzbaur had requested for his secret project. When General Magruder authorized Lubbock to obtain a cutter for Creuzbaur at the end of April, the engineer may very well have been close to putting the final pieces together to launch his own bold raid on the blockaders off Galveston. Although the evidence supports the existence of such a project, it does not appear that any such attack was ever attempted.[409]

On May 9, 1865, Robert Dunn was authorized to secure transportation from Houston to Shreveport. There was no stated reason for this trip. It may be that he was being sent to work on torpedo boat projects there. It may also be the case that he was simply going to Louisiana to assist with placing additional defensive torpedoes in the Red River. Whatever the reason, Dunn's movement at this point is one additional piece of confirmation that his work on the Lynchburg torpedo boat had largely come to a conclusion. The same order instructed Lieutenant John Phillips to "take command of the torpedo boat now being constructed on the bayou as soon as it is completed" and urged him to "devote his attention to such arrangements and preparations as may be necessary to insure its rapid completion." Two days later, nine more men were assigned to assist with "building torpedo boats."[410]

The last special order ever issued by General Magruder was written in Houston on May 22, 1865. It directed Commodore Leon Smith to turn over to Major R. P Rowley, an engineer, the steamer *Little Rebel* and "the engine brought in for the torpedo boat."[411] Four days later, the surrender of the Army of the Trans-Mississippi was signed in New Orleans. For all the frantic effort that was put in to completing torpedo boats during the last three months of the war, none of the boats ended up making the slightest difference to the war's outcome. In fact, no evidence has been located that they ever set out on a mission.

Although the boat at Lubbock's Mill never even had its engine installed, the torpedo boat at Lynchburg appears to have been much closer to completion. Indeed, it may have been functional to at least some limited extent. But as far as can be determined, the Lynchburg torpedo boat never deployed a single torpedo. If the boat ever had a name, it was not listed. If Lieutenant Phillips ever stepped aboard and formally took command, there is no record of the event.

The reader may be wondering why the Confederates that had been working "day and night" to finish a torpedo boat did not at least make some effort to use it. It is difficult to say. Perhaps the boat was never mechanically complete enough for use. Another explanation may lie in the fact that General Magruder could see the end of the war approaching and knew that he would soon be dealing with his enemy as a captive. Given that probable course of events, he may have recognized the counterproductive nature of launching a last desperate effort to inflict casualties among the people who would soon be deciding his fate. Instead, Magruder prudently elected to wait out the end of the war and not take any actions that might further jeopardize his personal situation.

EPILOGUE

On June 2, 1865, General Edmund Kirby Smith went on board the USS *Fort Jackson* at Galveston and signed papers ratifying the surrender terms that had already been agreed to by a subordinate in New Orleans the previous week. Fearing retribution, he then headed to Mexico to see what the postwar environment would produce. For the same reason, General "Prince John" Magruder chose to move his place of residence to Mexico to await the course of events.[412]

Edgar Singer returned to his home in Lavaca, where he quietly signed a parole of honor on July 8, 1865. Under his signature, where an officer's rank was typically displayed, he added merely that he had been the commander of "Singer's Special Service Company." It is understandable that he avoided much detail about this "special service" given the number of "shoot on sight" orders that had been issued for those involved with building and installing torpedoes.[413]

Many of Singer's men followed their commander's lead by coming back to Lavaca and signing simple paroles. J. D. Braman signed his parole the same day as Singer and gave exactly the same description of his "special service" during the war.[414] Robert W. Dunn had actually beaten the other two men home. He signed his parole in Lavaca on June 22 with a subtle note of levity, referring to his unit simply as "Prof. Singer's Special Service Co., C.S.A."[415]

Although Singer would go on to achieve a fair measure of success, the postwar era was not particularly kind to the other members of the Singer "special service" group. John Fretwell, who became grand master of the Masonic Order in Texas shortly after the war, ran a hotel called the San Antonio

House in Lavaca for a few years before ending his life in Mobile virtually penniless. After running a store for a few years in Lavaca, J. D. Braman moved to Galveston and tried to start a cotton factor business. That business is noted in the 1875 city directory, but by 1876 it seems to have closed and become the subject of litigation. Braman survived long enough to be briefly mentioned in a 1909 Galveston newspaper article about the submarine *Hunley* and its Texas connections. Little is known about the postwar lives of the other men who worked with Singer. It is ironic that men who had been a part of so many military accomplishments during the war never really managed to achieve much public distinction after the end of that conflict.[416]

"Prof. Singer," as Braman fondly referred to his former chief in his surrender papers, did a great deal of traveling after the war. Like his illustrious uncle, Singer continued to be an active inventor. He obtained an 1870 patent for a cotton-seed hulling machine while in New Orleans. In 1874, he moved to Marlin, a small town in Falls County, Texas, where he obtained an 1875 patent for brick molds. In 1876, Singer was assigned rights to cotton baling patents that showed his residence as Houston. By 1879, Singer was again living in Marlin, where he obtained a patent relating to cotton bale ties. Interestingly, none of Singer's postwar inventions related to weapons or sewing machines. Perhaps he avoided those fields to avoid drawing attention to himself and his actions during the war.[417]

In addition to inventing agricultural and construction products, Singer went into the mining business. He had first investigated the business in 1879 by going to Leadville, Colorado, where a significant silver deposit had been discovered the previous year. Singer responded to an inquiry from a Galveston newspaper, saying that there were now at least three hundred Texans there and that some of them had struck "big bonanzas." His initial mining results were promising and, in 1890, Singer incorporated the Land & Mineral Company in Lampasas with three partners. The company's capital was reported to be $500,000, showing that Singer's personal wealth had soared remarkably since the end of the war.[418]

Singer and his company soon had extensive mining operations in Colorado. In 1900, Singer was interviewed by an El Paso newspaper. Although he was seventy-four by then, the reporter said he was still as active as a man of fifty. If he wasn't so old, Singer joked, "he would take himself and a tent" into the mountains and continue to "rough it while prospecting." Although he was still evaluating new mining opportunities, Singer confessed that he was now looking for a warmer place to spend the winters.[419]

Singer told the El Paso reporter that his search for minerals in a warmer climate had led him to study ten railway maps of Mexico. He then admitted that he had gone from Texas into Mexico for a brief period shortly after signing his parole in 1865. "It was at the time when thousands of the Confederate soldiers thought that it would be impossible to live in the states." "Many of us," Singer noted, "took our portable belongings and fled to the land [Mexico] now rich in ore." Singer's niece remembered her uncle saying that on one occasion after the war he had been shown a wanted poster issued during the conflict, which offered a five-thousand-dollar reward for his apprehension. Once the pressure passed and it seemed possible to escape punishment, Singer quickly ended his exile and returned to Texas.[420]

Throughout his travels and mining ventures, Singer had steadfastly maintained a residence in Marlin. Calling it his "health resort," Singer noted proudly to the El Paso reporter that Marlin had a well that produced great quantities of heated water with remarkable curative powers. The water not only cured rheumatism, but it also rejuvenated the digestive organs. As far as Singer was concerned, Marlin "beats Hot Springs."[421]

The newspaper articles that reported on Singer's mining success and patents made no mention of his connection with Civil War torpedoes or the secret service. Although Singer's connection to the torpedo had been exposed in Northern newspapers as early as 1864, that aspect of his service had been largely ignored or forgotten shortly after the war. The mines with which Singer was now publicly associated were in Colorado—not the ones that had blown up USS *Tecumseh* in Mobile Bay.[422]

Singer's lack of military notoriety began to change shortly after the turn of the century. In 1905, Singer went north to visit the place where he had grown up in Illinois. In Belvidere, Singer met with his cousin, Joseph B. Pettey, whom he had not seen in sixty-one years. The local newspaper noted that the two men's mothers had been sisters and that both men descended from a common ancestor who had fought in the American Revolution. The reporter could not resist pointing out that Singer "was the only member of a large family which in any of its branches became associated with the Confederacy."[423]

Captain Pettey had served as an ensign in Admiral Porter's fleet. This contrasted with Singer, the reporter observed, who had invented the diabolical device that caused the loss of so many seamen and might have killed his cousin. The newspaper recited that, "It is now conceded that E. C. Singer was the first inventor of [a] mechanism for the explosion of submarine torpedoes, and that his genius first made them first possible of use." Orders had been issued that torpedo builders should be shot on sight. For this reason, the article observed, it was not until the last general amnesty that men like Singer were restored to citizenship.[424]

The two cousins shared an interesting wartime story with the Illinois reporter. At one point in the war, cotton traders had been permitted to pass relatively freely through Union and Confederate lines. One of these traders remarked to Captain Pettey that he had encountered his cousin, Singer, deep behind enemy lines near Jackson, Mississippi. Pettey told the trader to tell Singer the next time he saw him that he wanted his cousin to come pay him a visit. Pettey said that the trader later returned and reported that he had seen Singer and passed along his message. The trader reported that Singer "was very much obliged but thought under the circumstance he was pretty well off where he was and that he guessed he would defer his visit until some more prudent occasion."[425]

In the reporter's presence, Pettey asked Singer if the trader had accurately repeated his answer. Singer laughed and said that yes, it was entirely correct. The reporter noted the genuine affection between the two cousins and commented that in 1905, forty years after the end of the war, "all the bitterness of the tremendous war has entirely vanished and only the force of circumstances placed the visitor of yesterday [Singer] upon the opposite side."[426]

In 1910, five years after his meeting with Pettey, Singer's search for a winter residence eventually led him to build a house on Harbor Island, which is in Red Fish Bay opposite the Texas city of Aransas Pass. He was in the process of building that house, at the age of eighty-five, when he fell from the roof. The injury fractured his collar bone, broke two ribs, and caused him serious internal injuries. This was probably the beginning of the end for Singer's health. It is also at this point that Singer determined to look for a wider platform to go on the record and finally tell some of his group's remarkable wartime story.[427]

In 1916, a San Antonio reporter named Horace N. Hill interviewed Edgar Collins Singer, who was at that time ninety-one years old. His initial intention was to talk to Singer about the torpedo he had invented, not knowing

E. C. Singer at age 91.
San Antonio Express, July 13, 1916.

of his connection to the submarine *Hunley*. As Singer revealed the full scope of his work during the war, Hill was astonished. On July 30, 1916, Hill published a lengthy article titled "Texan Gave World First Successful Submarine Vessel" in the *San Antonio Express*. The article featured two pictures of Singer, one taken at age ninety-one and one taken forty-six years before, in 1870. The article began with a headline statement in bold print: "In Buffalo Bayou, Half a Century and More Ago, Captain Singer, Still Living, Successfully Tested His Invention Which Confederate Government Then Used With Terrible Effect on Federal Navy—Singer's Idea Is Now Sinister Scythe of the Seas for Warring Nations."[428]

Much of what we know about the early history and operations of the Singer group comes from this remarkable article. It is fortunate that Singer agreed to the interview when he did. Just three years later, at the age of ninety-four. he died at his home in Marlin. Singer was buried in Marlin at Calvary Cemetery. His simple grave marker makes no mention of his military service or accomplishments.[429]

As Singer's long postwar story illustrates so dramatically, there was just something about the climate of Texas that led that state's Civil War inventors to lead long and productive lives. San Jacinto veteran and inventor Lucien Hopson, for example, encountered only limited success selling his curiously-shaped projectile to the Confederacy during the war. But it seems clear that Hopson's ideas were worth exploring. After the war, the inventor received two US patents for his projectiles. The first patent (305,002), received in 1884, was for a "ball and driver." This appears to have been for the small ball that so impressed the Confederate Ordnance Department in 1861. The second patent (313,075), which Hopson received in 1885, was for a triangular projectile that matched the description of his earlier Confederate patent. Although John Mercer Brooke initially dismissed Hopson's invention as ineffective, Brooke himself drew a sketch of its unique shape in his private journal and noted that it might eventually be more effective if it were cupped at the base and fired from one of his rifles.[430]

Whether Hopson's projectile was actually used by anyone during the Civil War is difficult to say. In July 1885, the *New York Times* published a story about Hopson and his connection as an "old soldier" to the upcoming fiftieth anniversary of the Texas Revolution. That flattering article stated in passing that Hopson's new 1885 US patent covered the same projectile design as his now worthless Confederate patent. Hopson told reporters at the time of his interview that his projectile had been used with success by Confederate batteries in Charleston. He also suggested that the Southern government was so pleased with the results that it had paid him a bonus to keep it secret. Never modest when it came to promoting his ideas, the eighty-two-year-old Hopson boasted to reporters that his steel-headed triangular projectile was still "the most accurate and instantaneous shot in naval and army warfare ever invented."[431]

In 1866, the state of Texas recognized Hopson's military service by granting him two separate tracts of land. He lived in Lampasas for many years after the war. In 1896, at the age of ninety-two, Hopson died in Austin. He is buried in the Texas State Cemetery.[432]

Like Hopson, the Austin group of inventors, including Robert Creuzbaur and Caleb Littlepage, went on to have productive careers while developing new ideas in a variety of fields. It was not always easy. After the war, Littlepage initially had difficulty making a living. In 1869, he took his family down to British Honduras, where he joined former Confederates attempting to become successful planters. This did not turn out to be an effective strategy, and Littlepage was soon back in the United States promoting his inventions.[433]

Littlepage would go on to secure five US patents to go with the two he had obtained before the war. Although one of the patents was for an electric foot-warmer, the other four related to saws and methods of forming saw teeth. Littlepage traveled extensively to promote his saw inventions. During the course of his travels, Littlepage developed an interest in spiritualism and began attending séances. A collection of his papers in Austin includes a spirit photograph of Littlepage and an unidentified female "spirit," as well as a "magnetized letter" from a New York medium.[434]

Subsequent to Littlepage's death in 1876, his family assigned all of his inventions and patents to Robert Creuzbaur in return for 50 percent of whatever profit he could generate from them. When he reviewed the inventions in 1880, Creuzbaur was initially interested in developing an idea for a "Latitude Indicator" that Littlepage had originated. Although Creuzbaur said he intended to spotlight the latitude idea in a nautical periodical, he had so many of his own projects in play that it does not appear to have led to anything significant.[435]

Like Littlepage, many former Confederates chose to pursue safety and opportunities in places like British Honduras, Mexico, or other areas even farther south. Always a contrarian, Creuzbaur chose to go in the opposite direction. After the war, Creuzbaur moved to New York, where he served as engineer for a number of prominent civic projects. As later events would prove, Creuzbaur was by far the most prolific of the former Confederate inventors. According to the author's count, after the war, Creuzbaur secured at least twenty-nine additional patents. While none of his patents related directly to the military subjects he had specialized in during the war, many did involve steam engines and boats.[436]

Although Creuzbaur's obituary declared that the inventor had died "in full enjoyment of his mental powers," *Scientific American* later questioned this assessment in an article about a motor patent application that had taken a record twenty-four years to be granted. When a reporter researched the history of the case, he was informed by the Creuzbaur family that "during the progress of the case, the inventor grew old and extremely eccentric, and the family delayed prosecution of the case until after his death, so that they might be able to handle the patent when issued, without obstruction or interference by him."[437]

One of the eccentricities that may have so particularly annoyed Creuzbaur's family was the inventor's tendency to write scathing letters to public figures complaining about the treatment of his ideas. In 1891, for example, Creuzbaur wrote an insulting letter to Thomas Edison demanding that Edison invest at least $500 in his syndicate to produce a "non-exhaust motor."[438] In 1899, he wrote a letter to the editor of the *New York Times* objecting to a stray comment that a writer had made about "liquid air."[439]

In 1911, he wrote a letter to Theodore Roosevelt complaining about the US Navy's failure to conduct serious tests of his "Pneumatic Static Ship Propulsion" system. In this letter, written just six months before he died, Creuzbaur demanded that Roosevelt appoint two "progressive" engineers to review his "PSSP" propulsion design. If they did not find anything objectionable, the inventor argued, Roosevelt would be obligated to use his influence to force the navy to incorporate the system in its vessels. Roosevelt declined.[440]

In an earlier section of this book, the author referred to Creuzbaur as the "Captain Nemo of Texas." Noting Jules Verne's fascination with the Civil War and the close parallels of the *Nautilus* mission and the commerce raiding of CSS *Alabama*, the author suggested that Verne may have been greatly influenced by that conflict. Is there any possibility that Verne knew about Creuzbaur and his *Avenger* project? Could Creuzbaur have been a partial influence for the Captain Nemo character?

Although the author has located no direct evidence supporting a connection, there are two tantalizing details that could potentially suggest such a possibility. In April 1867, Jules Verne made his one and only transatlantic voyage. He arrived in New York and visited the area for a period lasting about a week. During his visit, Verne toured Brooklyn, where Creuzbaur lived and worked. No evidence has yet been located of any meeting between the two men.[441]

The second potential connection between Verne and Creuzbaur is even less direct. At one point in *Twenty Thousand Leagues*, the protagonist, Professor Aronnax, receives a formal invitation from Captain Nemo to participate in an underwater hunt. Aronnax describes the note as being "written in clear bold handwriting, a little Gothic-looking and reminiscent of German writing."[442] This is an odd description for a communication from Nemo, who is later revealed in the book *Mysterious Island* to have been the son of an Indian raja. It would not, however, be an odd description for something written by Robert Creuzbaur, a German cartographer who wrote virtually everything in a beautiful script that resembled German calligraphy.

Creuzbaur would probably have thought of the eccentric Captain Nemo as a kindred soul. Although he always regarded himself as an engineer and practical scientist, Creuzbaur had consistently operated on the fringe of scientific thought. For example, he was an avid believer in the use of copper wires as dowsing rods to locate water. He wrote to the *New York Sun* in 1877 and explained that because water distributed electrical energy beneath the earth, a skillful operator like himself could detect and locate subtle differences in current through a copper wire dowsing rod. Before dismissing this claim entirely, it is interesting to note that a skeptical Maine resident reported in 1951 that Creuzbaur had almost forty years previously used his rod to precisely fix the position of a water well for him. Creuzbaur told the landowner that at the site he identified, three channels of water would be discovered about eight feet down. The well was dug, and three channels were located at a depth that was only one foot deeper than Creuzbaur had predicted.[443]

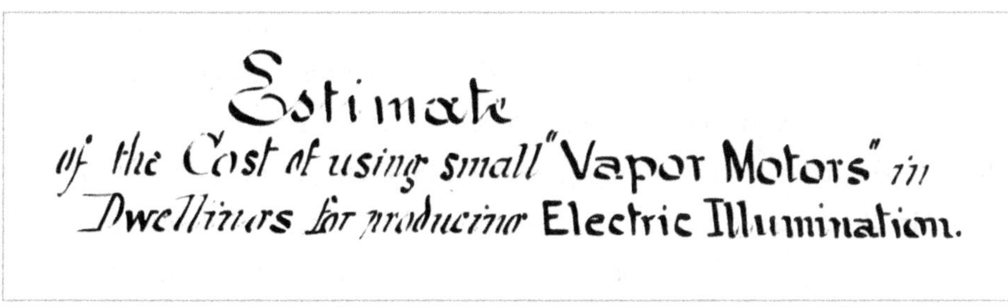
Estimate
of the Cost of using small "Vapor Motors" in Dwellings for producing Electric Illumination.

Detail from letter from Robert Creuzbauer to Thomas Alva Edison, November 6, 1878. Thomas A. Edison Papers, School of Arts and Sciences, Rutgers University.

Creuzbaur always tried to invent cutting-edge devices and was drawn to approaches others viewed as unproductive. He had shown that during the Civil War by relentlessly pursuing his radical designs for the proposed warships *Sea King* and *Avenger*. As he turned eighty, Creuzbaur decided that it was finally time to turn his attention to aeronautics. The inventor started his studies with the core belief "that the only successful flying machine will be one that will closely imitate the birds."[444]

After conducting a detailed examination of birds and their wings, in 1909, the eighty-six-year-old inventor unveiled his design for a flying machine he called the *Volant*. The name may be a tribute to French balloonist Jean Pierre Blanchard, who in the late 1700s attempted to invent a *vaisseau volant* ("flying vessel"). Shaped like a parachute with a triangular sail, Creuzbaur's airship was to be powered by a new propeller design and feature the same non-exhaust steam motor he had unsuccessfully tried to sell to Thomas Edison. He claimed that *Volant* would be "far more efficient per square foot than the Wright Brothers type." Indeed, Creuzbaur predicted that because of its unique design, *Volant* would soon take to the skies and "soar like a bird." Creuzbaur said that he was so confident in his design that if he could just get some capitalist to build it, he would be happy to serve as a passenger in it and compete in the upcoming Hudson-Fulton contest for flying machines. Despite his enthusiasm, it does not appear that *Volant*—or its inventor—ever got off the ground. Creuzbaur died in 1911 at the age of eighty-eight.[445]

On September 13, 1912, almost a year after his death, Robert Creuzbaur's patent for a motor was finally granted. This was the patent that he had applied for in 1888 and Creuzbaur's family had delayed prosecuting. To give some measure of the inventing climate that Creuzbaur experienced during his long life, Creuzbaur's first air chamber patent in 1860 was number 32,595. His last patent in 1912 was number 1,037,842. More than a million inventions were patented during Creuzbaur's inventing life. Although many things in society had changed enormously during the fifty-two years that had passed since his first invention, some of the drawings of Creuzbaur's motor in the 1912 patent are strikingly similar to the drawings that the Captain Nemo of Texas used to promote his *Avenger* vessel in 1862.[446]

Creuzbaur did not live long enough to see anyone attempt to build the flying machine he proposed. It may surprise readers to learn that as inventive as Texans were, the author has been unable to locate any evidence that they ever seriously experimented with balloons or flying machines in Texas during the war. But there was one postwar Texan, Adolphus E. Morse, who was closely associated with what has been called the Confederate Balloon Corps. While General Magruder was fighting the Peninsula Campaign in July 1862, the nineteen-year-old Morse was part of a team conducting reconnaissance from the balloon *Gazelle*, which was towed down the James River by CSS *Teaser*, the same vessel used in the testing of Creuzbaur's underwater cannon. After *Teaser* and that balloon were captured on July 4, 1862, the Confederates built another balloon at Charleston, in which Morse ascended on a number of missions in 1863. After the war, in 1872, Morse and his wife moved to Texas. He died in 1914 at the age of seventy-one and is buried in Oakwood Cemetery, Corsicana. In 2013, a monument and marker were installed there for Morse and the Confederate Balloon Corps. The marker states that "it is highly probable Lieutenant Morse was the last of any military balloonists to ascend skyward during the final stages of the [Civil War]." A scrap of the captured balloon *Gazelle* is preserved in the collection of the National Air and Space Museum in Washington, DC.[447]

Lieutenant Morse made it far higher into the sky than any of the Confederate rockets manufactured in Texas. The reader will probably not be surprised to learn that neither Captain George H. Schroeder, who unsuccessfully attempted to manufacture rockets in 1864, nor Captain John S. Greer, who unsuccessfully attempted to lead a battery to fire them, ever had anything more to do with rockets after the war. After returning to civilian life, Schroeder apparently did branch out from repairing sewing machines. An article in an 1888 newspaper reports that he had arrived in La Grange and opened a gun and locksmith business. He died there in 1897 and is buried in a La Grange cemetery.[448]

Captain Greer ended his days in Corpus Christi, where he was active in Democratic politics. He served both as justice of the peace and county commissioner. His financial situation was sufficiently secure that it enabled him to take a two-month-long trip to Oregon in 1880. His 1886 obituary contains a detailed recitation of his Mexican-American War service but merely mentions in passing that he had been a Confederate ordnance officer during what it referred to as the "late unpleasantness." It makes absolutely no mention of his connection to the only dedicated rocket battery ever formed in Texas.[449]

General John Bankhead Magruder, the ringmaster of the Texas circus who had tried to add Greer's rockets as one of his featured acts, headed to Mexico after the war. He would never again hold an important military command. When the French-sponsored regime he served met a bloody end, Magruder returned to the United States, where he lectured to make ends meet and lived in relative poverty. "Prince John" Magruder did not live long enough to join other Confederate generals in publishing his memoirs. This is unfortunate. Because of the wide variety of his wartime experiences, they would undoubtedly have made for good reading. He died of a heart condition in Houston in 1871. His body was later moved to the Episcopal Cemetery in Galveston, where it lies today under a large obelisk erected in 1894.[450]

Located not far away from Magruder's monument in Galveston is the grave of Commodore Thomas B. Chubb, who ran the Goose Creek shipyard and was so passionate about attempting to complete the torpedo boat. The story of how he came to be buried there is a bit confusing because of the similarity of two names. Commodore Thomas B. Chubb had a son named Thomas Henry Chubb. The younger Chubb had been born in New England but spent most of his early life with his father in Texas. Son Thomas H. Chubb served in the crew of the *Royal Yacht* during the war and was captured late in the conflict when that unfortunate vessel was unsuccessfully turned into a blockade runner. After the war, he contracted yellow fever in Galveston and was advised by a physician to seek a cooler northern climate to aid in his recuperation. He ended up in Post Mills, Vermont, and soon urged his family to join him.[451]

Thomas B. Chubb elected to join his son in Post Mills and in 1869 surprised his neighbors by opening a lodge there called the Commodore House, which catered to his friends and other Southern travelers. Also in 1869, the elder Chubb married Martha A. Sturgis, the widow of a Union officer. Although Commodore Chubb died in Vermont in 1886, he requested to be buried with a Confederate flag, and his body was returned to Galveston for that purpose. Chubb's Civil War home, constructed in 1859, still stands at 1417 Sealy Avenue in Galveston.[452]

After luring his father and family to join him, Thomas H. Chubb decided to make Vermont his permanent home. Serving on a blockade runner had been interesting, but he now found himself desperately in search of a business that could provide him with a living. After a few false starts, he hit upon the idea of manufacturing high-quality bamboo fishing rods. Perhaps this choice was inspired by his exposure to fishing in Texas or his exposure to creative Texans like Creuzbaur and Littlepage. Whatever the source of his inspiration, Chubb soon discovered that he had a natural talent for inventing better fishing rods and reel mechanisms. His patented inventions were successful, and his products were soon in high demand. By 1883, Chubb's advertisement in the *American Angler* journal boasted that his facility was the "Largest Fishing Rod Factory in the World." After an 1891 fire, Chubb elected to sell his entire remaining business and retire.[453]

In 1910, Captain Thomas H. Chubb, as the former fishing rod manufacturer now styled himself, had a premonition that his death was approaching. He even predicted that his funeral would take place on the following Sunday. Chubb's prophecy proved accurate, and he died that same week of what was described at the time as "apoplectic shock." Like his father, Chubb requested that he be buried in a coffin with his head resting on a Confederate flag. It would probably have been difficult to locate such a flag in Vermont almost

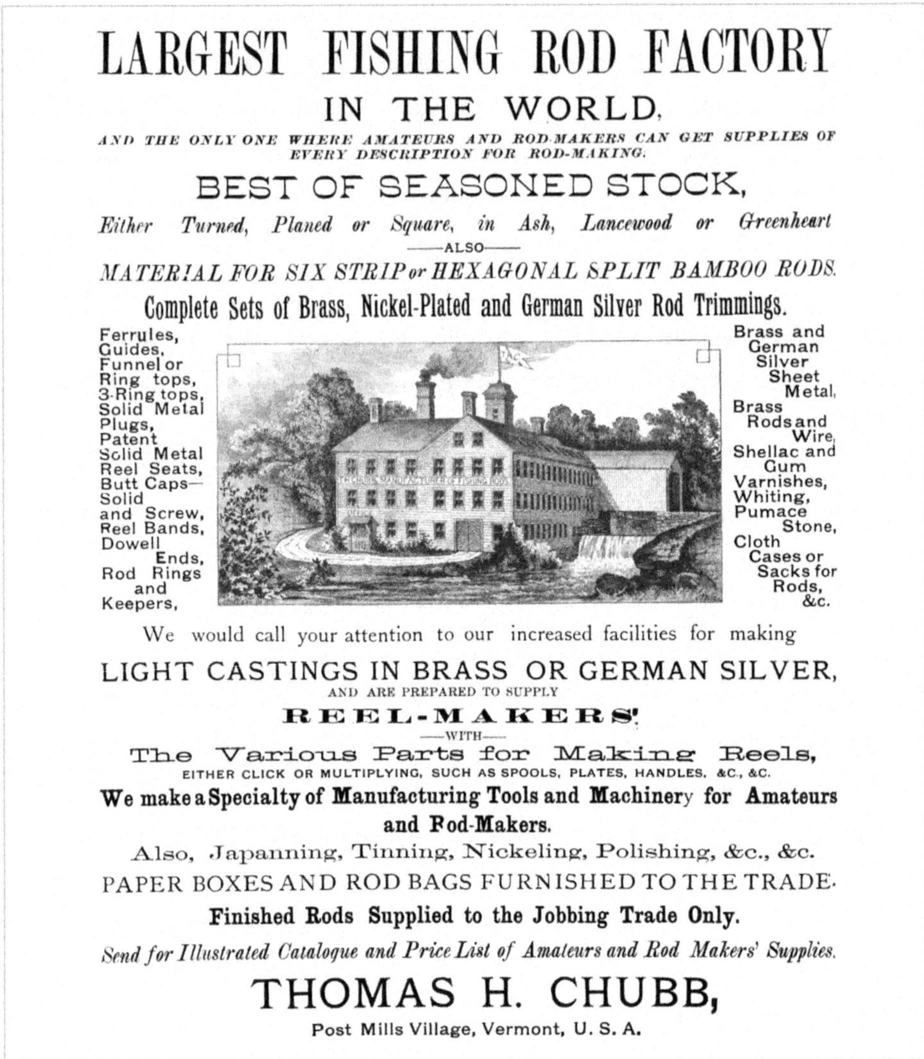

Advertisement from the *American Angler*. November 10, 1883.

fifty years after the war. Fortunately, Chubb had kept such a flag, possibly from the *Royal Yacht*, and his request was honored. The circumstances concerning Chubb's death and burial as an unreconstructed rebel were considered so unusual in New England that his obituary was later published in the *New York Tribune*.[454]

Unlike the Chubbs, who had gone north after the war, two Texas inventors returned from waiting out the war in the opposite camp. Phidello W. Hall, the Union cavalryman who obtained a Confederate patent for his revolving battery before escaping to Kentucky, returned to Calvert, Texas, shortly after the war and there became active in politics as what was then termed a "scalawag" (radical Republican). Hall became one of the most active participants in Texas Republican politics in the immediate postwar period. One historian has called Hall "the most despised of all the radical candidates" in Robertson County.[455]

Lacking many candidates who met the technical requirements to qualify for office, Hall was appointed district attorney for Robertson County in 1867. Two years later he was appointed postmaster. He was elected to the Texas Senate in 1870, where he served on the Militia Committee. Hall served in a political office during the heated Reconstruction period in Texas and was involved in many confrontations and controversies.[456]

Perhaps because he was so intensely involved in political activities, Phidello Hall never succeeded in securing a US patent for the breech-loading gun that was the subject of his 1861 Confederate patent. Instead, he secured three patents for combination and permutation locks in 1873–74. His last patent, granted in 1875, was for a postage-stamp holder. Remarkably, one of these small holders has survived to the present, where it is the smallest item in the collection of the Historical Society of Montgomery County, Pennsylvania. Hall died in 1888 and is buried in the historic Old Cottonwood Cemetery near Cross Plains, Texas.[457]

One of the most unusual settlers to appear in Texas after the end of the war was Mordecai P. Hunnicutt, the Union spy who reported the possible existence of a Confederate submarine in Texas. He settled in Waco, where he became head of the police force. Hunnicutt became one of the first captains in the State Police but encountered difficulties dealing with state officials. He was accused of killing a boy named Eugene Carter in 1870 and was convicted of the crime in 1875. The conviction was later reversed on appeal. After a retrial, Hunnicutt was acquitted. He died in Waco in 1891.[458]

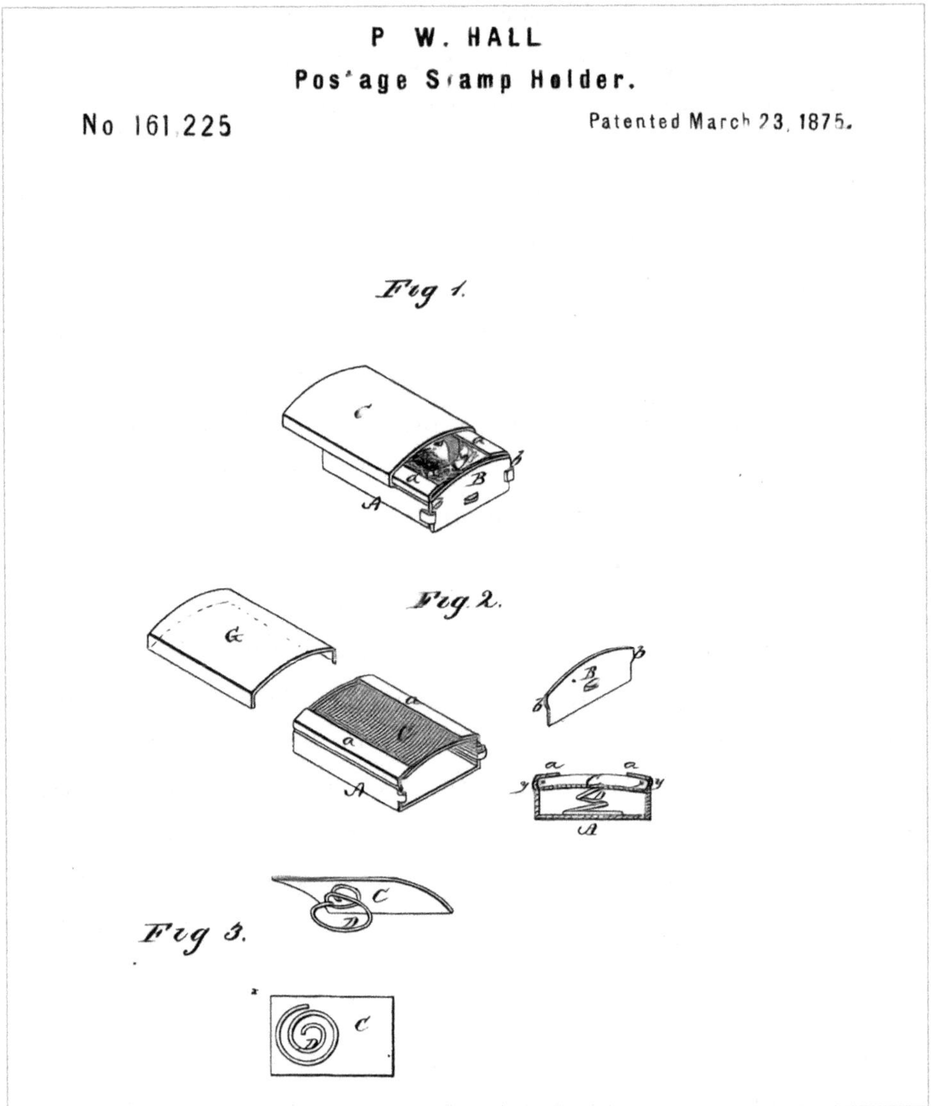

Drawing from US Patent No. 161,225, issued to P. W. Hall for postage-stamp holder, March 23, 1875. US Patent and Trademark Office, Alexandria, Virginia.

Like Hunnicutt and Phidello Hall, Gail Borden Jr., one of the only Texas inventors to provide inventions to Northern armies during the war, found the postwar era a good time to reacquaint himself with the Lone Star State. Like

Edgar Singer, Borden was inclined to spend winters in Texas because of its more hospitable climate. Borden, however, was not content to merely move to one of the existing Texas cities. Instead, he would design what might today be called a planned community. Soon after the war, he began building homes for himself and his family at "Bordenville" (later shortened to "Borden"), where he eventually built a meatpacking facility in 1872. In addition to a sawmill and copperware factory, the inventor also built a school for White children and a freedmen's school for Black children.[459]

Gail Borden died in Borden in 1874 at the age of seventy-three. His body was returned to New York City, where he was buried at a site he had chosen in Woodlawn Cemetery. Initially, only a granite milk can marked the inventor's grave. Eventually, a more detailed monument was added. It contained the inspirational lines "I tried and failed, I tried again and again, and succeeded." This could have been the epitaph for many Civil War Texas inventors.[460]

As Borden's monument so eloquently notes, many inventions fail, sometimes through no fault of the inventors or their work. Although inventors like Borden, Singer, and Creuzbaur had long and productive lives, the same could not be said about the torpedo boat projects underway in the Houston area at the end of the war. On June 19, 1865, Major General Gordon Granger arrived in Galveston with his staff. At a building on the Strand, Major Frederic W. Emery issued a series of orders, including General Order No. 3. That order is today celebrated as the basis for the national holiday known as "Juneteenth."[461]

The surrender terms signed by the Confederate Army of the Trans-Mississippi provided that all Confederate property, including war matériel, would be turned over to Union forces. As the quartermasters began taking inventories of the various ships and property turned over by the Confederates, there was one object that stood out: the torpedo boat that now lay partially sunk near Lynchburg. In a report dated June 21, 1865, John H. Sterrett, the former Confederate superintendent of steam transports serving on the transition team, recommended to his new Union superiors that the boat be raised and sent to the San Jacinto shipyard for inspection and repair. Because of a sudden and surprising ownership claim, that recovery operation was soon put on hold.[462]

Not long after Major Frederic Emery gave his preliminary approval to raise and repair the torpedo boat, former Singer operatives Dunn and Bradbury came forward and claimed that they were the true owners of the torpedo boat. This claim was probably the reason that the boat was not promptly raised to make it ready for sale. Although Emery did not know that Thomas Chubb had already received partial payment for the boat, he was rightly suspicious of this new and mysterious ownership claim. In a letter dated July 17, 1865, Emery demanded that the two men produce any and all papers and contracts relating to the construction of the torpedo boat. He also insisted that they submit a sworn statement as to the intended purpose of the vessel. This was clever. Emery knew that the men would be reluctant to submit a statement in the postwar environment admitting that their aim was to construct a ship whose sole purpose was killing Union sailors. No record of any response to Emery's demand has been located, suggesting that the builders did not pursue their ownership claim.[463]

On July 26, 1865, Captain and Assistant Quartermaster G. E. Atwood submitted his inventory of all the property that had been received from the Confederate government. He did not identify any *Hunley*-like submarines, nor did he list the second torpedo boat at Lubbock's Mill. He did, however, list a solitary torpedo boat at Lynchburg, which he described as being "in bad order." Atwood also noted his understanding that the boat had been "claimed by builders." The disputed builders claim was apparently withdrawn or otherwise resolved within the next few months. By November 29, 1865, Atwood's inventory listed the torpedo boat along with other former Confederate vessels without any notice of a claim by builders. A status report on former Confederate boats in January 1866 continued to describe it merely as "sunk in San Jacinto River."[464]

Disposing of the captured Confederate property was not a high priority. It took more than a year before the US Treasury Department decided to finally conduct a clearance sale for all that remained of the former Confederate vessels. The sale was conducted by George W. Dent, who had the distinction of being U. S. Grant's brother-in-law as well as supervising agent for the Treasury Department. Dent's newspaper advertisements for the sale prominently feature the steamboat *Col. Stell* and its equipment. To attract buyers, Dent described the *Stell* as being "in good running order." The notice then listed a

Sale of Government Property

WILL be sold on THURSDAY, the 12th July, at 10 A. M., at the corner of Strand and Tremont streets, in the city of Galveston, the following property:

Steamboat "Col. Stell," 264 tons burthen (new measurement), two high-pressure engines, cylinder 16 inches in diameter 5 feet stroke, "doctor" engines, &c. Her tackle, apparel and furniture, as she now lies, near Bean's Wharf, in good running order.

Steamboat "John F. Carr," as she now lies, sunk at Lynchburg.

Steamboat "Island City," as she now lies at Bean's Wharf, Galveston, together with her tackle, furniture and apparel.

ALSO,

Sloop "Mattie," now lying near Kuhn's Wharf.

Schooner "Nightingale," at LaVaca, in good order.

Schooner "Helena," at LaVaca.

Also, at same time and place, the wrecks of the following steamboats, viz:

Steamer "Mary Hill," 20 miles below Liberty.
"Orizaba," 8 miles below Liberty. [riv.
"Josiah H. Bell," near Orange, Sabine
"Little Britton," on Sabine river.
"Uncle Ben," near Sabine Pass.
"Clifton," near Sabine Pass. [riv.
"Bayou City," near LaGrange, Neches

The Engines, Machinery, &c.. of these boats are said to be good, and can be recovered at little cost.

Also, Saw-mill machinery, &c., &c., located at different points.

Also, Torpedo Boat, at Lynchburg.

Terms cash, in U. S. Treasury Notes.

By order of GEO. W. DENT,
Supervising Agent Treas. Dep't.

ALEX. N. SHIPLEY, Gov't Auct'r. Je28-tds

Advertisement of US government sale.
In the *Galveston Daily News*, July 10, 1866.

variety of other vessels like the steamboat *John F. Carr*, which was being sold "as she now lies, sunk at Lynchburg." The notice offers for sale or salvage the wrecks of seven steamboats, some of which had been prominent participants in Texas Civil War battles. Dent described the last auction item very simply: "Also, Torpedo Boat, at Lynchburg." No record has yet been located showing the results of this sale.[465]

The mysterious fate of the last torpedo boat is perhaps emblematic of the plans of Confederate Texans who hoped to make their state part of a new nation. In the end, the objects that were so boldly conceived and so cunningly designed would play no role in determining the outcome of the Civil War. Instead, their torpedo boats--and larger plans—would wind up in bad order, good for little more than being salvaged or scrapped.

The Texans of 1865 who supported Southern independence would have to plan for an entirely different future than the one they had envisioned so hopefully in 1861. They would have to reinvent themselves and their society. It would take time and would not be an easy process. The good thing about the future, however, is that by definition it provides the time and freedom necessary to allow dreams to come true. Instead of designing rockets, tanks, and submarines to be used in war, postwar Texans would start the long journey that would lead to designing rockets to go to the moon, revolutionize techniques to search for energy, and develop devices that enable humanity to explore the deepest secrets of the oceans and the cosmos. As Gail Borden's monument so eloquently points out, failure is sometimes just the first necessary step along the path that ultimately leads to enduring success.

NOTES

The following abbreviations are used in these notes:

BAL: Robert U. Johnson and Clarence C. Buel, eds., Battles and Leaders of the Civil War: Grant-Lee Edition, 4 vols. (New York: Century Co., 1887–1888; repr., Harrisburg, PA: Archive Society, 1991).

CMSR: Compiled Military Service Records maintained at the National Archives and Records Administration.

Confederate Citizens File: Confederate Citizens Papers Relating to Citizens or Business Firms, 1861–1865. National Archives and Records Administration, Record Group 109.

NARA: National Archives and Records Administration, Washington, DC.

OR: US War Department, The War of the Rebellion: A Compilation of the Official Records of the Union and Confederate Armies, 128 vols. (Washington, DC: Government Printing Office, 1880–1901), Series 1 (unless otherwise noted).

ORN: US Naval War Records Office, Official Records of the Union and Confederate Navies in the War of the Rebellion, 30 vols. (Washington, DC: Government Printing Office, 1894–1922), Series 1 (unless otherwise noted).

SHSP: Southern Historical Society Papers, 52 vols. (1876–1959; repr., n.p.: Broadfoot Publishing Co., 1990–92).

TSLAC: Texas State Library and Archives Commission, Austin, Texas.

USPTO: United States Patent and Trademark Office, Alexandria, Virginia.

Introduction

1 Larry Chang, ed., *Wisdom for the Soul: Five Millennia of Prescriptions for Spiritual Healing* (Washington, DC, Gnosphia, 2006), 250.

Chapter 1

2 US Patent No. 22,880, for water wheel, issued to C. V. Littlepage on February 8, 1859, USPTO; "Improved Water Wheel," *Scientific American*, November 1, 1860, 321; Caleb Van Ausdol Littlepage and Robert Creuzbaur, "Criticisms on the Experiments with Turbine Wheels at Philadelphia," *Scientific American*, August 25, 1860, 130–131; Littlepage and Creuzbaur, "Criticisms on the Experiments with Turbine Wheels at Philadelphia," *Scientific American*, September 1, 1860, 130–131.

3 Joe B. Frantz, "Borden, Gail, Jr.," *Handbook of Texas Online*, accessed December 20, 2023, https://www.tshaonline.org/handbook/entries/borden-gail-jr.

4 Joe B. Frantz, *Gail Borden: Dairyman to a Nation* (Norman: University of Oklahoma Press, 1951), 157.

5 Frantz, *Gail Borden*, 197–200.

6 Gail Borden Jr., *Letter of Gail Borden, Jr. to Dr. Ashbel Smith, Setting Forth an Important Invention in the Preparation of a New Article of Food, Termed Meat Biscuit* (Galveston: Gibson & Cherry, 1850).

7 Frantz, *Gail Borden*, 219.

8 Joe B. Frantz, "Gail Borden as a Businessman," *Bulletin of the Business Historical Society* 22, no. 4 (December 1948): 128–129.

9 Jeffry D. Wert, *Civil War Barons: Tycoons, Entrepreneurs, Inventors, and Visionaries Who Forged Victory and Shaped a Nation* (New York: Da Capo Press, 2018), 255; CMSR for Henry L. Borden, accessed March 25, 2024, https://www.fold3.com/image/9948381/borden-henry-l-page-1-us-civil-war-service-records-cmsr-confederate-texas-1861–1865; CMSR for John G. Borden accessed March 25, 2024, https://www.fold3.com/image/288600912?terms=g,john,borden.

10 "Abraham Lincoln, Inventor, 1849: A Spotlight on a Primary Source by Abraham Lincoln," Gilder Lehrman Institute of American History, accessed October 28, 2024, https://www.gilderlehrman.org/history-resources/spotlight-primary-source/abraham-lincoln-inventor-1849; US Patent No. 6469, granted May 22, 1849, USPTO; "Abraham Lincoln's Patent Model," Smithsonian National Museum of American History, accessed October 28, 2024, https://www.si.edu/object/abraham-lincolns-patent-model%3Anmah_213141.

11 Richard C. Rattenbury, "Colt Revolvers," *Handbook of Texas Online*, accessed July 23, 2023, https://www.tshaonline.org/handbook/entries/coltrevolvers.

12 John Grady, "Infernal Machines: Mine Warfare in the Civil War," On Point 18, no. 2 (Fall 2012), 7.

13 William C. Emerson, "Unfounded Hopes: A Design Analysis of the Confederate Ironclad Steamer CSS *Atlanta*," *Warship International* 32, no. 4 (1995): 367.

14 International Maritime Museum, Hamburg, Germany, "Experimental Submarine Fire Divers," accessed December 20, 2023, https://www.imm-hamburg.de/museum/ausstellungsrundgang/tour-of-the-exhibitions-english/deck-5-war-and-peace/experimental-submarine-brandtaucher/.

15 Joseph P. Sanchez, "Palo Alto, Battle of," *Handbook of Texas Online*, accessed December 20, 2023, https://www.tshaonline.org/handbook/entries/palo-alto-battle-of; National Park Service, Palo Alto National Historical Park, "Nations in Conflict: A Fight Over Texas," accessed December 20, 2023, http://npshistory.com/publications/paal/index.htm.

16 Mike Gruntman, *Blazing the Trail: The Early History of Spacecraft and Rocketry* (Reston, VA: American Institute of Aeronautics and Astronautics, 2004), 3–5.

17 Ralph W. Donnelly, "Rocket Batteries in the Civil War," *Military Affairs* 25, no. 2 (Summer 1961): 69–75; Paul D. Olejar, "Rockets in Early American Wars," *Military Affairs* 10, no. 4 (Winter 1946): 17–19, 23–32; Ralph W. Donnelly, "Rocketry in the 1860's," *Ordnance* 46, no. 252 (May–June 1962): 767.

18 Gruntman, *Blazing the Trail*, 555–562.

19 Gruntman, *Blazing the Trail*, 64.

20 Dr. Thomas P. Lowry, *Civil War Rockets* (n.p.: CreateSpace Independent Publishing Platform, 2012), 33–36; Donnelly, "Rocket Batteries in the Civil War," 77–79; Gruntman, *Blazing the Trail*, 67.

Chapter 2

21 United States Army, *American Military History* (Washington, DC: Center of Military History, United States Army, 1989), 192–193; National Park Service, "Tredegar Iron Works-Ironmaker to the Confederacy," accessed January 8, 2024, https://www.nps.gov/articles/tredegar-iron-works-ironmaker-to-the-confederacy.htm.

22 United States Census Bureau, "U.S. Census Bureau History," accessed December 20, 2023, https://www.census.gov/history/www/homepage_archive/2015/april_2015.html#:~:text=According%20to%20the%201860%20Census,of%20America%20had%208.7%20million; Edward T. Cotham, Jr., *Juneteenth: The Story Behind the Celebration* (Kerrville, TX: State House Press, 2021), 13.

23 Lynda L. Cryst, Barbara J. Rozek, and Kenneth H. Williams, eds., *The Papers of Jefferson Davis*, 14 vols. (Baton Rouge: Louisiana State University Press,

1971–2015), 7:195; "Sherman's Portable Breastwork," *Scientific American*, February 14, 1863, 104.

24 T. R. Havins, "Two Menefee-Sylvester Letters," *Southwestern Historical Quarterly* 59, no. 1 (July 1955): 69; L. W. Kemp, "Menefee, John Sutherland," *Handbook of Texas Online*, accessed December 20, 2023, https://www.tshaonline.org/handbook/entries/menefee-john-sutherland.

25 Cryst, Rozek, and Williams, *The Papers of Jefferson Davis*, 8:445.

26 Alex Roland, "Secrecy, Technology, and War: Greek Fire and the Defense of Byzantium, 678–1204," *Technology and Culture* 33, no. 4 (October 1992): 655–679; Brandt Heatherington, "Military Weapons: The Origin of the Combat Flamethrower," *Military Heritage*, August 2006, 8.

27 Biography of Lucien Hopson, Texas State Cemetery, accessed July 25, 2023, https://cemetery.tspb.texas.gov/pub/user_form.asp?pers_id=252; "Battle of San Jacinto," *The DeSmet (SD) Leader*, January 17, 1885, p. 3.

28 R. Jackson Knight, *Confederate Invention: The Story of the Confederate States Patent Office and its Inventors* (Baton Rouge: Louisiana State University Press, 2011), 273–274.

29 Invoice for Lucien Hopson, May 10, 1862, endorsed by Josiah Gorgas, Confederate Citizens File for Lucien Hopson, NARA; Office of Ordnance Payment Record for Lucien Hopson, August 1, 1862, Confederate Navy Subject File M1091, Record Group 45, NARA.

30 Letters received by Jefferson Davis, Cryst, Rozek, and Williams, *The Papers of Jefferson Davis*, 8:465–467.

31 Letters received by Jefferson Davis, Cryst, Rozek, and Williams. *The Papers of Jefferson Davis*, 8:465–467; George M. Brooke Jr., *Ironclads and Big Guns of the Confederacy: The Journals and Letters of John M. Brooke* (Columbia, SC: University of South Carolina Press, 2002), 115.

32 Letters received by Jefferson Davis, Cryst, Rozek, and Williams, *The Papers of Jefferson Davis*, 8:465–467.

33 "Letter from Matagorda," *Galveston Daily News*, August 20, 1868, p. 3; "System of Mutual Education," *Telegraph and Texas Register* (Houston), July 18, 1851, p. 1; Christina L. Gray, "Millican, TX," *Handbook of Texas Online*, accessed February 8, 2024, https://www.tshaonline.org/handbook/entries/millican-tx.

34 L. H. W. Johnson to S. B. Davis, Millican, TX, November 21, 1861, Confederate Citizens File for L. H. W. Johnson, Record Group 109, NARA.

35 Phidello W. Hall to Adjutant, 11th Kentucky Cavalry, Camp Wofford, March 10, 1864, CMSR for Phidello W. Hall.

36 Phidello W. Hall to Adjutant, 11th Kentucky Cavalry, Camp Wofford, March 10, 1864, CMSR for Phidello W. Hall.

37 Knight, *Confederate Invention*, 208.

38 "List of Confederate Patents," *Record of News, History and Literature* (Richmond), June 17, 1863, p. 7.

39 US Patent No. 36,836, issued to Richard J. Gatling on November 4, 1862, USPTO; US Patent No. 453,702, issued to H. S. Maxim on June 9, 1891, USPTO.

40 Phidello W. Hall to Adjutant, 11th Kentucky Cavalry, Camp Wofford, March 10, 1864, CMSR for Phidello W. Hall.

41 Phidello W. Hall to Adjutant, 11th Kentucky Cavalry, Camp Wofford, March 10, 1864, CMSR for Phidello W. Hall.

42 Phidello W. Hall to Adjutant, 11th Kentucky Cavalry, Camp Wofford, March 10, 1864, CMSR for Phidello W. Hall; Special Orders No. 257, War Department, Adjutant General's Office, Washington, DC, May 27, 1865, CMSR for Phidello W. Hall.

43 Confederate Citizens File for John G. Gooch, Record Group 109, NARA.

44 *Dallas Daily Herald*, Feb. 29, 1860, p. 2.

45 Mary Kate Hunter, "The Old Cemetery, the Shrine of Palestine," *The Tracings* 2, no. 2 (Fall 1998): 95.

46 Leonidas Polk, Caleb S. Ives, Benjamin Eaton, and Charles Gillett, "The Church in the Republic of Texas." *Historical Magazine of the Protestant Episcopal Church* 2, no. 2 (1933): 34–46.

47 Confederate Citizens File for John G. Gooch, Record Group 109, NARA.

48 L. Polk to J. P. Benjamin, Columbus, KY, October 10, 1861, ORN, 22:793.

49 *Register of Officers of the Confederate States Navy, 1861–1865* (Washington, DC: Government Printing Office, 1931), 23.

50 Earl J. Hess, *Civil War Torpedoes and the Global Development of Landmine Warfare* (Lanham, MD: Rowman & Littlefield, 2023), 15; John Grady, "Damn the Torpedoes," *New York Times*, February 6, 2012, accessed March 28, 2024, https://archive.nytimes.com/opinionator.blogs.nytimes.com/2012/02/06/damn-the-torpedoes/.

51 Leonidas Polk, *Leonidas Polk, Bishop and General*, ed. William M. Polk (New York: Longmans, Green and Co., 1915), 2:71; Hess, *Torpedoes and the Global Development of Landmine Warfare*, 16.

52 Certificate of Sackfield Maclin, San Antonio, TX, August 28, 1862, CMSR for C. V. Littlepage, Record Group 109, NARA; Contract between C. V. Littlepage and J. Gorgas, Ordnance Department, CSA, March 9, 1862, CMSR for C. V. Littlepage, Record Group 109, NARA; Knight, *Confederate Invention*, 213.

53 Knight, *Confederate Invention*, 208–229.

54 David C. Humphrey, "Austin, TX (Travis County)," *Handbook of Texas Online*, accessed December 20, 2023, https://www.tshaonline.org/handbook/entries/austin-tx-travis-county; Knight, *Confederate Invention*, 208–228; Andrew Forest Muir, "Inventions Patented by Texans, 1846–1861," *Southwestern Historical Quarterly* 62, no. 4 (April 1959): 552–554.

Chapter 3

55 David Madden, "Rediscovering Civil War Classics: Jules Verne's Civil War," *Civil War Book Review* 9, no. 2 (2007); accessed January 4, 2024, https://repository.lsu.edu/cgi/viewcontent.cgi?article=2603&context=cwbr.

56 John Lamb, "Jules Verne and the Heroes of Birkenhead," accessed January 4, 2024, https://julesverneandtheheroesofbirkenhead.co.uk/wp-content/uploads/2021/06/1-From-Birkenhead-to-Atlantis-The-Merseyside-Origins-of-Captain-Nemos-Nautilus-Copy-Copy-2.pdf; Alan Weston and Rebecca Koncienzcy, "Uncovering Links Between Birkenhead and the Father of Science Fiction," *Liverpool News*, July 31, 2022, accessed January 4, 2024, https://www.liverpoolecho.co.uk/news/liverpool-news/uncovering-links-between-birkenhead-father-24613705.

57 Andrew W. Hall and Edward T. Cotham Jr., "A Sharp Fight," *Houston History* 11, no. 2 (July 2014): 2–7.

58 Edward T. Cotham Jr., *Battle on the Bay: The Civil War Struggle for Galveston* (Austin: University of Texas Press, 1998), 38–40; Edward T. Cotham Jr., *Decisions of the Galveston Campaigns: The Twenty-One Critical Decisions That Defined the Operations* (Knoxville: University of Tennessee Press, 2024), 8–15.

59 "Robert Creuzbaur Dead," *Brooklyn Daily Eagle*, Oct. 26, 1911, p. 20; "Karlsruhe, Germany," Euro Cities, accessed December 21, 2023, https://eurocities.eu/cities/karlsruhe/.

60 "Robert Creuzbaur Dead," *Brooklyn Daily Eagle*, Oct. 26, 1911, p. 20; "Robert Creuzbaur at 86 Invents New Airship," *Brooklyn Daily Eagle*, May 2, 1909, p. 24: Joseph J. Mersman, *The Whiskey Merchant's Diary: An Urban Life in the Emerging Midwest* (Athens: Ohio University Press, 2007), 243, 252, 256.

61 "J. De Cordova's Map of the State of Texas," Bullock Texas State History Museum, accessed August 4, 2023, https://www.thestoryoftexas.com/discover/artifacts/cordova-map-state-of-texas; "The first Official Map of Texas—1849," Copano Bay Press, accessed August 4, 2023, https://copanobaypress-gallery.com/products/de-cordovas-map-of-texas-1849;

Frank H. Holcomb, *Landmark Maps of Texas* (Kerrville, TX: State House Press, 2024), 12, 199, 217.

62 Texas State Historical Association, "Creuzbaur, Robert," *Handbook of Texas Online*, accessed August 5, 2023, https://www.tshaonline.org/handbook/entries/creuzbaur-robert; Robert Creuzbaur, "Plan of the City of Austin" (1853), Map No. 00928, TSLAC.

63 Littlepage and Creuzbaur, "Criticisms of the Experiments with Turbine Wheels at Philadelphia," *Scientific American*, August 25, 1860, 130–131.

64 US Patent No. 32,595, granted June 18, 1861, USPTO.

65 Neil P. Chatelain, "Creuzbaur's Revolutionary Confederate Ironclad *Avenger*," *Civil War Navy: The Magazine*, Winter 2022, 56–61.

66 R. Creuzbaur to F. R. Lubbock, Travis County, TX, November 11, 1861, Texas Governor Sam Houston Records (should be filed with Lubbock papers but misfiled in Sam Houston papers collection), TX 002107, Box 2014/109–5, Folder 79, TSLAC.

67 R. Creuzbaur to F.R. Lubbock, Travis County, TX, November 11, 1861, TSLAC.

68 Statements of Francis R. Lubbock and James Brown in *House Journal of the Ninth Legislature, Regular Session, of the State of Texas, November 4, 1861–January 14, 1862*, comp. James M. Day (Austin: Texas State Library, 1964), 72–77.

69 Lubbock and James Brown, *House Journal of the Ninth Legislature*, 72–77.

70 Letter from Gov. F. R. Lubbock to W. von Rosenberg, J. M. Steiner, and J. Brown, November 12, 1861, Letterpress Book of Texas Gov. Francis R. Lubbock, Nov. 1861–April 1862, Papers of Texas Governor Francis R. Lubbock. No. 002109, TSLAC.

71 Statement of James Brown, *House Journal of the Ninth Legislature, Regular Session, of the State of Texas*, 77.

72 Statement of F. R. Lubbock, *House Journal of the Ninth Legislature, Regular Session, of the State of Texas*, 71.

73 Chapter IV, *General Laws of the Ninth Legislature of the State of Texas* (Houston: E. H. Cushing, 1862), 4–5.

74 Allen H. Mesch, *Ebenezer Allen: Statesman, Entrepreneur, and Spy* (Grapevine, TX: Waldorf Publishing, 2020), 1, 9–28.

75 Mesch, *Ebenezer Allen*, 64–67, 74–79.

76 Mesch, *Ebenezer Allen*, 116–173, 178–197; E. Allen to G. Lincecum, Galveston, TX, Nov. 10, 1853, Folder 35–0001, Ebenezer Allen Papers, Rosenberg Library, Galveston, TX; E. Allen to S. M. Williams, Galveston, TX, April 10, 1854, Entry 23–2956, Samuel May Williams Papers, Rosenberg Library, Galveston, TX.

77 John Grady, *Matthew Fontaine Maury: Father of Oceanography* (Jefferson, NC: McFarland & Co., 2015), 1–10.

78 Invoices dated April 21, May 3, 5, 15, and 30, 1862, contained in file labeled "(B Ordnance) BM-Mines and Torpedoes-Charleston-Miscellaneous," Naval Records Collection of the Office of Naval Records and Library, Subject Files for the Confederate States Navy, Record Group 45, NARA.

79 Invoices dated April 21, May 3, 5, 15, and 30, 1862, contained in file labeled "(B Ordnance) BM-Mines and Torpedoes-Charleston-Miscellaneous," Naval Records Collection of the Office of Naval Records and Library, Subject Files for the Confederate States Navy, Record Group 45, NARA.

80 Letter from E. Allen to the Chairman and Members of the Committee on Naval Affairs of the Senate, Richmond, VA, Sept. 26, 1862, CMSR for Robert Creuzbaur, Record Group 109, NARA.

81 Commander Thomas Edward Symonds, "Maneuvering Steam Rams and Iron-cased Ships," *The Times* (London), April 14, 1862, p. 11.

82 Commander Thomas Edward Symonds, "Maneuvering Steam Rams and Iron-cased Ships," *The Times* (London), April 14, 1862, p. 11.

83 Chatelain, "Creuzbaur's Revolutionary Confederate Ironclad *Avenger*," 54–58.

84 US Patent No. 7,644,675, awarded to Don Dongcho Ha for lateral thruster unit for marine vessels, January 12, 2010, USPTO.

85 United States Naval Undersea Museum, "Reflecting Light Through Periscopes," accessed January 20, 2024, https://www.history.navy.mil/content/dam/museums/undersea/education/Reflecting%20Light%20and%20Periscopes.pdf.

86 Jules Verne, *The Mysterious Island* (New York: Charles Scribner's Sons, 1920), 464.

87 Chatelain, "Creuzbaur's Revolutionary Confederate Ironclad *Avenger*," 57–59; Mesch, *Ebenezer Allen*, 213–219; Statement of Jefferson Davis, *Journal of the Confederate States of America, 1861–1865* (Washington, DC: Government Printing Office, 1905), 567.

88 Statement of William E. Martin in the Senate, December 17, 1862, *Reports and Resolutions of the General Assembly of the State of South Carolina Passed at the Annual Session of 1862* (Columbia, SC: Charles P. Pelham, State Printer, 1862), 209–210.

89 F. W. Pickens, Message No. 7, *Journal of the Senate of the State of South Carolina, Being the Session of 1862* (Columbia, SC: Charles P. Pelham, 1862), 73.

90 Statement of William E. Martin in the Senate, December 17, 1862, 210.

91 Excerpt from report of M. F. Maury in statement of William E. Martin in the Senate, December 17, 1862, 210.

92 Statement of William E. Martin in the Senate, December 17, 1862, 209; *Civilian and Gazette Weekly* (Galveston), October 9, 1860, p. 2.

93 Statement of William E. Martin in the Senate, December 17, 1862, 211–212.

94 Cara Vandergriff, "'Petticoat Gunboats': The Wartime Expansion of Confederate Women's Discursive Opportunities Through Ladies' Gunboat Societies" (master's thesis, University of Tennessee, 2013), accessed March 30, 2024, https://trace.tennessee.edu/utk_gradthes/1691/, 45–47.

95 Letter to Congress from E. Allen and J. R. Sprague, Charleston, SC, January 13, 1863, Confederate Citizens File for "Edgar [sic] Allen," Record Group 109, NARA.

96 Brooke, *Ironclads and Big Guns of the Confederacy*, 118, 125.

97 E.M. Seifert, "Evolution of the Torpedo," *Ordnance* 39, no. 209 (March–April, 1955): 722; Boris V. Drashpil, "Surface Torpedo Craft of the Imperial Russian Navy," *Warship International* 19, no. 3 (1982): 237; US Naval Undersea Museum, "The Remarkable Story of the Howell Torpedo," accessed August 12, 2023, https://navalunderseamuseum.org/howell/#:~:text=The%20Howell%20torpedo%20was%20the,first%20successful%20torpedo%20in%201866.

Chapter 4

98 Report of D. G. Farragut, Pensacola Bay, FL, October 15, 1862, ORN, 19:254–255.

99 Thomas M. Settles, *John Bankhead Magruder: A Military Reappraisal* (Baton Rouge: Louisiana State University Press, 2009), 2, 8, 11–17; Cotham, *Battle on the Bay*, 87; Civil War in the East, "West Point Officers in the Civil War," accessed December 31, 2023, https://civilwarintheeast.com/west-point-officers-in-the-civil-war/.

100 J. Mark Thompson, "Magruder, John Bankhead," in *Encyclopedia of the American Civil War*, ed. David S. Heidler and Jeanne T. Heidler (Santa Barbara, CA: ABC-CLIO, 2000), 3:1240–1241.

101 Paul D. Casdorph, *Prince John Magruder: His Life and Campaigns* (Chichester, NY: John Wiley & Sons, 1996), 87–91.

102 Settles, *John Bankhead Magruder*, 132–136, 158–161; Cotham, *Battle on the Bay*, 92; Leonard W. Riedel Jr., "John Bankhead Magruder and the Defense of the Virginia Peninsula, 1861–1862" (master's thesis, Old Dominion University, 1991), 100–115.

103 Riedel, "John Bankhead Magruder and the Defense of the Virginia Peninsula," 114–116; Cotham, *Battle on the Bay*, 92–93; Settles, *John Bankhead Magruder*, 173–175.

104 Jubal Early and Frank E. Vandiver, ed., *War Memoirs: Autobiographical Sketch and Narrative of the War Between the States* (Bloomington: Indiana University Press, 1960), 59.

105 John Grady, "Damn the Torpedoes," *New York Times*, February 6, 2019.

106 Hess, *Civil War Torpedoes and the Global Development of Landmine Warfare*, 21–29; W. Davis Waters, "'Deception is the Art of War': Gabriel J. Rains, Torpedo Specialist of the Confederacy," *North Carolina Historical Review* 66, no. 1 (January 1989): 29–37.

107 Baker P. Lee, "Magruder's Peninsula Campaign in 1862," SHSP 19 (January 1891): 64.

108 Settles, *John Bankhead Magruder*, 188–190.

109 Settles, *John Bankhead Magruder*, 196–198; Stephen W. Sears, *To the Gates of Richmond: The Peninsula Campaign* (New York: Ticknor & Fields, 1992), 176.

110 Sears, *To the Gates of Richmond*, 216–217.

111 D. H. Hill, "Lee's Attacks North of the Chickahominy," BAL, 2, pt. 1: 362.

112 R. E. Lee to J. B. Magruder, Headquarters, Army of Northern Virginia, June 29, 1862, OR, 11, pt. 2: 687.

113 R. E. Lee to W. H. Stevens, Headquarters, Army of Northern Virginia, June 5, 1862, OR, 11, pt. 3: 574.

114 R.E. Lee to J. Gorgas, Headquarters, Army of Northern Virginia, June 5, 1862, OR, 11, pt. 3: 574.

115 R. E. Lee to G. Minor, Richmond, VA, June 5, 1862, OR, 11, pt. 3: 575–576.

116 Brooke, *Ironclads and Big Guns of the Confederacy*, 93.

117 David H. Schneider, "Lee's Armored Car: Photo Sleuthing Reveals a Fearsome Weapon's True Origins," *Civil War Times Illustrated*, February 2011, 56–59. For an image drawn from memory of the rail gun showing less side protection, see Harry W. Miller, *Railway Artillery: A Report on the Characteristics, Scope of Utility, Etc. of Railway Artillery* (Washington, DC: Government Printing Office, 1921), 1:8, plate 1.

118 Brooke, *Ironclads and Big Guns of the Confederacy*, 94; Robert R. Hodges Jr., *American Civil War Railroad Tactics* (Oxford, UK: Osprey Publishing, 2009), 19–20; R. E. Lee to G. Minor, Richmond, VA, June 5, 1862, OR, 11, pt. 3: 575–576; R. E. Lee to S.R. Mallory, Dobbs House, VA, June 21, 1862, OR, 11, pt. 3: 610.

119 Report of J. B. Magruder, Richmond, VA, August 12, 1862, OR, 11, pt. 2: 664.

120 Joseph L. Brent, *Mobilizable Fortifications and their Controlling Influence in War* (Boston: Houghton, Mifflin & Co., 1885), 58.

121 Brent, *Mobilizable Fortifications and their Controlling Influence in War*, 58; John J. Eicher and David J. Eicher, *Civil War High Commands* (Stanford, CA: Stanford University Press, 2001), 591.

122 Cotham, *Battle on the Bay*, 96; Daniel H. Hill, "McClellan's Change of Base and Malvern Hill," *BAL*, 2, pt. 2: 394.

123 Settles, *John Bankhead Magruder*, 232–241.

124 Special Orders No. 237, October 10, 1862, 15 *OR*, 826; Settles, *Magruder*, 241.

125 Special Orders No. 237, October 10, 1862, 15 *OR*, 826; Settles, *Magruder*, 241.

126 A. L. Long, "Memoir of General John Bankhead Magruder," *SHSP* 12, no. 2 (March 1884): 110.

127 Edward T. Cotham Jr., *The Southern Journey of a Civil War Marine: The Illustrated Notebook of Henry O. Gusley* (Austin: University of Texas Press, 2006), 111–114; Aragorn Storm Miller, "Shea, Daniel D.," *Handbook of Texas Online*, accessed December 22, 2023, https://www.tshaonline.org/handbook/entries/shea-daniel-d.

128 Donald S. Frazier, *Cottonclads: The Battle of Galveston and the Defense of the Texas Coast* (Fort Worth, TX: Ryan Place Publishers, 1996), 31–32; Cotham, *Southern Journey of a Civil War Marine*, 114–115; J. R. Bartlett, *Memoirs of Rhode Island Officers Who Were Engaged in the Service of Their Country During the Great Rebellion of the South* (Providence, RI: Sidney S. Rider & Bro., 1867), 300.

129 Cotham, *Southern Journey of a Civil War Marine*, 114–115; G. E. Conklin to E. F. Gray, Lavaca, TX, November 1, 1862, *ORN*, 19:801.

130 Mark K. Ragan, *Confederate Saboteurs: Building the Hunley and Other Secret Weapons of the Civil War* (College Station: Texas A&M University Press, 2015), 8–9; Horace H. Hill, "Texan Gave World the First Successful Submarine Torpedo," *San Antonio Express*, July 30, 1916, p. 45.

131 Anonymous, "Singer, John V.," *Handbook of Texas Online*, accessed August 15, 2023, https://www.tshaonline.org/handbook/entries/singer-john-v.;1850; Randolph W. Farmer, "Singer, Edgar Collins," *Handbook of Texas Online*, accessed August 15, 2023, https://www.tshaonline.org/handbook/entries/singer-edgar-collins; "Passengers," *Galveston Weekly Journal*, December 10, 1852, p. 4.

132 "Passengers," *Galveston Weekly Journal*, December 10, 1852, p. 4; 1850 United States Federal Census for Lockport, IL, accessed August 15, 2023, https://www.ancestry.com/discoveryui-content/view/16712236:8054; Anonymous, "Singer, John V.," *Handbook of Texas Online*, accessed August 15, 2023, https://www.tshaonline.org/handbook/entries/singer-john-v.;1850 ; Randolph W. Farmer, "Singer, Edgar Collins," *Handbook of Texas Online*, accessed August 15, 2023, https://www.tshaonline.org/handbook/entries/singer-edgar-collins.

133 Anonymous, "Singer, John V.," *Handbook of Texas Online*, accessed August 15, 2023, https://www.tshaonline.org/handbook/entries/singer-john-v.; Bill Walraven, "Old box Sheds New Light on Singer Family Saga," *Corpus Christi Caller Times*, October 4, 1984, p. 17; R. G. Stillwell, "Son of Lost City's Founder Tells History of Island Settlement," *Brownsville Herald*, September 6, 1931, p. 5.

134 "Singer's Sewing Machine," *Scientific American*, November 1, 1851; US Patent No. 8,294, awarded to Isaac Merritt Singer of New York, NY, on August 12, 1851, USPTO; National Museum of American History, Smithsonian Institution, Washington, DC, "Isaac Singer's Sewing Machine Patent Model," Accession No. 48865, Catalog No. T06054.000, accessed March 31, 2024, https://www.si.edu/object/1851-isaac-singers-sewing-machine-patent-model%3Anmah_1071133.

135 Gary Hoover, "The Sordid Saga of Mr. Singer and his Sewing Machine," American Business History Center, accessed August 15, 2023, https://americanbusinesshistory.org/the-sordid-saga-of-mr-singer-and-his-sewing-machine/.

136 US Patent No. 1,151, issued to I. M. Singer for stone drill, May 16, 1839, USPTO; Ruth Brandon, *A Capitalist Romance: Singer and the Sewing Machine* (Philadelphia: J. B. Lippincott Co., 1977), 24–25; Hill, "Texan Gave the World First Successful Submarine Torpedo."

137 US Patent No. 26,130, dated November 15, 1859, awarded to E. C. Singer of Port Lavaca, Texas, USPTO.

138 David D. Porter, "Torpedo Warfare," *North American Review*, September–October, 1878, 213.

139 Hill, "Texan Gave World the First Successful Submarine Torpedo."

140 Cotham, *Battle on the Bay*, 105–111.

141 Cotham, *Battle on the Bay*, 113–115.

142 Cotham, *Battle on the Bay*, 113.

143 Cotham, *Battle on the Bay*, 116, 129.

144 Cotham, *Battle on the Bay*, 132.

145 Cotham, *Battle on the Bay*, 105–111.

146 Hodges, *American Civil War Railroad Tactics*, 20–22.

147 Cotham, *Battle on the Bay*, 119.

148 Getulius Kellersberger, *Memoirs of an Engineer in the Confederate Army of Texas*, trans. Helen S. Sundstrom (n.p., n.d.), 28–29.

149 W. P. Ballinger to P. O. Hébert, Office of Confederate States Receiver, Houston, TX, May 30, 1862, Confederate Citizens File for W. P. Ballinger, Record Group 109, NARA.

150 Cotham, *Battle on the Bay*, 151.

151 H. H. Bell to D. G. Farragut, Galveston, TX, January 24, 1863, ORN, 19:554.

152 D. G. Farragut to H. Bell, New Orleans, LA, February 6, 1863, ORN, 19:603.

153 Charles W. Hayes, *History of the Island and City of Galveston* (Cincinnati, OH, 1879; repr., Austin: Jenkins Garrett Press, 1974), 2:592.

154 Texas Genealogy Trails, "Biographies of Galveston County, Texas," accessed August 20, 2023, http://genealogytrails.com/tex/gulfcoast/galveston/bios_s.htm; Receipts dated December 4, 1861, and July 4, 1862, Confederate Citizen File for James P. Sherwood, Record Group 109, NARA.

155 E. P. Turner to J. Walker, Houston, TX, February 9, 1863, Letters Sent, District of Texas, New Mexico, and Arizona, December 1862–June 1863, Record Group 109, NARA; Russell Cushman, "Engineer, Soldier, Planter, Inventor and Nurseryman, George W. Durant," accessed August 18, 2023, http://russellcushman.blogspot.com/2013/11/major-george-w-durant-of-bryan-and.html.

156 "Evolution of the Tank: A Brief History of the Land Dreadnoughts and Their Increasing Efficiency in Battle," *Current History*, November 1919, 352; "Official History of the 'Tanks,'" *Current History*, January, 1918, 38.

157 "*The War Wagon*," accessed August 16, 2023, https://www.classicmoviehub.com/facts-and-trivia/film/the-war-wagon-1967/page/1/.

158 David Lustig, "Where Old Props Await Their Next Star Turn," *Los Angeles Times*, November 5, 1989; "*The War Wagon*," IMDB, accessed August 16, 2023, at https://www.imdb.com/title/tt0062472/; "*The War Wagon* Rolls in Mexico," *Los Angeles Times*, October 5, 1966.

Chapter 5

159 Hill, "Texan Gave World the First Successful Submarine Torpedo."

160 Hill, "Texan Gave World the First Successful Submarine Torpedo."

161 Ragan, *Confederate Saboteurs*, 19.

162 Ragan, *Confederate Saboteurs*, 19; Viktor Ernst Karl Rudolf von Scheliha, *A Treatise on Coast Defense* (London, UK: W Clowes and Sons, 1868), 228–230.

163 Von Scheliha, *A Treatise on Coast Defense*, 228.

164 Ragan, *Confederate Saboteurs*, 16, 19–21; Fretwells: Genealogy and Family History, "Dr. John Richard Fretwell, Confederate Inventor," accessed February 1. 2024, http://www.thefretwells.com/research/drjrfretwell.aspx.

165 US Patent No. 182,047, granted September 12, 1876, to C. P. Wyckoff and J. R. Fretwell for an Automatic Detaching Hook, USPTO; J. R. Fretwell to S.

Houston, Lavaca, TX, March 13, 1861, Texas Governor Sam Houston Records, TX 002107, Box 2014/109–5, Folder 75, TSLAC.

166 J. R. Fretwell to E. Clark, Lavaca, TX, September 22, 1861, Texas Governor Edward Clark Records, TX 002108, Box 2014/099–4, Folder 106, TSLAC; Kenneth R. Rutherford, *America's Buried History: Landmines in the Civil War* (El Dorado Hills, CA: Savas Beatie, 2020), 77.

167 John S. Barnes, *Submarine Warfare, Offensive and Defensive* (New York: D. Van Nostrand, 1869), 70–73.

168 Ragan, *Confederate Saboteurs*, 20–21.

169 Randolph W. Farmer, "Whitney, Benjamin Augustus," *Handbook of Texas Online*, accessed August 17, 2023, https://www.tshaonline.org/handbook/entries/whitney-benjamin-augustus.

170 Mark K. Ragan, "Singer's Secret Service Corps: A Group of Texas Friends Led by Edgar Singer Raised Havoc with Their Torpedoes and Helped Finance CSS Hunley," *Civil War Times*, November–December 2007, 30.

171 Ragan, *Confederate Saboteurs*, 21–22.

172 John C. Wideman, *The Sinking of the USS Cairo* (Jackson: University Press of Mississippi, 1993), x, 36–39, 102–104.

173 James M. Matthews, ed., "An Act to Provide and Organize Engineer Troops to Serve During the War," Approved March 20, 1863, *Public Laws of the Confederate States of America Passed at the Third Session of the First Congress* (Richmond, VA: R. M. Smith, 1863), 98–99; Hill, "Texan Gave World the First Successful Submarine Torpedo."

174 S. B. Buckner to B. A. Whitney, Mobile, AL, April 17, 1863, Confederate Citizens File for Whitney and Braman, Record Group 109, NARA; D. Ledbetter to B. A. Whitney, Engineer Office, Mobile, AL, July 17, 1863, Confederate Citizens File for Whitney and Braman, Record Group 109, NARA.

175 Isaac N. Brown, "Confederate Torpedoes in the Yazoo," BAL, 3:580; Ragan, *Confederate Saboteurs*, 31.

176 Ragan, *Confederate Saboteurs*, 35; Patent No. 200 for "Torpedo" issued to E. C. Singer on September 15, 1863, cited in Knight, *Confederate Invention*, 170–171, 222.

177 "Report of a Commission on Singer's Torpedo," Von Scheliha, *A Treatise on Coast Defense*, 225–227.

178 Isaac N. Brown, "Confederate Torpedoes in the Yazoo," BAL, 3:580.

179 Report of John G. Walker, Vicksburg, MI, July 22, 1863, ORN, 25:283; Extract from log of USS *Kenwood*, July 13, 1863, ORN, 25:286.

180 D. D. Porter to G. Welles, Off Vicksburg, July 14, 1863, ORN, 25:282–283.

181 I. N. Brown to Brigadier General Chalmers, Lexington, MS, July 17, 1863, ORN, 25:290.

182 Entry for USS *Baron De Kalb* (sternwheel casemate gunboat), US Naval History and Heritage Command, accessed August 17, 2023, https://www.history.navy.mil/research/histories/ship-histories/danfs/b/baron-de-kalb-i.html; Michael Halleran, M.M., "USS *Baron De Kalb*: The Masonic Ironclad," accessed August 17, 2023, http://www.phoenixmasonry.org/masonicmuseum/uss_baron_dekalb_the_masonic_ironclad.htm; Richard F. Muth, "A Masonic Secret Weapon: The H. L. Hunley," *Knight Templar Magazine*, accessed August 17, 2023, http://www.knightstemplar.org/KnightTemplar/articles/20141127.htm.

Chapter 6

183 Brian Hicks, *Sea of Darkness: Unraveling the Mysteries of the* H. L. Hunley (Ann Arbor, MI: Spry Publishing, 2014), 61–68.

184 Ben M., "Historical Marker: The *Hunley*." Clio: Your Guide to History. January 5, 2017. accessed August 26, 2023, https://theclio.com/entry/29848; Jack O'Brien, "Where was the *Hunley* Built?" *Gulf South Historical Review* 21, no. 5 (Fall 2005): 29–48.

185 Hicks, *Sea of Darkness*, 94–98.

186 Hicks, *Sea of Darkness*, 98–99; Mark K. Ragan, *Submarine Warfare in the Civil War* (Cambridge, MA: Da Capo Press, 2002), 110–111.

187 Hill, "Texan Gave World the First Successful Submarine Torpedo;" Ragan, *Submarine Warfare in the Civil War*, 111; Ragan, *Confederate Saboteurs*, 28; Richard F. Muth, "A Masonic Secret Weapon: The H. L. Hunley," *Knight Templar Magazine* archive, accessed August 21, 2023, http://www.knightstemplar.org/KnightTemplar/articles/20141127.htm.

188 Hill, "Texan Gave World the First Successful Submarine Torpedo."

189 Hill, "Texan Gave World the First Successful Submarine Torpedo."

190 *St. Louis Directory for 1860* (St. Louis: R. V. Kennedy & Co., 1860), 549; John Thomas Scharf, *History of Saint Louis from the Earliest Periods to the Present Day* (Philadelphia: Louis H. Everts & Co, 1883), 2:1158.

191 C. Williams to Gov. W. H. Gist, St. Louis, MO, November 20, 1860, Confederate Citizens File for C. Williams, Record Group 109, NARA; C. Williams to J. J. Pettus, St. Louis, MO, November 26, 1860, Mississippi Department of Archives and History, accessed March 31, 2024, https://cwrgm.org/item/mdah_757–930–11–06.

192 Charles Babbage, "Submarine Navigation," *Illustrated London News* (June 23, 1865): 623–624.

193 National Park Service, "USS Triton Sail Park," accessed January 13, 2024, https://www.nps.gov/places/000/uss-triton-sail-park.htm.

194 Mark K. Ragan, *Submarine Warfare in the Civil War* (Cambridge, MA: Da Capo Press, 2002), 115.

195 Hicks, *Sea of Darkness*, 135.

196 P. G. T. Beauregard to Quartermaster and Railroad Agents on Line from Charleston, Charleston, SC, August 7, 1863, OR, 28, pt. 2: 265.

197 Robert S. Neyland and Heather G. Brown, H. L. Hunley *Recovery Operations* (Washington, DC: US Naval History and Heritage Command, 2016), 19.

198 T. Jordan to B. A. Whitney, Charleston, SC, August 15, 1863, OR, 28, pt. 2: 285; Milton F. Perry, *Infernal Machines: The Story of Confederate Submarine and Mine Warfare* (Baton Rouge: Louisiana State University Press, 1965), 99.

199 Knight, *Confederate Invention*, 158, 219.

200 J. B. Clark to J. B. Magruder, Richmond, VA, June 27, 1863, CMSR for Robert Creuzbaur, Record Group 109, NARA.

201 Ragan, *Submarine Warfare in the Civil War*, 115–117.

202 A. L. Rives to E. Kirby Smith, OR, 22, pt. 2: 973.

203 Ragan, *Confederate Saboteurs*, 33.

204 Knight, *Confederate Inventions*, 280.

205 A. L. Rives to E. Kirby Smith, Engineer Bureau, August 20, 1863, OR, 22, pt. 2: 973–974.

206 Notice by War Department, CSA, Richmond, VA, August 21, 1863, OR, 22, pt. 2: 973–974.

207 A. L. Rives to E. Kirby Smith, Engineer Bureau, September 15, 1863, OR, 22, pt. 2: 1017.

208 Knight, *Confederate Inventions*, 221.

209 Hill, "Texan Gave World the First Successful Submarine Torpedo."

210 Neyland and Brown, H. L. Hunley *Recovery Operations*, 21–22.

211 Neyland and Brown, H. L. Hunley *Recovery Operations*, 22; H. L. Hunley to P. G. T. Beauregard, Charleston, SC, September 19, 1863, Confederate Citizens File for Horace L. Hunley, Record Group 109, NARA.

212 R. Creuzbaur to Stephen D. Yancey, Houston, TX, September 21, 1863, CMSR for R Creuzbaur, Record Group 109, NARA.

213 Edward T. Cotham Jr., *Sabine Pass: The Confederacy's Thermopylae* (Austin: University of Texas Press, 2004), 125–148.

214 R. Creuzbaur to Stephen D. Yancey, Houston, TX, September 21, 1863, CMSR for Robert Creuzbaur, Record Group 109, NARA; List of Engineer Officers,

District of Texas, New Mexico, and Arizona, Galveston, TX, November 7, 1863, CMSR for Robert Creuzbaur, Record Group 109, NARA.

Chapter 7

215 Edward H. Wiser, "A Rough, Wet Ride: The Civilian Genesis of the American Motor Torpedo Boat" (PhD diss., Florida State University, 2009), 23–37.

216 Johnny Dwayne Littlefield, "*David* and the *David*-Class of American Civil War Era Torpedo Boats of Charleston, South Carolina" (PhD diss., Texas A&M University, 2020), 76–81.

217 P. G. T. Beauregard to S. Cooper, Charleston, SC, October 13, 1862, ORN, 13:812–813.

218 R. Thomas Campbell, *Hunters of the Night: Confederate Torpedo Boats in the War Between the States* (Shippensburg, PA: Burd Street Press, 2000), 53–60.

219 W. T. Glassell, "Reminiscences of Torpedo Service in Charleston Harbor by W. T. Glassell, Commander, Confederate States Navy," SHSP 4, no. 5 (November 1877): 225–235; Campbell, *Hunters of the Night*, 61–65; Ragan, *Submarine Warfare in the Civil War*, 150–152.

220 Robert S. Solomon, C.S.S. David: *The Story of the First Successful Torpedo Boat Attack in Naval Warfare* (Columbia, SC: R. L. Bryan Co., 1970).

221 Johnny Dwayne Littlefield, "*David* and the *David*-Class of American Civil War Era Torpedo Boats of Charleston Harbor," 101–116; Ragan, *Submarine Warfare in the Civil War*, 150–152.

222 Campbell, *Hunters of the Night*, 55–56, 68, 81, 103.

223 "Remarks of General Beauregard, C.S. Army, Relative to Ironclad Gunboats," Charleston, SC, November 14, 1863, ORN, 15:694–695.

224 J. F. Gilmer to F. D. Lee, Savannah, GA, December 25, 1863, Letters and Telegrams Sent and Endorsements on Letters Received by Engineers Bureau of the Department of South Carolina, Georgia, and Florida, Chapter III, vol. 9, p. 88, Record Group 109, NARA.

225 J. S. Barnes to S. P. Lee, James River, VA, May 24, 1864, ORN, 9:601; Campbell, *Hunters of the Night*, 92–93.

226 J. H. Upshur to S. P. Lee, Off Newport News, VA, April 9, 1864, ORN, 9:593; Report of G. Gansevoort, J. Fyffe, and J. W. Stimson, Newport News, VA, April 12, 1864, ORN, 9:599–600; H. Davidson to S.R. Mallory, Turkey Island, April 11, 1864, ORN, 9:603. Campbell, *Hunters of the Night*, 96–100.

227 Campbell, *Hunters of the Night*, 103–114.

Chapter 8

228 Charles P. Stone to Adjutant General of the Army, New Orleans, LA, November 27, 1863, ORN, 9:411.

229 A copy of this letter is contained in a File labeled "1863-Stone, Charles P.," File No. G487, Records of the Adjutant General's Office, Record Group 94, NARA. The original has not been located and may no longer exist.

230 File labeled "1863-Stone, Charles P.," File No. G487, Record Group 94, NARA.

231 CSA Patent No. 211 awarded to C. Williams of St. Louis, MO, on October 25, 1863, cited in Knight, *Confederate Invention*, 222.

232 Mesch, *Ebenezer Allen*, 229–232.

233 Mesch, *Ebenezer Allen*, 229–232; "Sudden and Mysterious Death," *Richmond Examiner*, October 16, 1863; "Obituary," *Richmond Examiner*, October 17, 1863, p. 2.

234 Mesch, *Ebenezer Allen*, 232–234.

235 Mesch, *Ebenezer Allen*, 234–236.

236 Mesch, *Ebenezer Allen*, 236.

237 J. F. Gilmer to J. A. Seddon, Charleston, SC, October 15, 1863, Letters and Telegrams Sent and Endorsements on Letters Received by Engineer Bureau of the Department of South Carolina, Georgia and Florida, Chapter II, vol. 9, 57–58, Record Group 109, NARA.

238 J. F. Gilmer to J. A. Seddon, Charleston, SC, October 15, 1863, Letters and Telegrams Sent and Endorsements on Letters Received by Engineer Bureau of the Department of South Carolina, Georgia and Florida, Chapter II, vol. 9, 57–58, Record Group 109, NARA.

239 Neyland and Brown, H. L. Hunley *Recovery Operations*, 23–25.

240 Neyland and Brown, H. L. Hunley *Recovery Operations*, 23–25.

241 Ragan, *Confederate Saboteurs*, 164.

242 Perry, *Infernal Machines*, 101–103.

243 CSA Patent No. 211 awarded October 25, 1863, to C. Williams, cited in Knight, *Confederate Invention*, 222.

244 C. Williams to J. F. Gilmer, Richmond, VA, October 27, 1863, Confederate Engineer Bureau Miscellaneous Papers, Record Group 109, Entry 27, Box 1, NARA (hereafter "Williams Gilmer Letter").

245 Williams Gilmer Letter.

246 Williams Gilmer Letter.

247 Williams Gilmer Letter.

248 Williams Gilmer Letter.

249 J. McClintock to M. F. Maury, undated, Matthew Fontaine Maury Papers, General Correspondence, 1825 to 1910, mss31682, box 46, Image 173–181, Library of Congress.

250 Williams Gilmer Letter.

251 The letters received and endorsement files of the Department of South Carolina, Georgia, and Florida, reflect the receipt of a letter from C. Williams dated November 23, 1863, containing a "communication to the Proprietors of the Submarine Torpedo Boat at Charleston." The chief of staff referred the communication to Lieutenant George E. Dixon on November 27, 1863. Record Group 109, NARA.

252 Charles P. Stone to Adjutant General of the Army, New Orleans, November 27, 1863, ORN, 9:411.

253 Edward R. S. Canby to Secretary of the Navy, Washington, DC, January 18, 1864, ORN, 9:411.

254 Andrew W. Hall, "Mystery of the Confederate Deep," *Civil War Monitor* 3, no. 4 (Winter 2013): 52–55; "Black Powder Blast Effects on the Confederate Submarine *Hunley*," Information Paper Prepared by the US Navy, August 28, 2017, Naval History and Heritage Command, accessed March 31, 2024, https://www.history.navy.mil/research/underwater-archaeology/sites-and-projects/ship-wrecksites/hl-hunley/black-powder-blast-effects-hunley.html#:~:text=It%20has%20been%20concluded%20that,more%20modern%20military%2Dgrade%20explosives; Ragan, *Confederate Saboteurs*, 83–84.

Chapter 9

255 V. Sulakowski to J. Kellersberg, OR, 26, pt. 2: 298–299; Hess, *Civil War Torpedoes*, 65.

256 Stephen A. Dupree, *Planting the Union flag in Texas: The Campaigns of Major General Nathaniel P. Banks in the West* (College Station: Texas A&M University Press, 2008), 70–71.

257 D. Bradbury to J. Duff, Victoria, TX, January 9, 1864, OR, 34, pt. 2: 854.

258 D. Bradbury to J. Duff, Victoria, TX, January 9, 1864, OR, 34, pt. 2: 854.

259 D. Bradbury to J. Duff, Victoria, TX, January 9, 1864, OR, 34, pt. 2: 854.

260 J. Barto Arnold III, "Fort Esperanza," *Handbook of Texas Online*, accessed December 25, 2023, https://www.tshaonline.org/handbook/entries/fort-esperanza.

261 W. R. Bradfute to E. P. Turner, Lavaca, TX, November 24, 1863, OR, 26, pt. 1:445; W. R. Bradfute to E. P. Turner, Fort Esperanza, TX, November 27, 1863, OR, 26, pt. 1: 446.

262 D. Bradbury to J. Duff, Victoria, TX, January 9, 1864, OR, 34, pt. 2: 854.

263 Lester N. Fitzhugh, "Saluria, Fort Esperanza, and Military Operations on the Texas Coast, 1861–1864," *Southwestern Historical Quarterly* 61, no. 1 (July 1957): 97.

264 C. C. Washburn to N. P. Banks, Matagorda Island, TX, November 30, 1863, OR, 26, pt. 1: 416–417.

265 J. T. Baker to C. J. Allen, Boston, MA, October 2, 1865, in W. R. King, *Torpedoes: Their Invention and Use, From the First Application to the Art of War to the Present Time* (Washington, DC: United States Navy Department, 1866), 5–6.

266 J. T. Baker to C. J. Allen, Boston, MA, October 2, 1865, in King, *Torpedoes: Their Invention and Use*, 5–6, Plate A.

267 Hess, *Civil War Torpedoes*, 64.

268 Hess, *Civil War Torpedoes*, 64–65; William H. Chenery, *The Fourteenth Regiment, Rhode Island Heavy Artillery (Colored) in the War to Preserve the Union, 1861–1865* (1898, repr., New York: Negro Universities Press, 1969), 22.

269 Letter from George Wheeler to Dear Malinda, in Camp on Matagorda Bay, December 3, 1863, Typescript, No. 2005.189, George Wheeler Papers, Pearce Civil War Collections Museum, Navarro College, Corsicana, TX.

270 National Park Service, "Battle Unit Details for the 34th Regiment, Iowa Infantry," accessed August 30, 2023, https://www.nps.gov/civilwar/search-battle-units-detail.htm?battleUnitCode=UIA0034RI; Map of Fort Esperanza prepared by Enos Reed, 34th Iowa, Texas State Library and Archives Commission, Texas State Archives Map Collection, AC Number 00014a.

271 D. Bradbury to J. Duff, Victoria, TX, January 9, 1864, OR, 34, pt. 2: 854–855.

272 C. C. Washburn to N. P. Banks, Matagorda Island, November 30, 1863, OR, 26, pt 1: 416.

273 R. W. Dunn to J. B. Magruder, Houston, TX, April 6, 1864, Confederate Citizens file for Robert W. Dunn, Record Group 109, NARA.

274 W. T. Sherman to J. B. Steedman, Big Shanty, GA, June 23, 1864, OR, 38, pt. 4: 579.

275 Unsigned letter dated August 1863 that appears to be in Robert Creuzbaur's handwriting, Richmond, VA, BM-Mines and Torpedoes File, Subject Files for the Confederate States Navy, Record Group 45, NARA.

276 Unsigned letter dated August 1863 that appears to be in Robert Creuzbaur's handwriting, Richmond, VA, BM-Mines and Torpedoes File, Subject Files for the Confederate States Navy, Record Group 45, NARA.

277 A. C. Matthews to Captain Caldwell, Cedar Bayou, TX, March 30, 1864, OR, 34, pt. 2: 783.

278 Hayes, *Island and City of Galveston*, 2:610.

279 Ben C. Stuart, "First Submarine Torpedo Vessel," *Galveston Daily News*, August 29, 1909, p. 17.

280 J. E. Slaughter to J. B. Magruder, Velasco, TX, December 28, 1863, Letters Received, District of Texas, New Mexico, and Arizona, December 1, 1862–April 30, 1864, Record Group 109, NARA.

Chapter 10

281 Bobby J. McKinney, *Confederates on the Caney: An Illustrated Account of the Civil War on the Texas Gulf Coast* (Rosenberg, TX: Mouth of Caney Publication, 1994), 1–2; Dupree, *Planting the Union flag in Texas*, 70–71, 77–79.

282 R. Creuzbaur to E. P. Turner, Houston, TX, November 5, 1863, CMSR for Robert W. Creuzbaur, Record Group 109, NARA.

283 R. Creuzbaur to E. P. Turner, Houston, TX, November 5, 1863, CMSR for Robert W. Creuzbaur, Record Group 109, NARA.

284 H. T. Douglas to E. P. Turner, Headquarters, Engineering Department, Trans-Mississippi Department, November 20, 1863, "Henry T. Douglas" File, Fourth Confederate Engineer Troops, A-R, Record Group 109, NARA, accessed December 17, 2023, https://www.fold3.com/image/153592891.

285 *Civilian and Gazette* (Galveston), July 9, 1861, p. 4.

286 Kellersberger, *Memoirs*, 33.

287 Kellersberger, *Memoirs*, 33.

288 Kellersberger, *Memoirs*, 33.

289 Kellersberger, *Memoirs*, 33.

290 Kellersberger, *Memoirs*, 33.

291 Special Order, issued by Major General John B. Magruder, Houston, TX, December 1, 1863, CMSR for G. H. Schroeder, Record Group 109, NARA.

292 Requisition by G. H. Schroeder, Engineer Department, Houston, TX, December 10, 1863, CMSR for G. H. Schroeder, Record Group 109, NARA.

293 Special Order, issued by Major General John B. Magruder, Houston, TX, December 1, 1863, CMSR for G. H. Schroeder, Record Group 109, NARA; Donnelly, "Rocket Batteries of the Civil War," 86; "Death of Capt. John S. Greer," *Corpus Christi Weekly Caller*, August 22, 1886, p. 4.

294 J. S. Greer to S. D. Yancy, Galveston, TX, February 9, 1864, CMSR for John S. Greer., Record Group 109, NARA.

295 "Notice to Volunteers," *Houston Daily Telegraph*, April 22, 1864, p. 4.

296 Donnelly, "Rocket Batteries in the Civil War," 87.

297 J. S. Greer to T. F. Drayton, Camp at River Spring, June 9, 1864, CMSR for John S. Greer, Record Group 109, NARA.

298 Kellersberger, *Memoirs*, 34.

299 Kellersberger, *Memoirs*, 34.

300 Kellersberger, *Memoirs*, 34.

301 Kellersberger, *Memoirs*, 34.

302 Kellersberger, *Memoirs*, 34.

303 Kellersberger, *Memoirs*, 34.

304 Kellersberger, *Memoirs*, 34.

305 Listing on Worthpoint site for "C. S. Hale Rocket, Texas Rocket Battery, San Antonio Texas 1863/64," accessed September 5, 2023, https://www.worthpoint.com/worthopedia/s-hale-rocket-texas-rocket-battery-1885251825.

Chapter 11

306 Special Orders No. 271, December 14, 1863, Charleston, SC, OR, 28, pt. 2: 553.

307 Information obtained from the examination of deserters from the enemy, Charleston, SC, January 7, 1864, ORN, 15:227–233; Neyland and Brown, H. L. Hunley *Recovery Operations*, 31.

308 Order of J. A. Dahlgren to Union blockading fleet at Charleston, Off Morris Island, SC, January 7, 1864, ORN, 15:226–227.

309 James H. Tomb, "Submarines and Torpedo Boats, C.S.N.," *Confederate Veteran* 22, no. 4 (April 1914): 169; Campbell, *Hunters of the Night*, 76–77.

310 Tom Chaffin, The H. L. Hunley: *The Secret Hope of the Confederacy* (New York: Hill & Wang, 2008), 170; Hicks, *Sea of Darkness*, 282–283.

311 Hall, "Mystery of the Confederate Deep," 52–53; Ragan, *Submarine Warfare in the Civil War*, 178–181.

312 Neyland and Brown, H. L. Hunley *Recovery Operations*, 34; Hicks, *Sea of Darkness*, 327–329.

313 Neyland and Brown, H. L. Hunley *Recovery Operations*, 35; Hicks, *Sea of Darkness*, 334.

314 Ragan, *Submarine Warfare*, 197; Hall, "Mystery of the Confederate Deep," 54–56.; Matthew D. Collette and Ken Nahshon, "Investigating the Loss of H. L. *Hunley*," Paper presented at the SNAME Maritime Convention, Bellevue, Washington, USA, November 2016., accessed December 25, 2023, https://www.history.navy.mil/content/dam/nhhc/browse-by-topic/War%20and%20Conflict/civil-war/Collette_Nahshon_Hunley.pdf.

315 Hicks, *Sea of Darkness*, 334–335; Ragan, *Submarine Warfare*, 199–200; Christopher D. Rucker, "The Myth of the *Hunley's* Blue Lantern," *Civil War Monitor*, October 8, 2012, accessed December 31, 2024, https://www.civilwarmonitor.com/the-myth-of-the-h-l-hunleys-blue-lantern/.

316 Hicks, *Sea of Darkness*, 188–190; Friends of the Hunley, "The Search for the *Hunley*," accessed December 25, 2023, https://www.hunley.org/the-search-and-recovery/.

Chapter 12

317 Ragan, *Confederate Saboteurs*, 90.

318 T. E. Courtenay to H. E. Clark, Richmond, VA, January 19, 1864, ORN, 26:186–187.

319 J. D. Braman (misspelled as Breaman in the Official Records) to his wife, Mobile, AL, March 3, 1864, ORN, 26:187–189.

320 Ragan, *Confederate Saboteurs*, 107–110, 113.

321 B. J. Sage (misidentified as B. J. Page in the Official Records) to "my friends," no date or place, ORN, 26:192.

322 General Order No. 184, Alexandria, LA, March 20, 1864, ORN, 26:184.

323 D. Porter to G. Welles, Alexandria, LA, March 20, 1864, ORN, 26:185–186.

324 D. Porter to Provost Marshal, St. Louis, MO, March 21, 1864, Off Alexandria, LA, ORN, 27:103; Thatcher and Thatcher, *Confederate Coal Torpedo*, 48–49; C. S. Bell to P. Tallon, St. Louis, MO, November 17, 1864, Entry 36, Correspondence, Reports, Appointments and Other Records Relating to Individual Scouts, Guides, Spies and Detectives: Records of the Provost Marshal General's Bureau, Record Group 110, NARA.

325 R. W. Dunn to J. B. Magruder, Houston, TX, April 6, 1864, Confederate Citizens File for R. W. Dunn, Record Group 109, NARA, accessed November 27, 2023, https://www.fold3.com/image/30874156; Ragan, *Confederate Saboteurs*, 114–115.

326 R. W. Dunn to J. B. Magruder, Houston, TX, April 6, 1864, Confederate Citizens File for R. W. Dunn, Record Group 109, NARA, accessed November 27, 2023, https://www.fold3.com/image/30874156; Ragan, *Confederate Saboteurs*, 114–115.

327 R. W. Dunn to J. B. Magruder, Houston, TX, April 6, 1864, Confederate Citizens File for R. W. Dunn, Record Group 109, NARA, accessed November 27, 2023, https://www.fold3.com/image/30874156; Ragan, *Confederate Saboteurs*, 114–115.

328 Thomas O. Selfridge, "The Navy in the Red River," BAL 4, pt 1: 362.

329 Thomas O. Selfridge, "The Navy in the Red River," BAL 4, pt 1: 363–364.

330 Porter, *The Naval History of the Civil War*, 512; Joiner, *Red River Campaign*, 120–122.

331 Joiner, *Red River Campaign*, 122–123.

332 Joiner, *Red River Campaign*, 125.

333 Charles E. Pearson and Thomas C. C. Birchett, *History and Archaeology of Two Civil War Steamboats: The Ironclad Gunboat USS* Eastport *and the Steamer* Ed. F. Dix (Baton Rouge, LA: Coastal Environments, 2001), 108.

334 D. Porter to W. T. Sherman, Alexandria, LA, April 16, 1864, ORN, 26:62.

335 Report of S. Phelps, Alexandria, LA, April 28, 1864, ORN, 26:79.

336 Report of S. Phelps, Alexandria, LA, April 28, 1864, ORN, 26:79.

337 Report of S. Phelps, Alexandria, LA, April 28, 1864, ORN, 26:79.

338 David D. Porter, *Incidents and Anecdotes of the Civil War* (New York: D. Appleton and Co., 1885), 239.

339 Charles E. Pearson, "Great Expectations for an Ill-Fated Ironclad," *Naval History Magazine*, February 2017, accessed November 27, 2023, https://www.usni.org/magazines/naval-history-magazine/2017/february/great-expectations-ill-fated-ironclad; Pearson and Birchett, *History and Archaeology of Two Civil War Steamboats*, 108.

340 Paul Brueske, *The Last Siege: The Mobile Campaign* (Philadelphia: Casemate Publishers, 2018), xv–xvi.

341 John C. Waugh, *Last Stand at Mobile* (Abilene, TX: McWhiney Foundation Press, 2001), 19–20.

342 Ragan, *Confederate Saboteurs*, 129–130; Perry, *Infernal Machines*, 159.

343 V. Scheliha to J. F. Gilmer (telegram), ORN, 21:559; Perry, *Infernal Machines*, 159–161.

344 Waugh, *Last Stand at Mobile*, 44.

345 S. R. Mallory to J. D. Bulloch, Richmond, VA, April 19, 1864, ORN, series 2, 2:627–628; W. P. Williamson to S. R. Mallory, Richmond, VA, April 16, 1864, ORN, series 2, 2:628.

346 S. R. Mallory to J. D. Bulloch, Richmond, VA, July 18, 1864, ORN, series 2, 2:688–689.

347 S. R. Mallory to J. D. Bulloch, Richmond, VA, July 18, 1864, ORN, series 2, 2:688–689.

348 J. D. Bulloch to S. R. Mallory, Liverpool, UK, September 16, 1864, ORN, series 2, 2:723–725; J. D. Bulloch to S. R. Mallory, Liverpool, UK, January 26, 1865, ORN, series 2, 2:790–791; Kevin J. Foster, "The Diplomats Who Sank a Fleet: The Confederacy's Undelivered European Fleet and the Union Consular Service," *National Archives Prologue Magazine*, Fall 2001, accessed January 2, 2024, https://www.archives.gov/publications/prologue/2001/fall/confederate-fleet#f29.

349 G. J. Rains to J. A. Seddon, Richmond, VA, November 18, 1864, OR, 42, pt 3: 1219–1220.

350 W. H. Macomb, Roanoke River, NC, December 11, 1864, ORN, 11:160–161.

351 W. H. Macomb, Roanoke River, NC, December 11, 1864, ORN, 11:160–161.

352 W. H. Macomb, Roanoke River, NC, December 11, 1864, ORN, 11:160–161.

353 W. H. Macomb, Roanoke River, NC, December 11, 1864, ORN, 11:160–161.

354 J. H. Gillis to H. K. Thatcher, Mobile Bay, March 30, 1865, ORN, 22:71.

355 W. M. Gamble to H. K. Thatcher, Mobile Bay, March 29, 1865, ORN, 22:72; R. W. Gifford to H. K. Thatcher, Mobile Bay, April 4, 1865, ORN, 22:73; W. Burk to G. Welles, Mobile Bay, April 4, 1865, ORN, 22:74.

356 N. M. Dyer to H. K. Thatcher, Blakely River, April 2, 1865, ORN, 22:72–73; E. P Colby to N. M. Dyer, Blakely River, April 2, 1865, ORN, 22:74.

357 David D. Porter, "Torpedo Warfare," *North American Review*, September–October 1878, 228.

358 Porter, "Torpedo Warfare," *North American Review*, September–October 1878, 231–232.

359 Porter, "Torpedo Warfare," *North American Review*, September–October 1878, 229.

360 Porter, "Torpedo Warfare," *North American Review*, September–October 1878, 228.

361 *Tri-Weekly Telegraph* (Houston), January 23, 1865, p. 4.

362 *Tri-Weekly Telegraph*, January 23, 1865, p. 4.

Chapter 13

363 H. T. Douglas to R. W. Dunn, Shreveport, LA, May 25, 1864, Letters Received by the District of Texas, New Mexico, and Arizona from Headquarters of the Department of the Trans-Mississippi, Record Group 109, NARA; Special Orders No. 123, Shreveport, LA, May 19, 1864, Special Orders of the Department of the Trans-Mississippi Received by the District of Texas, New Mexico, and Arizona, 1864, Record Group 109, NARA.

364 Katherine Brash Jeter, ed., *A Man and His Boat: The Civil War Career and Correspondence of Lieutenant Jonathan H. Carter, CSN* (Lafayette, LA: Center for Louisiana Studies, University of Southwestern Louisiana, 1996), 117, 130.

365 Aragorn Storm Miller, "Creuzbauer, Edmund," *Handbook of Texas Online*, accessed January 16, 2024, https://www.tshaonline.org/handbook/entries/creuzbauer-edmund; Alwyn Barr, "The Battle of Calcasieu Pass," *Southwestern Historical Quarterly* 66, no. 1 (July 1962): 59–67.

366 Barr, "Battle of Calcasieu Pass," 59–67.

367 Special Orders No. 173, Houston, TX, June 21, 1864, Special Orders of District of Texas, New Mexico, and Arizona, April–June, 1864, Record Group 109,

NARA; Special Orders No. 190, Houston, TX, July 8, 1864, Special Orders of District of Texas, New Mexico, and Arizona, July–September, 1864, Record Group 109, NARA.

368 *Galveston City Directory 1859–1860* (Galveston, TX: W & D Richardson, 1859–60), 81.

369 D. Bradbury to L. G. Aldrich, Houston, TX, June 15, 1864,Confederate Citizens File for D. Bradbury, Record Group 109, NARA.

370 D. Porter to F. M. Ramsay, Mound City, June 25, 1864, ORN, 26: 438–439.

371 E. C. Singer to Major Barton, Houston, TX, August 14, 1864, Camp Rogers, Confederate Memorial Literary Society, Virginia Museum of History and Culture, Richmond, Virginia.

372 Special Order No. 120, Houston, TX, April 30, 1865, Special Orders of the District of Texas, New Mexico, and Arizona, March 1865–May 1865, Record Group 109, NARA; Ragan, *Confederate Saboteurs*, 150, 152, 156–157, 174–176, 181–182; J. G. Walker to H. T. Douglas, Anderson, TX, December 2, 1864, Letters Sent in the Field, District of Texas, New Mexico, and Arizona, September 1864–May 1865, Record Group 109, NARA; Trevia Wooster Beverly, "Confederate Naval Works on Goose Creek," Application for Historical Marker approved July 15, 2006, accessed December 26, 2023, https://www.baytownhistory.org/images/Application_-_Confederate_Naval_Works.pdf.

373 J. Kellersberger to H. Willke, Houston, TX, August 19. 1864, CMSR for Julius Kellersberg, Sappers and Miners A-K, Record Group 109, NARA, accessed December 18, 2023, https://www.fold3.com/image/185343947.

374 R. Creuzbaur to Capt. A. R. Jones, Houston, TX, August 31, 1864, CMSR for Robert Creuzbaur, Record Group 109, NARA, accessed December 18, 2023, https://www.fold3.com/image/119181524.

375 J. G. Walker to H. T. Douglas, Anderson, TX, December 2, 1864, Letters Sent in the Field, District of Texas, New Mexico, and Arizona, September 1864–May 1865, Record Group 109, NARA.

376 J. G. Walker to H. T. Douglas, Anderson, TX, December 2, 1864, Letters Sent in the Field, District of Texas, New Mexico, and Arizona, September 1864–May 1865, Record Group 109, NARA.

377 Diana J. Kleiner, "Chubb, Thomas B.," *Handbook of Texas Online*, accessed January 1, 2024, https://www.tshaonline.org/handbook/entries/chubb-thomas-b.

378 Cotham, *Battle on the Bay*, 42–49; Norman Brown, ed., *Journey to Pleasant Hill: The Civil War Letters of Captain Elijah P. Petty*, 2 vols. (San Antonio: University of Texas Institute of Texas Cultures, 1982), 1:44.

379 J. G. Walker to H. T. Douglas, Anderson, TX, December 2, 1864, Letters Sent in the Field, District of Texas, New Mexico, and Arizona, September 1864–May 1865, Record Group 109, NARA.

380 H. Close to T. Jack, Galveston, TX, January 21, 1865, Confederate Citizens File for Hiram Close, Record Group 109, NARA; W. A. Freret to J. G. Walker, Shreveport, LA, December 13, 1864, Letters Received by the District of Texas, New Mexico, and Arizona from Headquarters of the Trans-Mississippi Department, January 1864–May 1865, Record Group 109, NARA.

381 J. G. Walker to H. T. Douglas, Anderson, TX, December 2, 1864, Letters Sent in the Field, District of Texas, New Mexico, and Arizona, September 1864–May 1865, Record Group 109, NARA; Special Order No. 101, Houston, TX, Anderson, TX, December 20, 1864, Special Orders of the District of Texas, New Mexico, and Arizona, March 1865–May 1865, NARA.

382 J. G. Walker to W. A. Freret, Houston, TX, December 29, 1864, Letters Sent in the Field, District of Texas, New Mexico, and Arizona, September 1864–May 1865, Record Group 109, NARA.

383 J. G. Walker to W. A. Freret, Houston, TX, December 29, 1864, Letters Sent in the Field, District of Texas, New Mexico, and Arizona, September 1864–May 1865, Record Group 109, NARA.

384 W. A. Freret to J. G. Walker, Shreveport, LA, January 10, 1865, CMSR for William A. Freret, NARA.

385 W. A. Freret to J. G. Walker, Shreveport, LA, January 14, 1865, Letters Received by the District of Texas, New Mexico, and Arizona from Headquarters of the Trans-Mississippi Department, January 1864–May 1865, Record Group 109, NARA; W. A. Freret to J. G. Walker, Shreveport, LA, February 9, 1865, Letters Received by the District of Texas, New Mexico, and Arizona from Headquarters of the Trans-Mississippi Department, January 1864–May 1865, Record Group 109, NARA; W. A. Freret to J. G. Walker, Shreveport, LA, January 31, 1865, Letters Received by the District of Texas, New Mexico, and Arizona from Headquarters of the Trans-Mississippi Department, January 1864–May 1865, Record Group 109, NARA.

386 Ragan, *Confederate Saboteurs*, 152.

387 Special requisition No. 40 by W. A. Freret dated February 9, 1865, approved by J. G. Walker, Houston, TX, CMSR for Will A. Freret, NARA.

388 J. G. Walker to T. Chubb, Houston, TX, February 21, 1865, Letters Sent in the Field, District of Texas, New Mexico, and Arizona, September 1864–May 1865, Record Group 109, NARA.

389 J. G. Walker to T. Chubb, Houston, TX, February 21, 1865, Letters Sent in the Field, District of Texas, New Mexico, and Arizona, September 1864–May 1865, Record Group 109, NARA.

390 Letter from H. S. Lubbock to Messrs. Baker, Hutchins, and others, Houston, TX, November 15, 1863, Texas Governor Francis R. Lubbock Papers, Box 2–22L/15A, Folder 3, TSLAC.

391 Letter from H. S. Lubbock to Messrs. Baker, Hutchins and others, Houston, TX, November 15, 1863, Texas Governor Francis R. Lubbock Papers, Box 2–22L/15A, Folder 3, TSLAC.

392 Memorial for Sgt. Mordecai Peebles Hunnicutt, Find a Grave, accessed February 6, 2024, https://www.findagrave.com/memorial/47947746/mordecai-peebles-hunnicutt; "NCOs: The MI Tradition," United States Army, Fort Huachuca, Arizona, accessed on February 6, 2024, https://studylib.net/doc/18378061/the-united-states-army---fort-huachuca--az; Edwin C. Fishel, *The Secret War for the Union: The Untold Story of Military Intelligence in the Civil War* (New York: Houghton Mifflin Co., 1996), 461–463.

393 Fishel, *The Secret War for the Union*, 463, 493; Peter G. Tsouras, *Major General George H. Sharpe and the Creation of American Military Intelligence in the Civil War* (Philadelphia: Casemate Publishers, 2018), 120–121, 169.

394 M. P. Hunnicutt to E. R. S. Canby, Morgan County, OH, September 19, 1864, Union Citizens File for M. P. Hunnicutt, Publication No. M345, Catalog No. 2133278, Record Group 109, NARA.

395 Receipt signed by M. P. Hunnicutt in New Orleans, LA, December 17, 1864, Letters Received by the Commission Branch of the Adjutant General's Office, 1863–1870, Frank W. Marston file, File No. M89, Record Group 94, NARA; Ragan, *Confederate Saboteurs*, 151, 155.

396 Ragan, *Confederate Saboteurs*, 154–155.

397 Ragan, *Confederate Saboteurs*, 160–161.

398 A. M. Jackson to C. T. Christensen, New Orleans, LA, March 13, 1865, ORN, 22:103–105.

399 A. M. Jackson to C. T. Christensen, New Orleans, LA, March 13, 1865, ORN, 22:103–104.

400 Special Order No. 83, Houston, TX, March 24, 1865, Special Orders, District of Texas, New Mexico, and Arizona, March–May 1865, Record Group 109, NARA.

401 Report of H. Wilson to H. K. Thatcher, Galveston, TX, March 27, 1865, ORN, 22:124–125.

402 W. R. Boggs to J. B. Magruder, Shreveport, LA, April 10, 1865, Letters Received

by the District of Texas, New Mexico, and Arizona from Headquarters of the Trans-Mississippi Department, January 1864–May 1865, Record Group 109, NARA; *Register of Officers of the Confederate States Navy*, 108.

403 Special Order No. 115, Houston, TX, April 25, 1865, Special Orders, District of Texas, New Mexico, and Arizona, March–May 1865, Record Group 109, NARA.

404 R. W. Dunn to J. B. Magruder, Houston, TX, April 28, 1865, Letters Received by the District of Texas, New Mexico, and Arizona from Headquarters of the Trans-Mississippi Department, January 1864–May 1865, Record Group 109, NARA; Ragan, *Confederate Saboteurs*, 174–175; Telegram from R. W. Dunn to E. Douglas, Houston, TX, April 29, 1865, Telegrams Sent, District of Texas, New Mexico, and Arizona, July 1864–May 1865, Record Group 109, NARA.

405 R. W. Dunn to J. B. Magruder, Houston, TX, April 28, 1865, Letters Received by the District of Texas, New Mexico, and Arizona from Headquarters of the Trans-Mississippi Department, January 1864–May 1865, Record Group 109, NARA; Ragan, *Confederate Saboteurs*, 174–175; Special Order No. 120, Houston, TX, April 30, 1865, Special Orders, District of Texas, New Mexico, and Arizona, March–May 1865, Record Group 109, NARA.

406 Special Order No. 120, Houston, TX, April 30, 1865, Special Orders, District of Texas, New Mexico, and Arizona, March–May 1865, Record Group 109, NARA.

407 Special Orders No. 191, Special Orders, District of Texas, New Mexico, and Arizona, July–September 1864, Record Group 109, NARA.

408 R. Creuzbaur to A. R. Jones, Ordnance Foundry, Houston, TX, August 31, 1864, CMSR for Robert Creuzbaur, Record Group 109, NARA.

409 Special Order No. 63, Houston, TX, March 4, 1865, Special Orders, District of Texas, New Mexico, and Arizona, March–May 1865, Record Group 109, NARA; Special Order No. 84, Houston, TX, March 25, 1865, Special Orders, District of Texas, New Mexico, and Arizona, March–May 1865, Record Group 109, NARA.

410 Special Order No. 129, Houston, TX, May 9, 1865, Special Orders, District of Texas, New Mexico, and Arizona, March–May 1865, Record Group 109, NARA; Special Order No. 131, Houston, TX, May 11, 1865, Special Orders, District of Texas, New Mexico, and Arizona, March–May 1865, Record Group 109, NARA.

411 Special Order No. 142, Houston, TX, May 22, 1865, Special Orders, District of Texas, New Mexico, and Arizona, March–May 1865, Record Group 109, NARA.

Epilogue

412 Cotham, *Battle on the Bay*, 182.

413 "Records related to E. C. Singer," Papers of and Relating to Military and Civilian Personnel, Adjutant General's Office, War Records Office, Record Group 109, NARA.

414 "Records related to J. D. Braman," Papers of and Relating to Military and Civilian Personnel, Adjutant General's Office, War Records Office, Record Group 109, NARA.

415 "Records related to R. W. Dunn," Papers of and Relating to Military and Civilian Personnel, Adjutant General's Office, War Records Office, Record Group 109, NARA.

416 Jack E. Beeler, "The John R. Fretwell Officer Jewels," accessed December 31, 2024, http://lavacalodge.org/the-john-r-fretwell-officer-jewels/; Advertisement for San Antonio House, *The Houston Transcript*, August 24, 1867, p. 6; "Dr. John Richard Fretwell, Confederate Inventor," Fretwells Genealogy and Family History, accessed December 9, 2023, http://www.thefretwells.com/research/drjrfretwell.aspx; W. A. Fayman and T. W. Reilly, *Galveston City Directory, 1875–1876* (Galveston, TX: n.p., 1875), 32, 99; Ben C. Suart, "First Submarine Torpedo Vessel," *Galveston Daily News*, August 29, 1909; Ragan, *Confederate Saboteurs*, 185–186.

417 Knight, *Confederate Invention*, 309–310; US Patent No. 164,198, for Improvement in Brick Molds, issued to Edgar C. Singer of Marlin, Texas, on May 17, 1875, USPTO; US Patent No. 223,071, for Improvement in Bale -Ties, issued to Edgar C. Singer of Marlin, Texas, on December 30, 1879, USPTO.

418 *Galveston Daily News*, July 20, 1879, p. 3; *Sunday Gazette* (Denison, TX), July 5, 1891, p. 2.

419 *El Paso Daily Times*, March 7, 1900, p. 8; *El Paso Daily Times*, March 8, 1900, p. 7.

420 *El Paso Daily Times*, March 8, 1900, p. 7; "Niece of Torpedo Inventor Visits Galveston," *Galveston Tribune*, May 16, 1921, p. 2.

421 *El Paso Daily Times*, March 8, 1900, p. 7.

422 "The Rebel Torpedoes," *Pittsburgh Daily Commercial*, April 21, 1864, p. 3.

423 "War Times Recalled," *Belvidere (IL) Daily Republican*, August 10, 1905, p. 2.

424 "War Times Recalled," *Belvidere Daily Republican*, August 10, 1905, p. 2.

425 "War Times Recalled," *Belvidere Daily Republican*, August 10, 1905, p. 2.

426 "War Times Recalled," *Belvidere Daily Republican*, August 10, 1905, p. 2.

427 *Aransas Pass Progress*, June 3, 1910, p. 3.

428 Horace N. Hill, "Texan Gave World First Successful Submarine Torpedo," *San Antonio Express*. July 30, 1916, p. 45–46.

429 "Inventor of Torpedo Dies," *Houston Post*, May 1, 1919, p. 13; Randolph W. Farmer, "Singer, Edgar Collins," *Handbook of Texas Online*, accessed December 10, 2023, https://www.tshaonline.org/handbook/entries/singer-edgar-collins.

430 United States Patents issued to Lucien Hopson for Projectiles, No. 305,002 Sept. 9, 1884, and No. 313,075, issued March 3, 1885, USPTO; Brooke, *Ironclads and Big Guns of the Confederacy*, 115.

431 "General Washington News," *The Courier-Journal* (Louisville, KY), July 9, 1885, p.1; "Tales That are Told," *New York Times*, July 10, 1885, p.4; "Mr. Lucien Hopson," *Evening Star* (Washington, DC), July 14, 1885, p.4; "An Old Mexican Soldier," *Capital* (Annapolis, MD), July 25, 1887, p. 3.

432 Entry for Lucien Hopson, Records of the Texas State Cemetery, Austin, TX, accessed December 26, 2023, https://cemetery.tspb.texas.gov/pub/user_form.asp?pers_id=252.

433 "Guatemala—South America," *Vermont Record and Farmer*, July 8, 1870, p. 7; Donald C. Simmons Jr., *Confederate Settlements in British Honduras* (Jefferson, NC: McFarland & Co., 2001), 154.

434 Caleb V. Littlepage papers, AR.2016.007, Austin History Center, Austin Public Library, Austin, TX.

435 Caleb V. Littlepage papers, AR.2016.007, Austin History Center, Austin Public Library, Austin, TX; Knight, *Confederate Invention*, 130.

436 Knight, *Confederate Invention*, 160–161.

437 Knight, *Confederate Invention*, 160–161; "Robert Creuzbaur Dead," *Brooklyn Daily Eagle*, October 26, 1911, p. 20; "An Application Long Pending," *Scientific American*, October 12, 1912, p. 308.

438 Letter from Robert Creuzbaur to Thomas A. Edison, New York City, October 6, 1891, Thomas A. Edison Papers, School of Arts and Sciences, Rutgers University.

439 Robert Creuzbaur, "Liquid Air Defended," *New York Times*, May 29, 1899, p. 6.

440 Letter from Robert Creuzbaur to Theodore Roosevelt, Brooklyn, New York, April 4, 1911, Theodore Roosevelt Papers, Library of Congress.

441 Williiam Butcher, *Jules Verne: The Definitive Biography* (New York: Thunder's Mouth Press, 2006), 175–181; "Passengers Arrived," *Commercial Advertiser* (New York), April 10. 1867, p. 4.

442 Jules Verne, *Twenty Thousand Leagues Under the Sea*, trans. William Butcher (Oxford, UK: Oxford University Press, 1998), 100.

443 "The Use of the Divining-Rod," *Advertiser Courier* (Hermann, MO), July 6, 1877, p. 2; Edwin A. Moore, "All in a Lifetime," *Portland (ME) Press Herald*, July 14, 1851, p. 8.

444 "Robert Creuzbaur at 86 Invents New Airship," *Brooklyn Daily Eagle*, May 2, 1909, p. 24.

445 "Jean Pierre Blanchard," The British Balloon Museum and Library, accessed December 30, 2024, https://www.bbml.org.uk/jean-pierre-blanchard/; "Robert Creuzbaur at 86 Invents New Airship," *Brooklyn Daily Eagle*, May 2, 1909, p. 24; "Robert Creuzbaur Dead," *Brooklyn Daily Eagle*, October 26, 1911, p. 20.

446 US Patent No. 1,037,842, granted September 3, 1912, for a motor to Helen M. Creuzbaur, Carrie Creuzbaur, and Grace C. Nichols, executors of the Estate of Robert Creuzbaur, USPTO.

447 "Lieutenant Adolphus E. Morse of Corsicana, Navarro County, Texas," accessed February 7, 2024, https://txnavarr.genealogyvillage.com/biographies/m/Morse_Adolphus_E.htm. This website also includes two excellent newspaper articles on Morse written in 2010 by C. Robert Keathley and Dana Stubbs for the *Corsicana Daily Sun*. For an article about the *Gazelle* and its place in history, see Thomas Paone, "The Most Fashionable Balloon of the Civil War," accessed February 7, 2024, https://airandspace.si.edu/stories/editorial/most-fashionable-balloon-civil-war.

448 "La Grange in 1888," *La Grange Journal*, February 23, 1933, p. 4; Find a Grave results for Capt. George H. Schroeder, La Grange, Texas Cemetery, accessed January 14, 2024, https://www.findagrave.com/memorial/search?firstname=george&middlename=h&lastname=schroeder&birthyear=&birthyearfilter=&deathyear=1897&deathyearfilter=&location=&locationId=&memorialid=&mcid=&linkedToName=&datefilter=&orderby=r&plot=&page=1#sr-97218189.

449 "Nueces County," *Galveston Daily News*, March 6, 1877, p. 2; "Corpus Christi," *Galveston Daily News*, September 10, 1882, p. 1; "Death of Capt. John S. Greer," *Corpus Christi Weekly Caller*, August 22, 1886, p. 4.

450 Cotham, *Battle on the Bay*, 187–188; Casdorph, *Prince John Magruder*, 299–300, 311, 314–316; Settles, *John Bankhead Magruder*, 295–304.

451 Thetford Vermont Historical Society, "Thomas Chubb's Fish Rod Factory," accessed January 1, 2024, https://www.thetfordhistoricalsociety.org/Chubb.html.

452 Texas Genealogy Trails, Genealogy Trails History Group, entry for Chubb, Commodore Thomas, accessed January 1, 2024, http://genealogytrails.com/tex/gulfcoast/galveston/bios_c.htm; Thetford, Vermont Historical Society, "Thomas Chubb's Fish Rod Factory," accessed January 1, 2024, https://www.thetfordhistoricalsociety.org/Chubb.html.

453 Thomas H. Chubb, Advertisement for Thomas H. Chubb Fishing Rod Factory, *American Angler*, November 10, 1883, 304; Thetford Vermont Historical Society, "Thomas Chubb's Fish Rod Factory," accessed January 1, 2024, https://www.thetfordhistoricalsociety.org/Chubb.html.

454 "Captain Chubb, formerly of Confederate Navy, Passes Away in Vermont," *New York Tribune*, July 10, 1910, p. 7.

455 Dale Baum, *Counterfeit Justice: The Judicial Odyssey of Texas Freedwoman Azeline Hearne* (Baton Rouge, LA: Louisiana State University Press, 2009), 144.

456 Patsy McDonald Spaw, ed., *The Texas Senate: Civil War to the Eve of Reform, 1861–1889* (College Station, TX: Texas A&M University Press, 1999), 145; W. J. Barker, comp., *Directory of the Members of the Thirteenth Legislature of the State of Texas* (Austin: State Journal Printer, 1873), 1; W. Richardson, *The Texas Almanac for 1870 and Emigrant's Guide to Texas* (Galveston, TX: Galveston News, 1870), 197; Entry for Phidello William Hall, Legislative Reference Library of Texas, accessed January 3, 2024, https://lrl.texas.gov/legeleaders/members/memberDisplay.cfm?memberID=4369.

457 Knight, *Confederate Invention*, 266–267; US Patent No. 161,225, issued June 22, 1875, to P. W. Hall for improvement in postage-stamp holder, USPTO; Karen Ploch, Curator, Historical Society of Montgomery County, "P. W. Hall," accessed December 20, 2023, https://hsmcpa.org/index.php/component/k2/item/248-p-w-hall; "Old Cottonwood Cemetery," accessed January 3, 2024, https://www.hmdb.org/m.asp?m=79977.

458 Walter P. Webb, *The Texas Rangers: A Century of Frontier Defense* (Austin: University of Texas Press, 2008), 220; Barry A. Crouch and Donaly E. Brice, *The Governor's Hound: The Texas State Police, 1870–1873* (Austin: University of Texas Press, 2011), 36, 55–56; *Memorial and Biographical History of McLennan, Falls, Bell and Coryell Counties* (Chicago: Lewis Publishing Co., 1893), 113–114.

459 Joe B. Frantz, "Borden, Gail, Jr.," *Handbook of Texas Online*, accessed December 11, 2023, https://www.tshaonline.org/handbook/entries/borden-gail-jr.; Jeff Carroll, "Borden, TX," *Handbook of Texas Online*, accessed December 11, 2023, https://www.tshaonline.org/handbook/entries/borden-tx.

460 Franz, *Gail Borden*, 275–276.

461 Cotham, *Juneteenth*, xii.

462 Cotham, *Juneteenth*, 149; Endorsement by F. W. Emery on letter from John H. Sterrett, Superintendent of Steam Transports, Galveston, TX, June 21, 1865, Headquarters, Division of the Gulf, District of Texas, Record Group 393, pt. 2, NARA.

463 F. W. Emery to Dunn & Bradbury, Headquarters, (Union) District of Texas, July 17, 1865, Letters sent, Division of the Gulf, District of Texas, p. 28–29, Record Group 393, pt. 2, NARA.

464 Report of G. E. Atwood Galveston, TX, July 26, 1865, OR, 48, pt 2: 1121; "Statement of Captured, Abandoned, and Confiscable property received by G. W. Dent, Special Agent, US Treasury Department at Galveston, Texas during the month of January 1866," Record Book of Official Transactions of Supervising Agent George W. Dent, January 1866–March 1866, Record Group 366, p. 50–51, NARA.

465 "Sale of Government Property," *Galveston Daily News*, July 10, 1866, p. 4.

SOURCES CONSULTED

Manuscript Collections

Austin History Center, Austin Public Library, Austin, Texas
- Caleb V. Littlepage Papers

Galveston and Texas History Center, Rosenberg Library, Galveston, Texas
- Ebenezer Allen Papers
- Samuel May Williams Papers

Library of Congress, Washington, DC
- Matthew Fontaine Maury Papers
- Theodore Roosevelt Papers

Pearce Civil War Collections Museum, Navarro College, Corsicana, Texas
- George Wheeler Papers

Rutgers University School of Arts and Sciences, New Brunswick, New Jersey
- Thomas A. Edison Papers

Texas State Library and Archives Commission, Austin, Texas
- Map of Fort Esperanza prepared by Enos Reed of Co. K, Thirty-Fourth Iowa Regiment
- Papers of Texas Governor Edward Clark
- Papers of Texas Governor Francis R. Lubbock
- Papers of Texas Governor Sam Houston
- Texas State Archives Map Collection

United States Naval Academy, Nimitz Library, Annapolis, Maryland
- Daniel D. T. Nestell Papers

University of North Carolina, Wilson Library, Chapel Hill, North Carolina
- Jeremy Francis Gilmer Papers

Virginia Museum of History and Culture, Richmond, Virginia
- Robert Knox Sneden Scrapbook (Virginia Historical Society Collection)
- Records of Camp Rogers (Confederate Memorial Literary Society Collection)

Wiggins Family Personal Collection
- Robert Creuzbaur Drawings and Papers

Government Documents

Barker, W. J., comp. *Directory of the Members of the Thirteenth Legislature of the State of Texas*. Austin: State Journal Printer, 1873.

General Laws of the Ninth Legislature of the State of Texas. Houston: E. H. Cushing, 1862.

Day, James M., comp. *House Journal of the Ninth Legislature, Regular Session, of the State of Texas, November 4, 1861–January 14, 1862*. Austin: Texas State Library, 1964.

National Archives and Records Administration. Records of the Adjutant General's Office. Record Group 94.

National Archives and Records Administration. Confederate Citizens Papers Relating to Citizens or Business Firms, 1861–1865. Record Group 109.

National Archives and Records Administration. Confederate Compiled Military Service Records. Record Group 109.

National Archives and Records Administration. Records of the Department of South Carolina, Georgia, and Florida. Record Group 109.

National Archives and Records Administration, Records of the District of Texas, New Mexico, and Arizona Records. Record Group 109.

National Archives and Records Administration, Records of the Fourth Confederate Engineer Corps. Record Group 109.

National Archives and Records Administration. Union Compiled Military Service Records. Record Group 94.

National Archives and Records Administration. Papers of and Relating to Military and Civilian Personnel. Adjutant General's Office. Record Group 109.

National Archives and Records Administration. Records of the Confederate Engineers Bureau. Record Group 109.

National Archives and Records Administration. Records of the Department of the Trans-Mississippi. Record Group 109.

National Archives and Records Administration. Records of the (Union) Division of the Gulf, District of Texas. Record Group 393.

National Archives and Records Administration, Records of the Engineers Bureau of the Department of South Carolina, Georgia, and Florida. Record Group 109.

National Archives and Records Administration. Naval Records Collection of the Office of Naval Records and Library. Subject Files for the Confederate States Navy. Record Group 45.

National Archives and Records Administration. Records of the Provost Marshal General's Bureau. Record Group 110.

Pelham, Charles P. South Carolina State Printer. *Reports and Resolutions of the General Assembly of the State of South Carolina Passed at the Annual Session of 1862*. 1862.

Public Laws of the Confederate States of America Passed at the Third Session of the First Congress. Richmond, VA: R. M. Smith, 1863.

US Government Printing Office. *Journal of the Confederate States of America, 1861–1865.* Washington, DC: Government Printing Office, 1905.

US Naval War Records Office. *Official Records of the Union and Confederate Navies in the War of the Rebellion.* 27 vols. Washington, DC: Government Printing Office, 1894–1922.

US Navy. *Register of Officers of the Confederate States Navy, 1861–1865.* Washington, DC: Government Printing Office, 1931.

US Patent and Trademark Office. US Patent Office Records.

US War Department. *The War of the Rebellion: A Compilation of the Official Records of the Union and Confederate Armies.* 128 vols. Washington, DC: Government Printing Office, 1880–1901.

Newspapers and Periodicals

Advertiser Courier (Hermann, Missouri)
Aransas Pass Progress (Aransas Pass, Texas)
Belvidere Daily Republican (Belvidere, Illinois)
Brooklyn Daily Eagle (Brooklyn, New York)
Brownsville Herald (Brownsville, Texas)
Capital (Annapolis, Maryland)
Civilian and Gazette Weekly (Galveston, Texas)
Commercial Advertiser (New York, New York)
Corpus Christi Caller Times (Corpus Christi, Texas)
Corpus Christi Weekly Caller (Corpus Christi, Texas)
Courier-Journal (Louisville, Kentucky)
Dallas Daily Herald (Dallas, Texas)
De Smet Leader (De Smet, South Dakota)
El Paso Daily Times (El Paso, Texas)
Evening Star (Washington, DC)
Examiner (Richmond, Virginia)
Galveston Daily News (Galveston, Texas)
Galveston Tribune (Galveston, Texas)
Galveston Weekly Journal (Galveston, Texas)
Harper's Weekly (New York, New York)
Houston Daily Telegraph (Houston, Texas)
Houston Post (Houston, Texas)

Houston Transcript (Houston, Texas)
Illustrated London News (London, UK)
La Grange Journal (La Grange, Texas)
Los Angeles Times (Los Angeles, California)
New York Times (New York, New York)
New York Tribune (New York, New York)
Pittsburgh Daily Commercial (Pittsburgh, Pennsylvania)
Portland Press Herald (Portland, Maine)
Record of News, History and Literature (Richmond, Virginia)
San Antonio Express (San Antonio, Texas)
Scientific American (New York, New York)
Sunday Gazette (Denison, Texas)
Telegraph and Texas Register (Houston, Texas)
Times (London, UK)
Tri-Weekly Telegraph (Houston, Texas)
Vermont Record and Farmer (Brattleboro, Vermont)

Published Primary Sources

Borden, Gail Jr. *Letter of Gail Borden, Jr. to Dr. Ashbel Smith, Setting Forth an Important Invention in the Preparation of a New Article of Food, Termed Meat Biscuit*. Galveston, TX: Gibson & Cherry, 1850.

Brent, Joseph L. *Mobilizable Fortifications and their Controlling Influence in War*. Boston: Houghton, Mifflin & Co.,1885.

Brooke, John M. *Ironclads and Big Guns of the Confederacy: The Journals and Letters of John M. Brooke*. George M. Brooke Jr., ed. Columbia: University of South Carolina Press, 2002.

Brown, Isaac N. "Confederate Torpedoes in the Yazoo." BAL 3:580.

Brown, Norman. *Journey to Pleasant Hill: The Civil War Letters of Captain Elijah P. Petty*. 2 vols. San Antonio: University of Texas Institute of Texas Cultures, 1982.

Chenery, William H. *The Fourteenth Regiment, Rhode Island Heavy Artillery (Colored) in the War to Preserve the Union, 1861–1865*, 1898. Reprint, New York: Negro Universities Press, 1969.

Chubb, Thomas H. Advertisement for Thomas H. Chubb Fishing Rod Factory. *American Angler*, November 10, 1883, 304.

Congreve, William. *The Details of the Rocket System*. London: Whiting, Finsbury Place, 1814.

Cushing, W. B. "The Destruction of the *Albemarle*." In *Battles and Leaders of the Civil War*. 4 vols. New York: Century Co., 1887–1888. Reprint, Harrisburg, PA: Archive Society, 1991. 4:634–641.

Cryst, Lynda L., Barbara J. Rozek, and Kenneth H. Williams, eds. *The Papers of Jefferson Davis*. 14 vols. Baton Rouge: Louisiana State University Press, 1971–2015.

Early, Jubal. *War Memoirs: Autobiographical Sketch and Narrative of the War Between the States*. Edited by Frank E. Vandiver. Bloomington: Indiana University Press, 1960.

Fayman, W. A., and T. W. Reilly. *Galveston City Directory, 1875–1876*. Galveston, TX: n.p., 1875.

Galveston City Directory 1859–1860. Galveston, TX: W & D Richardson, 1859–1860.

Glassell, W. T. "Reminiscences of Torpedo Service in Charleston Harbor by W. T. Glassell, Commander, Confederate States Navy." *Southern Historical Society Papers* 4, no. 5 (November 1877): 225–235.

Havins, T. R. "Two Menefee-Sylvester Letters." *Southwestern Historical Quarterly* 59, no. 1 (July 1955): 69–72.

Hill, Daniel H. "Lee's Attacks North of the Chickahominy." *BAL* 2, pt. 1: 362.

Hill, Daniel H. "McClellan's Change of Base and Malvern Hill." *BAL* 2, pt. 2: 394.

Johnson, Robert U., and Clarence C. Buel, eds., *Battles and Leaders of the Civil War: Grant-Lee Edition*. 4 vols. New York: Century Co., 1887–1888. Reprint, Harrisburg, PA: Archive Society, 1991.

Kellersberger, Getulius. *Memoirs of an Engineer in the Confederate Army of Texas*, trans. Helen S. Sundstrom. n.p., n.d.

Lee, Baker P. "Magruder's Peninsula Campaign in 1862." *Southern Historical Society Papers* 19 (January 1891): 60–65.

Long, A. L. "Memoir of General John Bankhead Magruder." *Southern Historical Society Papers* 12, no. 2 (March 1884): 105–110.

Miller, Harry W. *Railway Artillery: A Report on the Characteristics, Scope of Utility, Etc. of Railway Artillery*. 2 vols. Washington, DC: Government Printing Office, 1921.

Polk, Leonidas. *Leonidas Polk, Bishop and General*. Edited by William M. Polk. 2 vols. New York: Longmans, Green and Co., 1915.

Porter, David D. *Incidents and Anecdotes of the Civil War*. New York: D. Appleton and Co., 1885.

Porter, David D. *The Naval History of the Civil War*. New York: Sherman Publishing Co., 1886.

Porter, David D. "Torpedo Warfare." *North American Review*, September–October 1878, 213–236.

Selfridge, Thomas O. "The Navy in the Red River." *Battles and Leaders of the Civil War*. 4 vols. New York: Century Co., 1887–1888. Reprinted, Harrisburg, PA: Archive Society, 1991: 4:362–366.

Tomb, James H. "Submarines and Torpedo Boats, C.S.N." *Confederate Veteran* 22, no. 4 (April 1914): 168–169.

Secondary Sources

Barnes, John S. *Submarine Warfare, Offensive and Defensive*. New York: D. Van Nostrand, 1869.

Barr, Alwyn. "The Battle of Calcasieu Pass." *Southwestern Historical Quarterly* 66, no. 1 (July 1962): 59–67.

Bartlett, J. R. *Memoirs of Rhode Island Officers Who Were Engaged in the Service of their Country During the Great Rebellion of the South*. Providence, RI: Sidney S. Rider & Bro., 1867.

Baum, Dale. *Counterfeit Justice: The Judicial Odyssey of Texas Freedwoman Azeline Hearne*. Baton Rouge: Louisiana State University Press, 2009.

Brandon, Ruth. *A Capitalist Romance: Singer and the Sewing Machine*. Philadelphia: J. B. Lippincott Co., 1977.

Brueske, Paul. *The Last Siege: The Mobile Campaign*. Philadelphia: Casemate Publishers, 2018.

Butcher, Williiam. *Jules Verne: The Definitive Biography*. New York: Thunder's Mouth Press, 2006.

R. Thomas Campbell. *Hunters of the Night: Confederate Torpedo Boats in the War Between the States*. Shippensburg, PA: Burd Street Press, 2000.

Casdorph, Paul D. *Prince John Magruder: His Life and Campaigns*. Chichester, NY: John Wiley & Sons, 1996.

Chaffin, Tom. *The* H. L. Hunley: *The Secret Hope of the* Confederacy. New York: Hill & Wang, 2008.

Chang, Larry, ed., *Wisdom for the Soul: Five Millennia of Prescriptions for Spiritual Healing*. Washington, DC: Gnosphia, 2006.

Chatelain, Neil P. "Creuzbaur's Revolutionary Confederate Ironclad *Avenger*." *Civil War Navy*, Winter 2022, 56–61.

Cotham, Edward T., Jr. *Battle on the Bay: The Civil War Struggle for Galveston*. Austin: University of Texas Press, 1998.

Cotham, Edward T., Jr. *Decisions of the Galveston Campaigns: The Twenty-One Critical Decisions That Defined the Operations*. Knoxville: University of Tennessee Press, 2024.

Cotham, Edward T., Jr. *Juneteenth: The Story Behind the Celebration*. Kerrville, TX: State House Press, 2021.

Cotham, Edward T., Jr. *Sabine Pass: The Confederacy's Thermopylae*. Austin: University of Texas Press, 2004.

Cotham, Edward T., Jr. *The Southern Journey of a Civil War Marine: The Illustrated Notebook of Henry O. Gusley*. Austin: University of Texas Press, 2006.

Crouch, Barry A., and Donaly E. Brice. *The Governor's Hound: The Texas State Police, 1870–1873*. Austin: University of Texas Press, 2011.

Donnelly, Ralph W. "Rocket Batteries in the Civil War." *Military Affairs* 25, no. 2 (Summer 1961): 69–93.

Donnelly, Ralph W. "Rocketry in the 1860's." *Ordnance* 46, no. 252 (May–June 1962): 767–69.

Drashpil, Boris V. "Surface Torpedo Craft of the Imperial Russian Navy." *Warship International* 19, no. 3 (1982): 236–66.

Dupree, Stephen A. *Planting the Union Flag in Texas: The Campaigns of Major General Nathaniel P. Banks in the West*. College Station: Texas A&M University Press, 2008.

Eicher, John J., and David J. Eicher. *Civil War High Commands*. Stanford, CA: Stanford University Press, 2001,

Emerson, William C. "Unfounded Hopes: A Design Analysis of the Confederate Ironclad Steamer CSS *Atlanta*." *Warship International* 32, no. 4 (1995): 367–387.

"Evolution of the Tank: A Brief History of the Land Dreadnoughts and Their Increasing Efficiency in Battle." *Current History*, November 1919, 352–355.

Fishel, Edwin C. *The Secret War for the Union: The Untold Story of Military Intelligence in the Civil War*. New York: Houghton Mifflin Co., 1996.

Fitzhugh, Lester N. "Saluria, Fort Esperanza, and Military Operations on the Texas Coast, 1861–1864." *Southwestern Historical Quarterly* 61, no. 1 (July 1957): 66–100.

Frantz, Joe B. *Gail Borden, Dairyman to a Nation*. Norman: University of Oklahoma Press, 1951.

Frantz, Joe B. "Gail Borden as a Businessman." *Bulletin of the Business Historical Society* 22, no. 4 (December 1948): 123–133.

Frazier, Donald S. *Blood on the Bayou: Vicksburg, Port Hudson, and the Trans-Mississippi*. Buffalo Gap, TX: State House Press, 2015.

Frazier, Donald S. *Cottonclads: The Battle of Galveston and the Defense of the Texas Coast*. Fort Worth, TX: Ryan Place Publishers, 1996.

Frazier, Donald S. *Tempest over Texas: The Fall and Winter Campaigns, 1863–1864*. Kerrville, TX: State House Press, 2020.

Grady, John. "Infernal Machines: Mine Warfare in the Civil War." *On Point* 18, no. 2 (Fall 2012): 6–14.

Grady, John. *Matthew Fontaine Maury: Father of Oceanography*. Jefferson, NC: McFarland & Co., 2015.

Gruntman, Mike. *Blazing the Trail: The Early History of Spacecraft and Rocketry*. Reston, VA: American Institute of Aeronautics and Astronautics, 2004.

Hall, Andrew W., and Edward T. Cotham Jr. "A Sharp Fight." *Houston History* 11, no. 2 (July 2014): 2–7.

Hall, Andrew W. "Mystery of the Confederate Deep." *Civil War Monitor* 3, no. 4 (Winter 2013): 49–57.

Hayes, Charles W., *History of the Island and City of Galveston*. 2 vols. Cincinnati, OH, 1879. Reprint, Austin: Jenkins Garrett Press, 1974.

Heatherington, Brandt. "Military Weapons: The Origin of the Combat Flamethrower." *Military Heritage*, August 2006, 8–11.

Heidler David S., and Jeanne T. Heidler, eds., *Encyclopedia of the American Civil War*. 5 vols. Santa Barbara, CA: ABC-CLIO, 2000.

Hess, Earl J. *Civil War Torpedoes and the Global Development of Landmine Warfare*. Lanham, MD: Rowman & Littlefield, 2023.

Hicks, Brian. *Sea of Darkness: Unraveling the Mysteries of the* H. L. Hunley. Ann Arbor, MI: Spry Publishing LLC, 2014.

Hodges, Robert R., Jr. *American Civil War Railroad Tactics*. Oxford, UK: Osprey Publishing, 2009.

Holcomb, Frank H. *Landmark Maps of Texas*. Kerrville, TX: State House Press, 2024.

Hunter, Mary Kate. "The Old Cemetery, the Shrine of Palestine." *The Tracings* 2, no. 2 (Fall 1998): 94–97.

Jeter, Katherine Brash, ed. *A Man and His Boat: The Civil War Career and Correspondence of Lieutenant Jonathan H. Carter, CSN*. Lafayette, LA: Center for Louisiana Studies, University of Southwestern Louisiana, 1996.

Joiner, Gary D. *The Red River Campaign: The Union's Final Attempt to Invade Texas*. Buffalo Gap, TX: State House Press, 2013.

King, W. R. *Torpedoes: Their Invention and Use, From the First Application to the Art of War to the Present Time*. Washington, DC: United States Navy Department, 1866.

Knight, H. Jackson. *Confederate Invention: The Story of the Confederate States Patent Office and its Inventors*. Baton Rouge: Louisiana State University Press, 2011.

Littlefield, Johnny Dwayne. "*David* and the *David*-Class of American Civil War Era Torpedo Boats of Charleston, South Carolina." PhD diss., Texas A&M University, 2020.

Lowry, Dr. Thomas P. *Civil War Rockets*. n.p: CreateSpace Independent Publishing Platform, 2012.

McKinney, Bobby J. *Confederates on the Caney: An Illustrated Account of the Civil War on the Texas Gulf Coast*. Rosenberg, TX: Mouth of Caney Publications, 1994.

Memorial and Biographical History of McLennan, Falls, Bell and Coryell Counties. Chicago, IL: Lewis Publishing Co., 1893.

Mersman, Joseph J. *The Whiskey Merchant's Diary: An Urban Life in the Emerging Midwest*. Athens: Ohio University Press, 2007.

Mesch, Allen H. *Ebenezer Allen: Statesman, Entrepreneur, and Spy*. Grapevine, TX: Waldorf Publishing, 2020.

Muir, Andrew Forest. "Inventions Patented by Texans, 1846–1861." *Southwestern Historical Quarterly* 62, no. 4 (April 1959): 552–554.

Neyland, Robert S., and Heather G. Brown. H. L. Hunley *Recovery Operations*. Washington, DC: Naval History and Heritage Command, 2016.

O'Brien, Jack. "Where was the *Hunley* Built?" *Gulf South Historical Review* 21, no. 5 (Fall 2005): 29–48.

"Official History of the 'Tanks.'" *Current History*, January 1918: 38–41.

Olejar, Paul D. "Rockets in Early American Wars." *Military Affairs* 10, no. 4 (Winter 1946): 16–34.

Pearson, Charles E., and Thomas C. C. Birchett. *History and Archaeology of Two Civil War Steamboats: The Ironclad Gunboat USS* Eastport *and the Steamer* Ed. F. Dix. Baton Rouge, LA: Coastal Environments, 2001.

Perry, Milton F. *Infernal Machines: The Story of Confederate Submarine and Mine Warfare*. Baton Rouge: Louisiana State University Press, 1965.

Polk, Leonidas I., Caleb S. Ives, Benjamin Eaton, and Charles Gillett. "The Church in the Republic of Texas." *Historical Magazine of the Protestant Episcopal Church* 2, no. 2 (1933): 34–46.

Ragan, Mark K. *Confederate Saboteurs: Building the* Hunley *and Other Secret Weapons of the Civil War*. College Station: Texas A&M University Press, 2015.

Ragan, Mark K. "Singer's Secret Service Corps: A Group of Texas Friends Led by Edgar Singer Raised Havoc with Their Torpedoes and Helped Finance CSS Hunley." *Civil War Times*, November–December 2007, 30–36.

Ragan, Mark K. *Submarine Warfare in the Civil War*. Cambridge, MA: Da Capo Press, 2002.

Richardson, W. *The Texas Almanac for 1870 and Emigrant's Guide to Texas*. Galveston, TX: Galveston News, 1870.

Riedel, Leonard W., Jr., "John Bankhead Magruder and the Defense of the Virginia Peninsula, 1861–1862." Master's thesis, Old Dominion University, 1991.

Roland, Alex. "Secrecy, Technology, and War: Greek Fire and the Defense of Byzantium, 678–1204." *Technology and Culture* 33, no. 4 (October 1992): 655–679.

Rutherford, Kenneth R. *America's Buried History: Landmines in the Civil War.* El Dorado Hills, CA: Savas Beatie, 2020.

Scharf, John Thomas. *History of Saint Louis from the Earliest Periods to the Present Day.* 2 vols. Philadelphi: Louis H. Everts & Co, 1883.

Schneider, David H. "Lee's Armored Car: Photo Sleuthing Reveals a Fearsome Weapon's True Origins." *Civil War Times Illustrated,* February 2011,: 56–59.

Sears, Stephen W. *To the Gates of Richmond: The Peninsula Campaign.* New York: Ticknor & Fields, 1992.

Seifert, E. M. "Evolution of the Torpedo." *Ordnance* 39, no. 209 (March–April 1955): 720–24.

Settles, Thomas M. *John Bankhead Magruder: A Military Reappraisal.* Baton Rouge: Louisiana State University Press, 2009.

Simmons, Donald C., Jr., *Confederate Settlements in British Honduras.* Jefferson, NC: McFarland & Co., 2001.

St. Louis Directory for 1860. St. Louis, MO: R. V. Kennedy & Co., 1860.

Solomon, Robert S. *C.S.S. David: The Story of the First Successful Torpedo Boat Attack in Naval Warfare.* Columbia, SC: R. L. Bryan Co., 1970.

Spaw, Patsy McDonald, ed. *The Texas Senate: Civil War to the Eve of Reform, 1861–1889.* College Station: Texas A&M University Press, 1999.

Thatcher, Joseph M., and Thomas H. Thatcher. *Confederate Coal Torpedo: Thomas Courtenay's Infernal Sabotage Weapon.* Fredericksburg, VA: Kenerly Press, 2011.

Tsouras, Peter G. *Major General George H. Sharpe and the Creation of American Military Intelligence in the Civil War.* Philadelphia: Casemate Publishers, 2018.

United States Army, *American Military History.* Washington, DC: Center of Military History, United States Army, 1989.

Verne, Jules. *The Mysterious Island.* New York: Charles Scribner's Sons, 1920.

Verne, Jules. *Twenty Thousand Leagues Under the Sea.* Oxford, UK: Oxford University Press, 1998.

Von Scheliha, Viktor Ernst Karl Rudolf. *A Treatise on Coast Defense.* London, UK: W Clowes and Sons, 1868.

Waters, Davis. "'Deception is the Art of War': Gabriel J. Rains, Torpedo Specialist of the Confederacy." *North Carolina Historical Review* 66, no. 1 (January 1989): 29–60.

Waugh, John C. *Last Stand at Mobile.* Abilene, TX: McWhiney Foundation Press, 2001.

Webb, Walter P. *The Texas Rangers: A Century of Frontier Defense.* Reprint, Austin: University of Texas Press, 2008.

Wert, Jeffry D. *Civil War Barons: Tycoons, Entrepreneurs, Inventors, and Visionaries Who Forged Victory and Shaped a Nation.* New York: Da Capo Press, 2018.

Wideman, John C. *The Sinking of the USS* Cairo. Jackson: University Press of Mississippi, 1993.

Wiser, Edward H. "A Rough, Wet Ride: The Civilian Genesis of the American Motor Torpedo Boat." PhD diss. Florida State University, 2009.

Digital Scholarship and Online Databases

Beeler, Jack E. "The John R. Fretwell Officer Jewels." http://lavacalodge.org/the-john-r-fretwell-officer-jewels/.

Ben M. "Historical Marker: The *Hunley*." Clio: Your Guide to History. January 5, 2017. https://theclio.com/entry/29848.

Beverly, Trevia Wooster. "Confederate Naval Works on Goose Creek." Application for Historical Marker, approved July 15, 2006. https://www.baytownhistory.org/images/Application_-_Confederate_Naval_Works.pdf.

The British Balloon Museum and Library, "Jean Pierre Blanchard," https://www.bbml.org.uk/jean-pierre-blanchard/.

The Civil War in the East, "West Point Officers in the Civil War." https://civilwarintheeast.com/west-point-officers-in-the-civil-war/.

Classic Movie Hub. "*The War Wagon*." https://www.classicmoviehub.com/facts-and-trivia/film/the-war-wagon-1967/page/1/.

Collette, Matthew D. and Ken Nahshon. "Investigating the Loss of *H. L. Hunley*." Paper presented at the SNAME Maritime Convention, Bellevue, Washington, November 2016. https://www.history.navy.mil/content/dam/nhhc/browse-by-topic/War%20and%20Conflict/civil-war/Collette_Nahshon_Hunley.pdf.

"The First Official Map of Texas—1849." Copano Bay Press. https://copanobaypress-gallery.com/products/de-cordovas-map-of-texas-1849.

"J. De Cordova's Map of the State of Texas." Bullock Texas State History Museum. https://www.thestoryoftexas.com/discover/artifacts/cordova-map-state-of-texas.

Cushman, Russell. "Engineer, Soldier, Planter, Inventor and Nurseryman, George W. Durant." http://russellcushman.blogspot.com/2013/11/major-george-w-durant-of-bryan-and.html.

Find a Grave. https://www.findagrave.com/.

Kevin J. Foster. "The Diplomats Who sank a Fleet: The Confederacy's Undelivered European Fleet and the Union Consular Service," *National Archives Prologue Magazine* 33, Fall 2001. https://www.archives.gov/publications/prologue/2001/fall/confederate-fleet#f29.

Fretwells: Genealogy and Family History. "Dr. John Richard Fretwell, Confederate Inventor." http://www.thefretwells.com/research/drjrfretwell.aspx.

Friends of the *Hunley*. "The Search for the *Hunley*." https://www.hunley.org/the-search-and-recovery/.

Gilder Lehrman Institute of American History. "Abraham Lincoln, Inventor, 1849: A Spotlight on a Primary Source by Abraham Lincoln." https://www.gilderlehrman.org/history-resources/spotlight-primary-source/abraham-lincoln-inventor-1849.

"Old Cottonwood Cemetery." https://www.hmdb.org/m.asp?m=79977.

Halleran, Michael M.M. "USS *Baron De Kalb*: The Masonic Ironclad." http://www.phoenixmasonry.org/masonicmuseum/uss_baron_dekalb_the_masonic_ironclad.htm.

Hoover, Gary. "The Sordid Saga of Mr. Singer and his Sewing Machine." American Business History Center. https://americanbusinesshistory.org/the-sordid-saga-of-mr-singer-and-his-sewing-machine/.

"The War Wagon." IMDB. https://www.imdb.com/title/tt0062472/.

International Maritime Museum, Hamburg, Germany, "Experimental Submarine Fire Divers." https://www.imm-hamburg.de/museum/ausstellungsrundgang/tour-of-the-exhibitions-english/deck-5-war-and-peace/experimental-submarine-brandtaucher/.

Lamb, John. "Jules Verne and the Heroes of Birkenhead." https://julesverneandtheheroesofbirkenhead.co.uk/wp-content/uploads/2021/06/1-From-Birkenhead-to-Atlantis-The-Merseyside-Origins-of-Captain-Nemos-Nautilus-Copy-Copy-2.pdf.

Madden, David. "Rediscovering Civil War Classics: Jules Verne's Civil War." *Civil War Book Review* 9, no. 2 (2007). https://repository.lsu.edu/cgi/viewcontent.cgi?article=2603&context=cwbr.

"Lt. Adolphus E. Morse of Corsicana, Navarro County, Texas." https://txnavarr.genealogyvillage.com/biographies/m/Morse_Adolphus_E.htm.

Motes, Thomas, "Pioneer Inventors, Sea Devils, and Infernal Machines: Submarine Development in the United States From the American Revolution Through the American Civil War." Master's thesis, University of South Alabama, 2022. https://jagworks.southalabama.edu/theses_diss/56

Muth, Richard F. "A Masonic Secret Weapon: The H. L. *Hunley*." *Knight Templar Magazine*. http://www.knightstemplar.org/KnightTemplar/articles/20141127.htm.

National Museum of American History, Smithsonian Institution. "Isaac Singer's Sewing Machine Patent Model." Accession No. 48865, Catalog No. T06054.000. https://www.si.edu/object/1851-isaac-singers-sewing-machine-patent-model%3Anmah_1071133.

National Park Service. "Battle Unit Details for the 34th Regiment, Iowa Infantry." https://www.nps.gov/civilwar/search-battle-units-detail.htm?battleUnitCode=UIA0034RI.

National Park Service. "Tredegar Iron Works-Ironmaker to the Confederacy." https://www.nps.gov/articles/tredegar-iron-works-ironmaker-to-the-confederacy.htm.

National Park Service. "USS *Triton* Sail Park." https://www.nps.gov/places/000/uss-triton-sail-park.htm.

Naval History and Heritage Command. Ship Histories. https://www.history.navy.mil/research/histories/ship-histories/.

Paone, Thomas. "The Most Fashionable Balloon of the Civil War." https://airandspace.si.edu/stories/editorial/most-fashionable-balloon-civil-war.

Pearson, Charles E. "Great Expectations for an Ill-Fated Ironclad." *Naval History Magazine*, February 2017. https://www.usni.org/magazines/naval-history-magazine/2017/february/great-expectations-ill-fated-ironclad.

"Phidello William Hall," Legislative Reference Library of Texas. https://lrl.texas.gov/legeleaders/members/memberDisplay.cfm?memberID=4369.

Ploch, Karen. Historical Society of Montgomery County. "P. W. Hall." https://hsmcpa.org/index.php/component/k2/item/248-p-w-hall.

Rucker, Christopher D. "The Myth of the *Hunley*'s Blue Lantern." *The Civil War Monitor*, October 8, 2012. https://www.civilwarmonitor.com/the-myth-of-the-h-l-hunleys-blue-lantern/.

Scafuri, Michael P. and Stephen Weise, "The H. L. *Hunley* Weapon System: Using 3D Modeling to Replicate the First Submarine Attack," 2014 Underwater Archaeology Proceedings, accessed October 30, 2024. https://www.academia.edu/28322590/The_H_L_Hunley_Weapon_System_Using_3D_Modeling_to_Replicate_the_First_Submarine_Attack?auto=download.

Smithsonian Institution, National Museum of American History. "Abraham Lincoln's Patent Model." https://www.si.edu/object/abraham-lincolns-patent-model%3Anmah_213141.

Texas Genealogy Trails. "Biographies of Galveston County, Texas." http://genealogytrails.com/tex/gulfcoast/galveston/bios_s.htm.

Texas State Cemetery. https://cemetery.tspb.texas.gov/.

Texas State Historical Association. *Handbook of Texas Online*. http://tshaonline.org/handbook.

Thetford, Vermont Historical Society. "Thomas Chubb's Fish Rod Factory." https://www.thetfordhistoricalsociety.org/Chubb.html.

United States Census Bureau. "U.S. Census Bureau History." https://www.census.gov/history/www/homepage_archive/2015/april_2015.html#:~:text=According%20to%20the%201860%20Census,of%20America%20had%208.7%20million.

United States Census Bureau. 1850 United States Federal Census for Lockport, IL. https://www.ancestry.com/discoveryui-content/view/16712236:8054.

United States Naval Undersea Museum. "Reflecting Light Through Periscopes," January 20, 2024. https://www.history.navy.mil/content/dam/museums/undersea/education/Reflecting%20Light%20and%20Periscopes.pdf.

United States Naval Undersea Museum. "The Remarkable Story of the Howell Torpedo." https://navalunderseamuseum.org/howell/#:~:text=The%20Howell%20torpedo%20was%20the,first%20successful%20torpedo%20in%201866.

United States Navy. Naval History and Heritage Command. "Black Powder Blast Effects on the Confederate Submarine *Hunley*," Information Paper Prepared by the US Navy, August 28, 2017. https://www.history.navy.mil/research/underwater-archaeology/sites-and-projects/ship-wrecksites/hl-hunley/black-powder-blast-effects-hunley.html#:~:text=It%20has%20been%20concluded%20that,more%20modern%20military%2Dgrade%20explosives.

Vandergriff, Cara. "Petticoat Gunboats': The Wartime Expansion of Confederate Women's Discursive Opportunities Through Ladies' Gunboat Societies." Master's thesis, University of Tennessee, 2013. https://trace.tennessee.edu/utk_gradthes/1691/, 45–47.

Weston, Alan, and Rebecca Koncienzcy. "Uncovering Links Between Birkenhead and the father of Science Fiction." *Liverpool News*, July 31, 2022. https://www.liverpoolecho.co.uk/news/liverpool-news/uncovering-links-between-birkenhead-father-24613705.

Williams, C. to J. J. Pettus. St. Louis, MO, November 26, 1860. Mississippi Department of Archives and History. https://cwrgm.org/item/mdah_757–930–11–06.

Worthpoint auction site listing for "C.S. Hale Rocket, Texas Rocket Battery, San Antonio Texas 1863/64." https://www.worthpoint.com/worthopedia/s-hale-rocket-texas-rocket-battery-1885251825rocket-battery-1885251825.

INDEX

G

H

M

www.ingramcontent.com/pod-product-compliance
Lightning Source LLC
LaVergne TN
LVHW010912280825
819315LV00018B/55
* 9 7 8 1 6 4 9 6 7 0 2 7 4 *